PLANNING THE MODERN PUBLIC LIBRARY BUILDING

Recent Titles in
The Libraries Unlimited Library Management Collection

PLANNING THE MODERN PUBLIC LIBRARY BUILDING

727. 824

Gerard B. McCabe and James R. Kennedy, editors

THE LIBRARIES UNLIMITED LIBRARY MANAGEMENT COLLECTION

A Member of the Greenwood Publishing Group

Westport, Connecticut • London

Library of Congress Cataloging-in-Publication Data

Planning for the modern public library building / edited by Gerard B.
McCabe and James R. Kennedy.
   p. cm.
  Includes bibliographical references and indexes.
  ISBN 1-313-32155-8
  1. Library buildings—planning. 2. Library buildings—Design and construction. 3.
Public libraries. I. McCabe, Gerard B. II. Kennedy, James R. (James Robert), 1943–.
Z679.5   2003
—dc21   2003051649

British Library Cataloguing in Publication Data is available.

Library of Congress Catalog Card Number: 2003051649
ISBN: 0-313-32155-8

First published in 2003

Libraries Unlimited
A Member of Greenwood Publishing Group, Inc.
88 Post Road West, Westport, CT 06881
www.lu.com

Printed in the United States of America

The paper used in this book complies with the
Permanent Paper Standard issued by the National
Information Standards Organization (Z39.48–1984).

10 9 8 7 6 5 4 3 2 1

CONTENTS

CONTENTS

CONTENTS

PREFACE

As an architect specializing in libraries, I have been caught up in the rapid changes affecting the planning and design of libraries, new technologies, computers, rethinking of services and mission, effective use of personnel, and the effects of all of these on the functional and the aesthetic plan. At no point in history have there been as many changes in every aspect of the library. The display, storage, movement, recording, and retrieval of books—and even the very nature of books—are in a state of flux.

Libraries had a major revolution once before, in the nineteenth century, changing a system that had been static since the time of the Greeks and Romans. Books over the preceding centuries were treasures kept in closed collections monitored by caretaker librarians. With the revolution, books for the first time were placed on open shelves, the result of Dewey's development of a classification system that placed books in a universal order. Each book was assigned digits that placed it in line among all books. The public flocked to the open library shelves, accessing unrestricted materials for every possible purpose, especially education—the truly free library was born, and access to information bettered and advanced our democratic societies.

Now we witness a second major revolution in information allowing infinite access to all information from anywhere. This revolution also centers on digits—great, long lines of bits read by microchips anywhere at any time. This access to universal information provides a broad betterment for the world and its people. The library of Dewey's day is gone forever, replaced by the new library as a center for all forms of information and an equally important hub of community activities.

In *Managing Planning*, my fellow colleagues and friends offer their individual wisdom, advice, and assistance to the reader in what Andrea Michaels terms the "ongoing reinvention" of the library. We plan for the next twenty years but are encouraged by Bill Sannwald to think about fifty years. We learn from the authors how to improve the planning processes, to gather support for library improvements, to become more effective through broader sharing of space with others and meeting the needs of youths and seniors, and to adopt the best of current technological changes available for our buildings. For further information, we are directed to other sources by Sandra Trezzo's annotated bibliography. All this is of value to readers seeking to gracefully and successfully plan a new or expanded library.

The bringing together of cost-effective and enhanced library services, and doing so by listening to the community and the experience of others, is a repeated theme of our authors. Another theme developed in Part VII by Donald Bergomi and Elisabeth Martin is that libraries capture the history, image, and spirit of the communities they serve. I believe we agree that libraries have a value beyond the sum of their parts when they are more than just warehouses. Understanding the heritage of libraries in general and the needs and image of the communities served is an important consideration in the planning process. The broadest and fullest use of libraries will be made if they are representative of our time and place in history, in the same way that the Carnegie libraries were representative of their time. According to the architect Le Corbusier, "There are living pasts and dead pasts. Some pasts are the liveliest instigators of the present, the best springboards into the future."[1] Let us draw upon the library's graceful architectural heritage, combine it with the available technologies of today, and create a new form of public building—open and free, wonderful, joy-inspiring places to join with our neighbors and children in finding information and guidance toward a better life. Let us dream the best library and find the way to build that dream.

Jay R. Carow, AIA, ALA
Chicago, November 5, 2002

1. Charles Edouard Jeanneret Le Corbusier, "When the Cathedrals Were White," quoted in *New York Times Magazine*, 11 November 2001, 23.

ACKNOWLEDGMENT

We wish to extend our thanks to independent editor and library consultant Mary-Elinor Kennedy for her wise perspective and narrative review.

INTRODUCTION

When we began our planning for this book, we discussed topics via email and in person at conferences. Both of us have library building experience, and we wanted to identify topics that would interest our clients and other librarians involved in planning for buildings. In our discussions, we reviewed what our individual consulting experiences had taught us, where there was a need for more information, and what we saw as future possibilities for libraries. In our prospectus for recruiting authors, we said, "The intent of this book is to offer public librarians insight into current activities in the sphere of building planning." Furthermore, we didn't want another handbook, and authors were to discuss issues from a management perspective. To recruit authors, we sought among colleagues and used the Internet. We believe we have found excellent people from the United States and Australia to write these chapters.

The subjects covered the range from planning basics to advanced technology. Not overlooked, however, are important subjects that relate to operating libraries, including marketing, landscaping, furniture selection, services for different age groups, and gathering support from the community.

In our experiences with renovating or expanding existing buildings, we found quite often that the children's spaces (and, even more, the spaces for young adults) were too small or virtually nonexistent. It was not unusual, in the late 1990s, to find the children's population undercounted in some communities. In a 1999 publication of the Annie E. Casey Foundation, William P. O'Hare (1999, 1) explained that the Bureau of the Census estimated that more than two million children were not counted in the 1990 census. Census 2000 did better. Although the new census figures have been helpful, the possibility exists that about one million children were missed (O'Hare 2001, 3). To plan spaces for varying age groups and especially for children and other young people, very accurate population figures for library service areas are quite essential.

Some issues that are important to library planning are usually left to later consideration. Marketing of the library collections and the library services is one such topic, but awareness of it is important to space design. Planning for landscaping of the exterior grounds shouldn't be put off for too long. It is part of the design that helps make the library building an inviting place.

As experienced consultants, both of us are sensitive to operating costs for library buildings. So some attention is given to energy efficiency, quality lighting at a reasonable cost, and even future prospects for power generation. At Storm Lake, Iowa (home to one of us), a geologic formation known as Buffalo Ridge begins and leads into Wisconsin. From this beginning, a series of windmill farms for power generation appears along the ridge. Awareness of power needs and the means for creating and conserving power are critical.

Hardwired computer services are being supplemented by wireless connectivity for computers. There is a need for better understanding of this new technology. Library dependence on computer-based procedures is increasing, and when computer technology is combined with other technologies, striking developments can occur (witness radio frequency identification systems for controlling circulation activity).

Last, some reports about experience in recent planning and the gathering of the human and other resources essential to the project can only be reassuring to those who are about to begin the process leading to improved library services and a building that operates successfully. Please read and enjoy this book. It was written for you.

Gerard B. McCabe, Catonsville, Maryland
James R. Kennedy, Storm Lake, Iowa

REFERENCES

A Kids Count Working Paper. Baltimore, MD: Annie E. Casey Foundation.

———. 2001. *The Child Population: First Data from the 2000 Census.* A Kids Count Report on Census 2000. Baltimore, MD: Annie E. Casey Foundation and the Population Reference Bureau.

O'Hare, William P. 1999. *The Overlooked Undercount: Children Missed in the Decennial Census.*

PART I
THE PLANNING BEGINS

1 EARLY PLANNING FOR A NEW LIBRARY

William W. Sannwald

A significant amount of planning and analysis is needed long before the first shovel of dirt is unearthed for a new library building at groundbreaking. A building does not just happen; rather, it is the result of a complex set of activities unique to each jurisdiction planning a library.

PROBLEMS WITH THE EXISTING BUILDING

Often the need for a new library building results from dissatisfaction with existing facilities, but sometimes this is difficult to recognize. Just as the lobster in a boiling pot doesn't realize what is taking place around it, most of us continue to work in library buildings that lack the resources needed to serve our customers. We gradually get used to the lack of space for users, staff, and collections and our inability to provide the technology that users need. Examining a number of factors that affect library service can help in assessing the adequacy of library buildings and in building a case statement for a new or renovated library.

Demographic Changes

Americans like to move—more than one out of ten move during a given year (Kotler and Armstrong 2001, 122–131). This has an impact on libraries as the number of people in a library service area either increases or decreases. The shift from city to suburb and from Rustbelt to Sunbelt has resulted in the development of sophisticated library systems such as those in Baltimore County, Maryland; Los Angeles County, California; and Hennepin County, Minnesota, to meet the needs of a rapidly growing population. A shift in services offered has occurred in central cities such as Detroit, where Clara Jones and Norman Maas developed the TIP program of community information and referral to meet their service populations' needs for basic information to successfully lead their lives (personal conversation with Clara S. Jones and Norman Maas).

The United States attracts immigrants as well. During the period from 1990 to 2000, minority groups accounted for approximately 70 percent of the growth of this country (Harrell 2002), and people moving into the country often gravitate to services offered by the public library. Gary Strong, director of the Queens Borough Public Library System in New York City, reports that the system has materials in over ninety languages to meet the needs of a very diverse population (Strong 2001).

Needs of public library users have changed through the years as well, and these changes have an impact on libraries. For example, new services such as computer labs, literacy programs, homework centers, and the library as a place have been added to meet the needs of a changing population, whereas some services such as reader's advisory and microform collections have been curtailed.

Collections

Having no more room to shelve books and media is an indicator that a physical change may be required to meet a growing collection. Collection obesity is sometimes the product of a librarian who is a book collector rather than a librarian. A collection development policy needs to be developed and implemented, and it should include a rigorous weeding program. In determining future collection space needs, the following issues should be examined:

- What is the current stack capacity of the library, and how much growth is available in existing stacks? Often, libraries run out of room for materials and convert other functional areas, such as seating and meeting rooms, into collection spaces.
- Does the library have open stacks? Closed stacks? A combination of the two? Closed stacks can often hold more volumes than open stacks because they can be packed to the limit, as staff will be accessing them.
- How many volumes are acquired each year? The number and variety of materials that libraries acquire today often make the job of holding and displaying materials more difficult, because libraries must deal with media and a wide variety of book formats.
- How many volumes are weeded each year? Weeding seems to be one of the things that librarians never find time to do, and yet the cost of holding materials on shelves is expensive. If a library can store approximately twelve books per square foot of space, which is a fairly accepted number, and the construction cost of a new building is $250 per square foot, the cost to house one book is almost $21 (an incentive to weed).
- Is auxiliary storage available? Having a low-cost storage location to house materials away from the library is a cost-effective way to retain important

materials that are not immediately needed. A system for library users to request and receive materials from remote storage in a timely manner is required.

- What impact will electronic resources have on the library? Libraries have been shifting from paper to electronics for reference and fact publications, but most readers still prefer paper for reading books and current magazines.
- Will electronics create a future need for more or less space? (Who knows? This will be determined by the speed of the shift to electronics.) Although an electronic version of a book or journal may require zero space, a reader sitting at a table requires approximately 20 square feet of space, and the same reader at an electronic workstation requires about 45 square feet.
- Will the library run parallel print and electronic systems? The answer is yes, to a great extent, for the immediate future.

Seating Capacity

As space grows short, seats are sometimes sacrificed for stacks and technology. It is illustrative to examine the seating plan or photos of the library on opening day and compare it to the present. There may also be changes in the pattern of use by the population served by the library, as well as a need for additional seating because of population growth.

Library as a Place

The public library is a place that belongs to everyone. New libraries often are arranged like bookstores, and many offer light refreshments that encourage customers to linger. Libraries are increasingly becoming places for interaction, and most newer ones have meeting spaces, seminar rooms, and sometimes performing-arts spaces and galleries. All of these activities and attractions make the library a desired destination and increase the square footage needs for new libraries.

Physical Problems in the Building

As they age, buildings develop physical problems that are beyond the scope of maintenance or renovation. One or more of the following problems may not require an immediate move to a new building, but these are often cues that a new building is desirable:

- Building conditions that are dangerous to users and staff or so expensive to mitigate and repair that they are not worth the effort. A building full of asbestos, or a serious structural problem, may hasten the move to a new library.
- Building systems (electrical, heating, ventilating, and air-conditioning [HVAC]; fire safety; etc.) that are outmoded or expensive to operate. As

the number of electrical units in a library increases, the capacity of a building to handle the additional load is taxed. Other systems may be so expensive and difficult to replace that, in the long run, a new building may be cheaper.

- An inflexible floor plan in that it does not meet changing service program needs. Libraries today have programs and activities such as homework centers, computer labs, and lifelong learning that were not in existence when many older buildings were built. Physical limitations may prevent a library from successfully establishing these activities.
- Difficulty in providing technology access (cables, wiring, etc.) to the existing space. Older buildings with thick concrete floors and columns often make it difficult to run power and data to parts of the building.
- A building that is not compliant with the Americans with Disabilities Act (ADA). Most buildings more than ten years old were not built to ADA standards and sometimes require costly alterations.

Site

Site problems may include the following:

- A location may no longer be accessible to the majority of users because of demographic movement in the service area. Many libraries in older communities have experienced population movement that resulted in the library's no longer being located in an area that easily serves most of the community.
- A location may be valuable for other activities, and the library's board may be forced or want to sell the property to owners who will use it for other purposes.
- The site may have environmental problems that could be dangerous, such as being in a flood zone or disclosure that the existing site was once a toxic waste site.
- A site may not provide adequate access through parking, public transportation, or other means of access.
- A location may not provide space needed for expansion on that site.

Standards or Guidelines

Usually, policymakers want to know if existing facilities are up to standards, and this is difficult because the Public Library Association (PLA) has not produced a statistical standard since 1967. Some states have a standard or guideline that requires so many square feet of library space for the service population, and most new libraries are in the range of 1 square foot per person served. Sizes of libraries have increased over the last twenty years due to technology, the library as a place, and larger children's rooms and homework centers.

THE BUILDING TEAM

If a decision is made to proceed with a new library, one or more building teams are formed to help move the library forward. Some groups that need to be considered in forming a team are the representatives from the governing authority or legal owners. The legal owners may be the administrative library board or, when the library is administratively part of a larger governmental agency, representatives of the authority where policy is established. Other members of the team may be representatives from the library administration and staff, Friends of the Library groups, and community interest groups. Other team members may be delegates of the jurisdiction's public works, personnel, legal, and financial experts, any other potential stakeholders, and (most important) the final customers—the library users. Usually, a smaller working group is formed from the larger group to expedite the building process, and their decisions are brought back to the larger group for review and approval. Whatever organization team or teams are formed, it is vital that only one person speak for the entire organization in dealing with consultants and contractors during the design and building process. It is also good to create teams whose members have skills and strengths that enhance each other.

Expect conflict with your internal team as well as with all those who will be involved in the project. Conflict is to be expected for a variety of reasons, and managing it will lead to a successful building. Issues that may cause conflict include the following:

- Lack of resources is usually at the top of the list as a conflict maker, because building needs are usually greater than the budget allocated to the project. Another resource issue may be that there is not sufficient staff to work on the project.
- Mutually exclusive goals are often part of a project. For example, the mayor may want to site the library in a location that the building team believes is not the best place for the library.
- Power differentials sometimes occur, such as when major donors exercise the "golden rule" in building design or function, threatening to take their money away if their desires are not met. Such situations require diplomacy to keep the donations and still meet the overall library needs.
- Role ambiguity occurs when people are not sure who has the authority over some aspects of the project. For example, who makes the final decision on various aspect of design? Is it the mayor, the board president, or someone else? This is why it is important to have only one person with authority to speak for the library team on the project, and to give that person authority to make decisions. It is to be hoped that the decisions made reflect the wishes of the group, and if there is some doubt on a particular item, a team meeting should be held.
- Sometimes library directors may find themselves in role conflict. An example of this is a situation in which what is best for the library may not be

what is best for the parent institution. The parent institution may want to place a police substation in the library, and the library team may believe that it is incompatible with the mission of the library.

- Incompatible personalities occur more often than we like to admit. Perhaps two members of the project team hate each other, and this spills over to their working relationship. It is sometimes jokingly suggested that all team members take a Myers-Briggs Type Indicator test as a basis for understanding each other.
- Unreasonable deadlines occur quite often in a building process. Rushing design phases before all have reached agreement, or opening the building before it is ready, may cause conflict.
- Unclear policies, standards, and rules are causes of conflict. Examples include situations in which it is not clear who decides if a change order is warranted or how a nonperforming subcontractor is to be handled. It is vital that the team meet to discuss all issues before the project starts.

NEEDS ASSESSMENT—GATHERING COMMUNITY SUPPORT

One of the first tasks of the building team is to determine what community needs and wants can be met by the new building and the program of library service offered in it. The PLA, through its *Planning for Results* (Nelson 2001) and other publications, provides forms and procedures for scanning a community to discover residents' library needs and wants. Using planning data, focus groups, surveys, and interviews, the building team will be able to determine the services the community needs and translate those services into a plan of library service.

Needs assessment is tied into two types of marketing activity: marketing research and planning. Marketing research is the collection and use of information for understanding community needs and wants, and making decisions to satisfy those needs and wants with the finite resources available to the library. Marketing planning is trying to anticipate future events and conditions and determine the courses of action necessary to achieve objectives.

Research looks at a number of factors such as geographic variables (where people live, how often they move, etc.), demographic characteristics (number of people, population projections, income, age segments, income, ethnicity), as well as psychographic factors such as different lifestyles in the community. This information is obtained through hard research such as surveys and reviewing census data, as well as softer research that includes focus groups and community meetings. Usually, this leads to a good understanding of what the community is and what it wants to be in the future. This future or community vision is the roadmap for the library in determining its plan of service. A note of caution is that the people who speak the most and loudest at community meetings or in response to surveys may not represent the entire community. The skill and judgment of the group collecting and interpreting the information is critical if the entire needs of the community are to be served. All stakeholders must be understood and their wants and needs addressed.

Planning looks at the needs and wants expressed by the community vision and determines a library plan of service to meet them. An honest assessment of the library's strengths, weaknesses, opportunities, and threats (SWOT analysis) will determine how capable the existing library is of satisfying the long-range community vision. This may lead to a need for a new or renovated library building, because the existing facility is incapable of meeting the new library plan of service. If this is the situation, the information gained through community analysis is often used to build a case for a new or renovated building.

It is important to involve library staff members in the planning process. They are closest to the customer, know what works and does not work in the existing building, and have a vital concern in the functionality of the new building. Programmers and architects, however, must balance some personal concerns voiced by staff with their overall experience and design sense.

LIBRARY PLAN OF SERVICE

Before community needs and wants are translated into space, the library should prepare a plan of service detailing how information from the needs assessment will be implemented in the new building. The plan of service logically flows from the needs analysis. For example, if it is discovered that unemployment is high in the library service area, this will probably call for a career center. If the library serves an area with lots of young children, the teen and youth services and programs will be important to the library.

Nolan Lushington, in *The Design and Evaluation of Public Library Buildings* (1991), provides information on how to translate library service plans (such as a service plan for a popular library) into the space, furniture, and fixtures required to provide the service.

HOW MUCH BUILDING IS NEEDED?

Based on community needs assessment, an estimate can be made of the spaces required to support the programs and services of the library. Projecting space requirements for library programs and services over at least a twenty-year and up to a fifty-year time span is the preferred method for determining the size of the building. If the library has done a good job of determining community needs and developed a plan of service to meet those needs, service can be translated into space.

A five-step approach may be used to determine community needs. The first issue is to determine the useful life of the building. Is the new space an interim solution, and if so, for how long? If an interim solution, how will this impact the future new or expanded building? Will the new building be added to the interim facility? Will stacks and furniture be reused? Another question concerns the time horizon in determining the useful life of the new or expanded building. Construction today should last more than fifty years, but variables other than construction durability often come into consideration, such as long-range population shifts and changing roles for the library. What library planner twenty years ago would have forecast the effects of computers on library service and the changes they have caused in library layout and construction?

Based on the plan of service, the programs and roles for the new library space must be decided and space requirements over the useful life of the building determined. These calculations should include the following:

- *Forecasting collection growth.* This will be determined by the library's budget, type of materials it acquires, circulation rates (percentages of the collection on the shelf), and weeding policy. Will the collection grow, stay the same, or perhaps even be reduced? Will the types of media change over the life of the building? All libraries should have a written collection policy that addresses these issues.
- *Forecasting seating requirements.* Most new libraries experience a surge of use after the building opens, and the question is, will the library continue to experience the increased in-house use of materials? Help in determining this should come from community analysis.
- *Forecasting technology growth (difficult, but not impossible).* The library may prepare for future changes by designing the building to be as flexible as possible through the use of cellular floors for power and data passage and an open floor plan for future rearrangements.
- *Forecasting staff needs.* This depends on how many service desks the new building will have and the projected increased workload. It is important early in design to lay out desks to get the maximum coverage with the fewest number of service points. A new building will generate more circulation and in-house use, and this increased workload may require additional staff.
- *Forecasting new programs.* What new programs will be added with the new building? If community analysis discloses a need for a large community room, this will definitely have an impact on the size of the building. When will the new programs be added, and how will they be added over the life of the building?
- *Forecasting discontinuing programs.* Will any existing programs be discontinued in the new building? Staff have often developed an attachment to existing programs, and their elimination sometimes is difficult to accomplish.

The third step is to determine how much space is required to support the library's plan of service. A number of steps help in this pre-building-program activity, and the following are recommendations for calculating space needs.

- Determine all programs that should be part of the library's plan of service, and the supporting spaces to support the programs. All program spaces needed to support the library's plan of service should be listed, including space for essential conveniences. If the library is going to have a meeting room for one hundred people, it will require washrooms, storage, an audiovisual-equipment closet, and other support elements for the meeting room. These all need to be listed to determine the size of the library.

- Once all the spaces required for the new building based on the library's plan of service are identified, use building planning aids to determine how much space each activity will require. Tools such as the Library Administration and Management Association's *Building Blocks for Library Spaces* (2001) and the California State Library's *Libris Design* database program will help determine the size needed to support programs and roles for each space. For example, determine the number of books and media that will be housed in the building over its useful life, the type and number of shelving units required to house the materials, and the aisle width required in the various areas of the library, then calculate the square footage required. This exercise should be done for all areas of the library, and electronic spreadsheets are an excellent way to total the spaces. The total will give you the library's gross square feet; it will also include a percentage of between 20 and 25 percent of the total space for all nonassignable spaces in the building, such as stairs and washrooms.
- Group all of the spaces required into sections in the library, and determine the relationship of each section to all the others. Bubble diagrams are a useful tool to illustrate space adjacencies in the building.

After all assignable and nonassignable spaces required to meet the library's plan of service are calculated, compare the total against local and regional standards. Some states have standards or guidelines of so many square feet per capita, and the PLA used to have a standard of 0.7 square feet per capita. The Wisconsin State Library, through the good work of Anders Dahlgren (1998), has facility guidelines stating that buildings shall support the library's service program, reflect the library's role in its community, accommodate changing technology, and reflect long-range planning based on community needs. The state library has a space needs worksheet that enables calculation of the size of library required for the community. My observation is that most public libraries being built today are closer to 1 square foot per capita, as noted in the previous section "Standards or Guidelines."

Another technique is to benchmark the proposed library against similar libraries in the same state, or nationally. The Public Library Data Service's annual statistical report (see PLA 2001) is an excellent source for benchmarking and best practices. Because the report is sorted by population, it is easy to benchmark against similarly sized jurisdictions and compare sizes of libraries.

If there is a variance from regional standards or from the benchmarked libraries, ask how significant it is, and what causes it. This information will help to determine if your library's planning is correct.

The final technique in calculating library size is to ask, how much can we afford? Unfortunately, sometimes this is the determining factor in space planning. In comparing costs against resources available, the following guidelines should be followed in estimating the cost of the building:

- Determine the construction cost (check with architect, institutional engineering staff, or local architect) to obtain cost per square foot.
- Calculate the architect's fee, which is usually a percentage fee (about 8 percent of total construction cost).

- Appoint a construction manager. Although construction management is not always legally required, it is highly recommended. This is for a person to oversee the construction of the project daily, which the architect does not include in his or her contract. The cost of a construction manager is usually a percentage fee of about 6 to 8 percent of total construction cost. Both architectural and construction management fees may vary based on size of project, consultant selected, and local conditions.
- Estimate furniture, fixture, and equipment costs at approximately $20 to $30 per gross square foot of total building space. This does not include shelving, which I prefer to include in the construction cost.
- Calculate miscellaneous fees (permits, demolition, etc.).

In calculating all these fees and costs, if the total is under the funds available, there is no problem. However, if the total cost estimate is over the funds available, it is time for value engineering or rethinking the project.

The best planning is a result of looking to needs, standards, benchmarking, and the funds available, with a weighting toward library needs. It is important to have a good understanding of all these factors in determining the scope and size of the proposed building project.

CONSULTANT SELECTION

A number of consultants must be selected in order to turn the dreams of the library into reality. The two primary consultants who will be involved throughout the entire process are the library building consultant and the architect.

The library building consultant is a person who has extensive library building experience and a good knowledge and understanding of the functional needs and requirements of library buildings. The consultant must have written and verbal communication skills to interact with all the library's stakeholders, and the political skills needed to listen to and respond to all the stakeholders. This person may be available on staff but is usually an outside consultant.

The library building consultant writes or helps in writing the building program, participates fully in all aspects of design, and represents the library as a link and interpreter to the architect and other design professionals. The architect is responsible for taking the library's building program and turning it into a graphic representation of what the building will be.

In selecting an architect, the building team should look at a number of traits. The most important trait is how well the architect listens and responds to client concerns. Creativity and technical competence are also important, as well as past experience, but some of the best buildings have come from architects who were designing their first libraries.

In selecting an architect, the following are some suggested questions to ask of the architect or the architect's references (McCarthy 1999, 95; Sannwald 2001, 8–12):

- Is the architect registered to practice in the state?
- Who will be the key contact in the firm during the entire design and construction process? Sometimes a firm will send their best salesperson or a star architect to an interview, and the commission is awarded to a person that you will never see again.
- Are all key personnel involved in the project from the architect's firm identified? The chief designer and project architect need to be identified, as well as any other personnel who will interact with the library.
- Is the architect's support team identified? Members of the support team include the landscape architect, civil engineer, structural engineer, sanitary engineer, mechanical engineer, electrical engineer, ADA compliance officer, and others.
- Are all members of the architect's team part of the firm, or are they subconsultants? Most subconsultants, such as the electrical engineer, have partnered with the architect for this project, but others, such as an interior designer, may be part of the firm.
- Does the architectural firm have the resources and time to devote to and complete the projected project?
- Does the architect have experience in working with public agencies and experience in working with libraries? If the architect has not worked with libraries, does the architect have a plan to become knowledgeable about library needs?
- Is the architect an empathetic listener, willing to understand and respond to library needs?
- Does the architect have written and verbal communication skills required for interacting with stakeholders?
- Does the architect have the political skills necessary to listen and respond to the concerns of all external and internal building-project stakeholders?
- Will the architect place library needs before design considerations? Remember that every architect, in pursuing a new commission, has already thought about how the building will look on the cover of *Architectural Record*.
- Does the architect have the ability to explain the reasons for a point of view and to persuade others of the importance of carrying out his or her recommendations?

After the architect is selected, the following are tasks that the architect is required to complete (McCarthy 1999):

- The architect will produce drawings and specifications that will set minimum standards of quality for the project.
- The architect will prepare drawings and specifications that will make the bids more meaningful. Construction bidders will have a common, understandable document to which they can refer in submitting bids or prices for the job.
- The architect will advise the client on the selection of materials and systems that are appropriate to the client's project.

- The architect will work to make sure the client receives protection of manufacturer's warrantees and contractor's guarantees of which the client might not be aware.
- If the client so chooses, the architect can observe the work to confirm that it is being done correctly and in conformance with specifications. The client only approves payments to the contractor after the architect has verified the completion and adequacy of the work. (A construction manager may also accomplish this function.)
- An architect's specifications should prohibit the use of any materials whose use is limited in certain locations by federal and/or state standards because of excessive flammability or other safety concerns.
- The architect will provide the client with a complete set of all documents used in the project. Using an architect will ensure that the client has adequate records of work done. Old drawings and specifications are invaluable when the client is considering an addition or remodeling.

THE BUILDING PROGRAM

The key to a great library is a great building program, which is the written representation of what the library wants and needs, and which reflects what it has and what it needs. Each area of the library must be detailed and described so that the architect can prepare drawings that transform the written word in graphical representations of what the building will be.

The building program is a vehicle to bring all of the library's stakeholders together on what the library building should be, because the program reflects their needs. Current and future library programs and activities are described in the program, and these help shape the physical building.

A good way to think of a program is as a cookbook for the architect, to make sure all the ingredients that the library needs are included. Just as a great cook can take basic ingredients and make a wonderful meal, an architect should be able to create an architecturally pleasing and functional building from the program. The program is also valuable as a check sheet for the library during the stages of design, development, and construction, to make sure that nothing has disappeared.

Some of the elements of a building program include an executive summary, background, objectives and methodology of the program, what other studies have occurred, and information about the community and the library as well as the proposed library site. A number of authors have done a good job in detailing the elements of a building program, including Raymond M. Holt (1989, 43), and Philip D. Leighton and David C. Weber (1999, 693–694).

Management Methods

It is also important to determine the management system that will be used to implement the planning and construction of the library. A number of architectural design and construction alternatives are available.

Design, bid, and build is the most common method. Here separate contracts are awarded for design and construction. The architect prepares a set of drawings, the project is advertised and the drawings made available to qualified contractors, and a contract is awarded to the lowest responsible bidder. A contract is a legally enforceable agreement, usually in written form, between the contractor and the library, and construction begins after execution of the contract.

Design-build pertains to an arrangement under which the library contracts directly with an owner to design and construct a building or project. Usually the contractor is the lead in the design-build process; the architect might be the lead under certain circumstances, however. Here, the owner has better control over costs but loses a lot of potential creativity by having the architect work for the contractor. It is not a popular way of working for most architects.

Turnkey projects are projects that a development team designs and builds according to a library's specifications. This process is similar to design-build, but the library has less control. It usually occurs when the library is part of a larger community development, and the developer is required to provide amenities such as libraries as part of his developments.

A twist on the design-build method that has become popular in some public works is a construction manager at risk. This is a construction delivery method in which a general contractor is brought on during the design phase to be part of the design team and to propose a guaranteed maximum price at or toward the end of the design development phase. If the owner accepts the guaranteed maximum price, this contractor will construct the facility. Proponents of the system argue that it causes the library less frustration and anxiety than other systems and tends to reduce or eliminate change orders.

Magic

Because of the digital revolution and the emergence of the library as a center of the community, this is a great time to be planning library buildings. The need is greater than ever as communities recognize that the library is indeed their link to both digital and analog information. Library buildings are the place where the information transfer takes place, and because of changing customer needs, buildings today have to be more flexible and adaptable than ever. The process of identifying a need for a library, forming a group of people to satisfy that need, programming the need into a library plan of service, and working with design professionals to turn the prose into three-dimensional objects is magic.

REFERENCES

Dahlgren, Anders C. 1998. *Public Library Space Needs: A Planning Outline*. Madison: Wisconsin Department of Public Instruction, Public Library Development.

Harrell, Gilbert D. 2002. *Marketing: Connecting with Customers*. Upper Saddle River, NJ: Prentice-Hall.

Holt, Raymond M. 1989. *Planning Library Buildings and Facilities: From Concept to Completion*. Metuchen, NJ: Scarecrow Press.

Kotler, Philip, and Gary Armstrong. 2001. *Principles of Marketing*. Upper Saddle River, NJ: Prentice-Hall.

Leighton, Philip D. and David C. Weber. 1999. *Planning Academic and Research Library Buildings*. 3rd ed. Chicago: American Library Association.

Lushington, Nolan. 1991. *The Design and Evaluation of Public Library Buildings*. Hamden, CT: Library Professional Publications.

McCarthy, Richard C. 1999. *Designing Better Libraries: Selecting and Working with Building Professionals*. 2d ed. Fort Atkinson, WI: Highsmith.

Nelson, Sandra 2001. *The New Planning for Results: A Streamlined Approach*. Chicago: American Library Association.

Public Library Association. 2001. *Statistical Report 2001*. Chicago: American Library Association.

Sannwald, William W. 2001. *Checklist of Library Building Considerations*. Chicago: American Library Association.

Strong, Gary. 2001. Telephone conversation with the author, 6 November.

SELECTED BIBLIOGRAPHY

American Library Association, Library Administration and Management Association, Buildings and Equipment Section, Functional Space Requirements Committee. 2001. *Building Blocks for Planning Functional Library Space*. Lanham, MD: Scarecrow Press.

Libris DESIGN. Sacramento, CA: California State Library. www.librisdesign.org.

2 BEFORE SIZING YOUR BUILDING, REINVENT IT: THINK NEW SERVICES, COLLECTIONS, AND EQUIPMENT

Andrea Arthur Michaels

In writing a prospectus for this book, editors and masters of understatement Gerard McCabe and James Kennedy commented that "continuing services require reinspection" as public librarians consider how to improve their buildings. At a time when, in some communities, even the need for the public library as a place is being debated and exponential change is occurring in nearly every area of endeavor, both reinspection and reinvention are essential components of the planning process. It is a time to question the traditional service paradigms and invent new ones to fit the future. Strategies to address change abound, but the importance of having a comprehensive vision and a clear understanding of the future of the library in each community cannot be overstated.

How does one understand the unknowable, the future? One way is a variation of the brainstorming process. The library planning team imagines some wildly different definitions (end states) of libraries and then describes scenarios that support those definitions via a Future Mapping® process (Leeman 1998). Just imagining the chain of events necessary to support the scenarios helps create a strategy to incorporate those end states into a melded strategy toward the future of libraries and even to suggest an action plan for a best future rather than a most likely future.

Will each public library continue to accumulate and circulate books primarily as bound volumes of paper? Will books be synonymous with reading in the mid-twenty-first century? Educators tell us that reading is the key to learning, and young people, in particular, should read and be read to. Is the library the best place for those activities? Might libraries provide as many interactive programs via the Internet as colleges provide distance education programs, programs that are available whenever people desire them? Would that level of availability reduce the need for a library building?

The paperless society certainly has not arrived as predicted, but young people are as comfortable scrolling as baby boomers are paging. Much, but not everything, is available on the Internet. Grade school, high school, and college students do most of their homework research on the Internet and spend increasing amounts of time playing computer games and communicating online. Although their Internet navigation skills may not yet be sophisticated and may not always elicit the best information, young people are quick to turn to the Internet for work and for pleasure, for information and entertainment. They can enjoy an ebook as comfortably as a paperback at the beach, in bed, or in a reading room. Their school assignments require computer input, output, and manipulation of data into a format that is readable, accurate, and presentable in myriad ways. Today's young people are those who will be responsible for funding the public library in the future. If the library is not relevant to their needs, all the sentimental memories of the libraries of the past will do nothing to fund the libraries of the future.

The Public Library Association's *Planning for Results: A Public Library Transformation Process* (Himmel and Wilson 1998, 2–9) recommends that all libraries undertake a planning process, imagine the most likely future, and create a vision statement. Then, continuing the step-by-step process and after scanning the community by citizens committees, community and library customer surveys, and suggestion boxes, the library planning committee selects service categories appropriate to the needs of its community and designs programs to meet those needs.

Whatever the approach to planning, in order to ensure that appropriate space and overall funds are eventually budgeted, the planning process must be a holistic one. It must be sufficiently detailed and imaginative. Certainly, in order to improve a building, the goals for its use must be fully articulated and the impact of those goals fully understood.

What are the limitations of the public library in providing Internet access and/or the use of computers for its customers? An increasing percentage of adults do their shopping and get their civic information online. Individual newspaper subscriptions are declining. Should each public library assume the cost of providing and maintaining the space as well as the equipment for the benefit of a few users who do not have Internet access? If so, what accommodations for the space, use, storage, and security of the equipment must be provided? If demographics and technologies change, or if library awareness campaigns are successful in bringing in new library customers, will foot or driving traffic to the library increase? It is generally assumed that additional space must accommodate an influx of people and equipment.

If the public library is to remain a destination or to become a community commons, a place for contemporary salons, a place synonymous with comfort and service—will the ambience that promotes its effectiveness require more generous or just better-planned and better-designed space? Does it make economic sense to expand public libraries as freestanding, limited-use facilities? What benefits may be achieved by co-locating with other institutions such as theaters, planetariums, museums, schools, or governmental entities? If public and academic libraries co-operate in collection management and storage, space and retrieval mechanisms must be provided in a manner that is time and space sensitive. If retrieval is auto-mated, the equipment must be accommodated in terms of weight and in terms of space. How do the projections of cost, maintenance, space, and weight of the mechanisms desired affect the library's overall goals?

How a library offers the services the planning team has selected will be de-pendent on the community, the library's budget, the skills of the staff, and/or the space available. The planning process should include (1) an analysis of the costs of staff, space, and collections to support the desired service categories; (2) an evaluation of the potential effectiveness of the new services proposed; and (3) an analysis of the efficiency and effectiveness of those proposed services that are presently being offered. Service should not be provided because of the ease of providing it or because the library is in the habit of providing it (Himmel and Wilson, 54).

Planning for Results defines effectiveness and efficiency as critical elements of excellence in library service and suggests, "If libraries are to achieve true excel-lence, they must first be effective in focusing their energies on the things that are the most important and then be efficient by doing those things in the most cost-effective ways" (Himmel and Wilson 1998, 41). After steps 1 through 3 of the planning process just described are accomplished, the planning team may move ahead with the subsequent and essential tasks to "determine available re-sources, identify activities necessary to meet objectives, and revisit the impact of the choices" (Himmel and Wilson, 41). Those tasks might well include an in-vestigation of current thinking in the realm of academic libraries to see what successes may be applicable in the public sector.

REINVENTION IN THE ACADEMIC SECTOR: RESPOND TO NEEDS, COLLECTIONS, AND EQUIPMENT

Over a decade ago, as a replacement for the traditional library catalog and a host of reference librarians ensconced at a large reference desk, the information commons, roving assistance, and a triage approach to assisting students and fac-ulty were introduced by notable academic libraries such as the Leavey Library at the University of Southern California in Los Angeles and the libraries of Es-trella Mountain Community College in Phoenix, Arizona, and George Mason University in Fairfax, Virginia. The underlying concept was that the keys to un-lock the door to information (the online catalog, stand-alone databases, and the Internet) were to be centrally located and easily manipulated by users via library-supplied computers.

These and other institutions recognized that students and faculty needed as-sistance in their search for information and that they also required software that could manipulate the information found. They recognized that students com-peted for time on the institutions' computers and were reluctant to leave those workstations in order to get help. As an organizational and design philosophy, the bulk of the library computers were grouped near the entry so that it would be easy for staff (including roving guides whose ranks include cross-trained staff of reference librarians, computer technologists from the academic computing or information technology (IT) department, and tutors) to monitor computer use and to provide help. The equipment would be easy to find, students could indicate their need for assistance by raising a hand or communicating online, and help could come to them. Cross-training of staff from the library, computing, and education departments ensured that students could experience quicker responses appropriate to their needs. Printers could be located in clusters of computer workstations, in on-site but out-sourced print shops capable of high-speed, high-quality printing, or (when funds permitted) at each computer.

Bound reference collections have been reduced in size as more materials are obtained electronically, and many reserve materials are digitized and made available online via the library's Web site rather than printed and circulated at a reserve desk. The space saved in the reduction of immediately accessible materials in paper format may be used to provide additional computers to access an even wider array of information. The space saved by reducing the size of the reference desk may be reallocated for scheduled, one-on-one consultation spaces shared by reference librarians.

Elsewhere, reinvention has taken place as librarians have overcome their fear of insect infestations and acceded to students' pleas for permitting food in the building, even in study areas. Vending areas morphed into food-court-type kiosks or gourmet coffee cafés. Transition spaces include sprawling lounge seats, music, and Internet access. Because education at all levels increasingly includes group assignments, many group studies for two, four, or more people are distributed throughout library buildings. Concerns about the potential of inappropriate behavior in these small spaces have been addressed by including one or more walls of floor-to-ceiling glass, and amenities include computer hook-ups or wireless systems, monitors for group review of video lessons or productions, white boards, and reconfigurable furniture. Librarians, such as those at Ferris State University in Big Rapids, Michigan, and Virginia Polytechnic Institute and State University in Blacksburg, also have teamed with educators to develop cooperative programs of teaching and learning. Library computer labs and classrooms have merged to become "collaboratories" where students may work with peers or professionals, in one-on-one and class situations, to produce or polish sophisticated presentations on state-of-the-art equipment for class assignments and for distance education.

As research collections continue to expand, partnerships with other similar institutions and disciplines demonstrate creative teamwork and sound fiscal management. Some academic institutions have for years accepted that their collections may be too large to have open access to every title, and they have used compact shelving, off-site storage, and paging systems to reduce construction and operating costs. For example, consortiums in California, in the District of Columbia and its environs, and in Minnesota share collections and off-site storage costs for seldom-needed materials while maximizing access to important resources. The just-in-case policy of book and periodical acquisition has been replaced or aug-mented by just-in-time and just-for-you practices. New high-density storage facil-ities such as those at the University of Nevada–Las Vegas, Eastern Michigan University, the University of Minnesota, and Harvard are among successful mod-els that permit a reduction in the overall square footage and operating costs while permitting rapid access to the institution's entire collection.

Virtual libraries now coexist with and enhance traditional library services at many major academic institutions. As campus buildings and dorms are connected to the Internet, so the libraries' resources have become virtually accessible twenty-four hours a day, seven days a week. Still, the academic research library remains the single most potent and visible symbol of an institution's commitment to excellence, and new and usually expanded academic libraries continue to appear across the United States. Ostensibly, with the ubiquitous Internet and stu-dent email accounts, with networked computer labs distributed throughout cam-puses, the requirement for study spaces could be reduced. Yet students request extended availability (even twenty-four-hour access) for actual library use as a quiet study hall and resource center. Some academic libraries even offer family study areas complete with data connections, printers, and children's materials as well as nearby restrooms and food service on an extended-hour basis.

Are there elements of the academic model that fit in with that for the com-munity at large? Obviously so, because joint-venture academic-public libraries are being built across the country. Florida led the way in creating joint facilities in Broward County Libraries and the Broward County Community College sys-tem. In 2002, NOVA Southeastern University opened a public-academic facil-ity. Notable among others, the City of San Jose, California, and San Jose State University are building a huge, new joint facility. In Arizona, the Scottsdale Li-brary has two successful partnerships: one with a high school and another with a middle school.

REINVENTION IN THE PUBLIC SECTOR: RESPOND TO COLLECTIONS, NEEDS, AND EQUIPMENT

The need to reinvent the public library is not new. Public libraries in the United States have responded to changes in information formats and technologies for years. Nearly as soon as audio and video technologies became available, public li-braries included those materials in their collections and provided the means to use them. Rooms dedicated to public use of long-playing records, audiotapes, slides, filmstrips, and 16-mm films then gave way to an even wider array of multimedia equipment. A host of special displayers for each type of media were often pur-chased and then stuffed into facilities ill prepared to accommodate them, particu-larly if no services or materials were eliminated. Meeting and training rooms became standard spaces in building programs and included the means of present-ing the various new technologies to a wide audience. As public interest in the technologies increased and the demand for equipment exceeded the enclosed spaces designated for its use, building designers often responded by reducing the number of full-height walls separating the technologies, collections, and reading areas to permit simple and responsive changes unfettered by barriers.

Libraries introduced the computer age to Americans. When many U.S. businesses were just beginning to include computers in their everyday operations, public libraries already had incorporated computer technology in staff areas and had demonstrated it to their users as COMCATs (computer output microfilm catalogs), OPACs (online public access catalogs), and computerized circulation records. Computerization allowed the public to quickly see the catalogs of hundreds of libraries and to then receive materials from the other side of the globe via Interlibrary Loan (ILL). Requests for public access to typewriters gave way to requests for basic programs for word processing and spreadsheets, to computers and printers. Then, as library users required instruction in the use of computers for the online library catalog and online or CD-ROM databases, the quiet library of the past gave way to the Quiet Room in a noisy library of the present.

Some reinventions that have become accepted practice include illuminated bookstore-type shelving and neon signs. Introduced to Baltimore County Public Libraries by Charlie Robinson (the now-retired director of the library system who is noted for innovative solutions), the approach instigated a nationwide trend of merchandising collections. Throughout the country, many libraries adjusted their collections to include more popular titles of books and movies. Other libraries, whose major roles included a concentration of collections and programs for preschool children, designed their children's collection areas as destinations, spaces that are inviting and attractive in and of themselves.

Many libraries saw opportunities to expand their Friends of the Library used-book-sale businesses to include gifts of museum-shop quality and food service vending to augment library budgets and attract visitors. Staff amenities have expanded to include break rooms with reclining lounge chairs, private departmental conference and training facilities, and showers and exercise facilities. Facilities and equipment for disabled users have been developed in concert with the spirit of the Americans with Disabilities Act. Special areas like Teen Central at the Phoenix Burton Barr Library have been funded and designed to attract young adults and visiting librarians.

Taking to heart the tenets of good planning, the Richmond Public Library's Ironwood Branch, just outside Vancouver, British Columbia, has exemplified innovative thinking and true reinvention. As described by Deputy Chief Librarian Cate McNeeley, the library system decided to put all previously held assumptions aside and to look anew at the library's role in the community. Their research indicated that many of their customers were to be found late at night in well-designed local bookstores sipping coffee, meeting people, and lounging with the latest bestsellers (that they were on waiting lists to receive at the library). So the Richmond Library created a compelling new destination that offered all that and more. By tapping into the retail trend of longer hours, food, and the optional convenience of self-service; by concentrating on staff strengths in accessing information, in training, and in cooperative programming, the Richmond libraries are now giving their customers what their customers wanted: more popular titles when they want them, a welcoming ambience, online conveniences of registration, renewals, and reservations, all with more personal service for less money in a smaller space than is traditional elsewhere. As a consequence, both circulation and library use are up, and the citizens and staff are happy.

Interestingly, the Richmond Library system found that the successes of the little 12,000-square-foot branch in attracting and keeping customers could be successfully replicated at its main Brighouse Branch, and it has revamped circulation, reference, new books, business resources, and computer areas systemwide. Customers presort their returns, retrieve their own holds, and use express-check equipment to quickly and privately check out their materials. The traditional circulation desk was replaced by a small "cards and accounts" station to handle on-site registration and overdue fines payment for customers who choose not to use the Internet for those same tasks. All fiction materials are displayed face out; new materials are showcased and accessible. Similarly, the reference/information desk was reduced in size, and all librarians are cross-trained. Each takes shifts monitoring the shelving and the reading and computing areas to offer help (à la Nordstrom's, an upscale department store chain), rather than waiting for customers to come to them to request assistance.

Although many U.S. librarians have visited the Ironwood Branch of the Richmond system—the self-proclaimed "Library of the Future"—and are using it as a model for their own new facilities, the most important lessons for each public library to apply are (1) to put its traditional assumptions aside, (2) to respond to the needs of its community now, (3) to use technology and the skills of staff to advantage, and (4) to create a planning and budgeting structure that will allow the library to continue to adapt as needs change.

The Richmond Library uses (and, in fact, developed) the new circulation and Internet technology to great effectiveness. Is the latest technology required to reinvent the library? Not necessarily. The Ironwood Branch, for example, circulates nearly a million items a year and still manages to get items from its collection (which includes seven different languages) back on the shelves within a few minutes of their return by having customers presort their returns, by eliminating double handling by staff, and by minimizing the distances that materials and personnel traverse in the return process.

Is self-checking necessary to institute a policy of self-service with holds? No. Even the short time that a circulation clerk would spend looking for the requested reserved item could be put to better use serving customers. Library-card numbers on the wrapped materials preserve privacy until given to the clerk, and computer-printed labels make the holds easy to find. Customers appreciate the speed and privacy of Richmond's express-check system, however.

PLANNING QUESTIONS FOR EVERY PROJECT: THINK BEYOND THE BOX

It is essential that librarians and programmers of new library facilities think more broadly and deeply than ever before and be prepared to go where others have not yet blazed a trail. It is relatively easy and ever so common to be itera-tive, to merely copy what has been done recently or what has been advertised as best practice. It is easier still to take the approach that, because funds for helpful new technologies are not available during the planning period, they will also not be available in the near future and that planning cannot adequately address potential change. It is simple to assume that a building must grow by roughly the same annual percentage as the growth of its book collection.

Each planning team should creatively answer the following questions:

1. Do larger libraries serve their communities better than smaller ones?
2. How is better service defined?
3. How essential is the primarily American benefit of browsing an open collection?
4. If less money is spent on the overhead of building and operating space, could the public be better served in other ways?
5. Is it really heresy to weed or compress the collections, reduce public ca-sual seating, or reassign staff? What are the customers' priorities?
6. What is the community's responsibility to provide equipment and soft-ware for public use in addition to standard Internet connections?
7. Should the public library provide uncensored free Internet access, as at an Internet café, to those who could not otherwise afford that access?
8. What partnerships could be developed to better husband the commu-nity's resources, reduce costs and ongoing expenses, and still ensure that the information needs of the community are met?
9. How can the building be initially affordable and sufficiently adaptable to prepare for a future of unknown needs?
10. Will the present community of users be the future community of users? (Describe the future community of users.)

SPACE REQUIREMENTS: UNDERSTAND ALL INFLUENTIAL FACTORS

Determining space needs is still a complex exercise, and it requires a thor-ough understanding of

- the services, collections, tasks, and technologies that will be resident in the library over the useful life of the facility;
- how human beings work, study, use technology, and socialize in each com-munity of users;
- the dynamics of diverse cultures using the same facility—such as when a high school library serves both the elderly and the very young, as well as teens, or when the research library serves the public;
- the role of space guidelines in programming;
- the service-value chain and how a well-programmed space may en-hance it;

- how to project area requirements;
- how to manage continual improvement and provide the adaptability to gracefully and economically respond to changing circumstances.

Because moneys for capital campaigns often appear to be more readily available than those for library systems that rethink, reorganize, or reinvent, the planning process often does not include a suitably specific determination of space needs. Later, during the building programming process, librarians typically explain to programmers what the library's role is, what the library's projected service categories are (what they'll do and how they'll do it), how crowded the existing conditions are, and how plans to increase the collection, attract more users, and provide better working conditions for staff indicate that more space is required. But the planning process should also include a simultaneous process of space analysis and needs assessment (a projection of space needs) before an overall project budget can be accurately projected.

Just as the planning team should analyze the activities necessary to fulfill the service objectives on a broad level, so should the team and each department examine in microscopic detail those existing operations that are to be included in the transformed library. Once the team imagines the very best, most effective, and most efficient manner for all operations and describes them, an operational plan, a space projection, and a budget can be developed to accomplish those objectives effectively.

Only a few years ago, librarians and planners assumed that, because of changes in life safety and accessibility codes, new libraries must be larger than the ones they replaced. Most public library buildings over twenty years old are crowded with materials and equipment. Requests for program, learning, and meeting places routinely exceed the designated spaces available, and building structure and furnishings usually limit the opportunities to use other spaces for such activities. Often the heating, ventilation, and air-conditioning system (HVAC), wiring, and lighting are outdated relative to the unprogrammed changes in service categories, in the additions of computers, merchandising displays, library services, and systems that have evolved since the buildings were completed. Whereas infrastructure spaces for HVAC have generally been reduced in size, more conditioned space for electrical and communication wiring is needed, offsetting the space savings in mechanical rooms.

The trend in the United States is to build ever-larger library facilities to support a growing number of services; but in Europe, Asia, and Canada, less space is allotted per person—for both customers and staff members. Should Americans learn to live with less? As more options become available to provide information, to develop partnerships, and to integrate new technologies to serve community needs, the more critical it is to approach each project on an individual and very creative basis. Perhaps the building, like the services, need only be transformed and not enlarged.

To gain an accurate understanding of existing practices, one must look, research, and understand the tasks, the equipment, and the human response. Old furnishings for staff and customers may not incorporate the appropriate human factors for best performance for use with current or anticipated services and equipment. Sometimes efficiency would be improved with less but more appropriate furniture, better ways of accomplishing necessary tasks, and a good housecleaning of all extraneous materials, furniture, and clutter. A thoughtful analysis of all tasks for efficiency and a potential change of procedures could elicit savings in time and space.

For instance, well before express-check systems were a viable option, the Emma S. Clark Library in Setauket, Long Island (New York), demonstrated an incredibly efficient and beautifully choreographed approach to check-in and reshelving. With a personal greeting (now touted as "Safeway service," after the supermarket chain) and with only two book trucks at a freestanding service desk that handled registration, checkout, and check-in, three impeccably trained circulation staff and a few pages managed to quickly handle all incoming and outgoing transactions and return the books to circulation. They wasted no time in double-handling anything. It was a no-excuses approach to customer service: Greet all customers by name, get them on their way with dispatch, and get returned materials back to the public in short order without consuming hundreds of square feet in so doing. Excellent supervision and training, coupled with high expectations of all staff, made the difference. They wasted neither time nor space.

In contrast is the current practice in another library system: Returning books move from the check-in desk to book trucks and then to shelves for sorting, where they may languish for days or weeks, ostensibly because pages cannot work from trucks unless all the materials are presorted and prearranged. The workspace for the staff is extremely cramped because of the interim holding shelving, and the result is that no task can be handled well.

EMPIRICAL RESEARCH: ANALYZE EXISTING SPACE AND PROJECTED OPERATIONS

To ensure a thorough understanding of the operations and spaces now used, chronicle the activities either in photographs or on video and use close examination of that record to evaluate the space, equipment, efficiency, and effectiveness of the process.

For example, the circulation service desk and workroom are a good place to start. Photograph the work surfaces from the front and back. Make certain that all cables and equipment are visible in overall and close-up views without staff or users in the picture. Additional photographs should illustrate both the staff and customer, with a typical large workload of outgoing and incoming materials. The photographs should clearly show the placement and size of all peripherals: computer scanner, sensitizer/desensitizer, control unit, central processing unit (CPU), receipt printer, and account printer; fax machine, telephone, and other equipment; telephone, cash register or cash drawer, and customer materials.

Measurements should be taken of each piece of equipment and notes made regarding power and wiring requirements. Additional photographs should illustrate the placement and size of staff support materials, including books, binders, library cards, registration materials, date-due slips or receipts, branch identifiers or other forms, manuals, storage containers for floppy disks and CDs or DVDs, paper files; waste containers, calendar, stamps, pens and pencils, and so on. The entire area should be measured and the results posted on a wall so that everyone begins to feel comfortable in visualizing square footage.

How are incoming materials handled? How would they be best handled? In a circulation workroom or at the service desk? Several libraries use frictionless tables (conveyors) to help move materials from book returns to return stations. What is the proper angle for those conveyors that will permit the weight of a light book or a CD to move down the conveyor without holding up the process? If the conveyor leads from a book return to a work surface, how does the accessible height of the book return mesh with the slope of the conveyor and the height of the work surface? Is an automated feed required to keep materials moving? How are materials stopped? How are receipts handled? How are items sorted or presorted? How many books or other materials will fit into the book return bin? What is the best size and cost of the return bins? (For instance, electronically adjustable bins can hold more books and reduce injuries, but they are expensive and require electrical outlets and more floor space than common depressible trucks.) What is the best way of handling those materials while checking them in? What can be done to speed the process and reduce physical strain? After the materials are checked in, what happens to them? What is the most efficient and safest way of getting them to the right branch or on the right shelves?

Similarly, if the library is considering new equipment or systems to circulate and secure library materials, visit another library using a new system, take photographs of an installation of said equipment as it is being used, and ask for recommendations as to how the system should be arranged or improved. What do the staff think are the best practices? Few manufacturers have literature or training materials that fully illustrate every component placed at its ergonomic best, all cables, all associated support materials and equipment, and a thorough step-by-step description of best operation. Photograph a technician on a typical maintenance call so that it is clear how equipment must be accessed or moved. Evaluate the light quantity or quality that is required to make repairs or read LCD/LED displays or diagnostic devices. Note the length of cables and how they feed through furniture to connect equipment. Note the number of outlets and circuits that are necessary, as well as minimum or maximum distances between equipment. Discuss every last nitty-gritty detail so that when you are ready to program and design specific spaces, each detail may be represented on a floor plan, and staff have a thorough understanding of what is involved.

Critically examine the workspaces and the work schedule of the staff. What type of spaces will permit staff to focus on the task at hand and to get variety in the work process? How do employees handle problems? What items or equipment in the workspace permit problems to be handled most effectively? Where is storage for daily tasks? How are supplies organized and monitored? Is the purchasing plan the most effective from the standpoint of both initial and long-term costs? Are present solutions the best solutions? Are present procedures the best procedures? What should be changed? How could it be changed?

Whereas the private sector in the United States has developed a means of giving employees a sense of ownership and control of their workspaces even as they are shared with others, most libraries provide all staff members with their own work surfaces, even though shifts may not overlap. In an effort to save space, however, often these work surfaces are too narrow or too shallow to be efficient. Consider how providing shared usable work areas and sufficient personal or project storage may be effective for the designated tasks. Also consider that shared equipment often means that a work surface must be provided for that equipment in addition to separate personal work surfaces. Could a change in shifts better serve customers and staff needs in both time and space?

Where does staff training take place? What type of equipment and furnishings are appropriate to the type of training considered? What incentives are available to staff to improve operations? Good service depends on good training, high expectations, and appropriate equipment, furnishings, and space to perform effectively.

Flowcharts of optimized operations combined with personnel organization charts can assist in graphically describing each functional area. Then, using *Building Blocks for Planning Functional Library Space* (American Library Association 2001) and thumbnail sketches of operations with dimensions applied, square footages may be assigned to tasks, personnel, and storage. These charts and sketches will later be useful in creating adjacency diagrams and building stacking plans.

What are the plans for the collection? What is the number of single-face sections needed in closed and in open shelving to serve the community? What is the preferred height of shelving for each portion of the open collection? Those figures should be double-checked with the height of the materials in the collection. Projections based on a volumes-per-square-foot formula do not take into account storage of nonstandard materials and handicap access to periodicals and other merchandised materials such as media, new books, and newspapers.

SUMMARY

These are challenging and exciting times. Although change is exponential, graceful and successful change may be most easily facilitated by thoughtful analysis and attention to detail during the planning process. The most common mistake made in connection with new or expanded library spaces or buildings is insufficiently detailed goals and insufficiently detailed space projections that would not permit the overall goals to be accomplished. The result is almost always an underfunded project.

Managing change is neither a small feat nor a small responsibility. Think creatively, and create a new standard for others to follow.

REFERENCES

American Library Association, Library Administration & Management Association, Buildings and Equipment Section, Functional Space Requirements Committee. 2001. *Building Blocks for Planning Functional Library Space*. Lanham, MD: Scarecrow Press.

Himmel, Ethel, and William James Wilson. 1998. *Planning for Results: A Public Library Transformation Process*. Chicago and London: American Library Association.

Leeman, Mike. 1998. "Future Mapping®: A Scenario-Based Approach to Engaging Key Business Management in Evaluating and Choosing the "Best" Future for an Enterprise from a Set of Strategic Alternatives." (Northeast Consulting Resources, Inc., Boston, MA) Slide presentation, Vision 2008: Mapping the Future of Libraries, 3M Innovation Workshop, Park Rapids, MN, 30 October–1 November.

SELECTED BIBLIOGRAPHY

Brawner, Lee B., and Donald K. Beck. 1996. *Determining Your Library's Future Size: A Needs Assessment and Planning Model*. Chicago and London: American Library Association.

Chepesiuk, Ron. 1998. "Internet College: The Virtual Classroom Challenge." *American Libraries* (March): 52–55.

Coffman, Steve. 1998. "What If You Ran Your Library Like a Bookstore?" *American Libraries* (March): 40–44.

Diess, Kathryn, and Joan Giesecke. 1999. "From Here to There: Moving to the Future Through Scenario Planning." *Library Administration and Management* 13 (2): 99–104.

Hardesty, Larry. 2000. "Do We Need Academic Libraries?" Position paper, Association of College and Research Libraries. www.ala.org/acrl/academiclib.html (accessed 21 January 2000).

Hawkins, Brian L., and Patricia Battin, eds. 1998. "The Unsustainability of the Traditional Library and the Threat to Higher Education." In *The Mirage of Continuity: Reconfiguring Academic Information Resources for the 21st Century*. Publication 75. Washington, DC: Council on Library and Information Resources, Association of American Universities, 129–153.

Kranich, Nancy. "Libraries Create Social Capital." *Library Journal* 126 (19): 40–41.

Leighton, Philip D, and David C. Weber. 2000. *Planning Academic and Research Library Buildings*. 3d ed. Chicago: American Library Association.

"Multi-Use Facilities: Converging Destinies, E-Merging Facilities." 1997. LAMA-BCUL program, American Library Association National Conference, San Francisco, 29 June.

Young, Jeffery R. 1997. "In the New Model of the Research Library, Unused Books Are Out, Computers Are In." *Chronicle of Higher Education* (17 October): A27–28.

3 GREENING THE LIBRARY: AN OVERVIEW OF SUSTAINABLE DESIGN

Alexander P. Lamis

INTRODUCTION

Sustainable design denotes a broad, philosophical approach that attempts to maximize the quality and utility of buildings while minimizing their impact on the surrounding environment. Successful design requires analysis of engineering systems: heating, cooling, air-conditioning, water usage, and lighting, as well as a thoughtful approach to the selection of materials of construction. Care must be taken in the siting of the building, understanding and taking advantage of the surrounding microclimate. Appropriate landscaping materials must be specified.

Sustainable design principles can be applied to all types of construction projects but are of particular importance to libraries. Libraries represent major investments by communities and institutions. They must last for a long time and often have limited funds available for maintenance. They are important symbols in communities and, as such, demonstrate the values embraced by those communities, which should include careful stewardship of environmental and material resources.

This chapter provides an overview of sustainable design approaches: their history, current strategies, and future prospects. Decision makers who are planning construction projects and renovations should be aware of environmental issues and be able to discuss project requirements with their design and engineering consultants. This will spur those responsible for the design of new libraries to develop more sustainable buildings.

It is only relatively recently that there has been a clear environmental imperative in building design. Historically, building has been a labor-intensive, handicraft process. The difficulty and expense of quarrying stone, cutting timber, and manufacturing glass and metals led to the use of indigenous materials and construction techniques that were long-lasting. This culture of scarcity limited the environmental damage caused by building activity. Before the development of mechanical air-conditioning in the early part of the twentieth century, buildings relied on passive design techniques to control the environment within a building: Massive walls reduced temperature variations, courtyards allowed lighting by natural rather than artificial means, and buildings were oriented to maximize the benefits and limit the problems associated with sunlight. Craftsmen developed regional building approaches over centuries. Traditional buildings provide environments that are still desirable today. A cloistered courtyard may be the most pleasant environment for reading yet created. Part of the sustainable approach consists of reevaluating and learning from the low-energy, durable, human-scaled environments built in the handicraft tradition.

Today, designers have analytical tools not available in the past. Machine power can be used to model our environment and to test design solutions virtually before they are constructed in reality. It is possible to model energy flows in buildings, to test lighting configurations, and to assess environmental impacts. It is now possible to see the wider environmental impact of local design decisions. The effects of manufacturing processes and transportation of materials to a construction site are becoming better understood. More often, environmental criteria are considered in specifications. Most important, designers are improving their awareness of the natural world and of the large impact the building industry has on it.

THE BUILDING SITE

The choice of an appropriate building site is an important decision in creating a sustainable library. Several criteria should be considered in choosing the site. How will library users get to the site? Will it be by car, bus, or by walking in the neighborhood? Sites that require that all patrons arrive by car represent less sustainable options than sites that are well served by bus, light rail, and other forms of public transport. In many suburban communities, where there is no practical alternative to driving to the library, the site should be close to other destinations such as supermarkets, drugstores, and schools, so that single-purpose trips can be minimized. Future demographic trends should be considered. Many formerly central libraries are now inconveniently situated. The creation of smaller neighborhood branches, especially in established pedestrian-oriented areas, should be considered. With the increasing use of computer networks, these local branches serve many of the same information needs as regional branches. Even smaller information stations, located in malls and in major shopping districts, can provide library services with minimal infrastructure requirements.

Adaptive Reuse Versus New Construction

Cities and, increasingly, suburban districts are filled with derelict and under-used buildings that could find new life as libraries, often at substantial cost savings over new buildings, and with the environmental benefit that substantially fewer resources are required for rehabilitation than new construction. Some of the most successful public libraries are found in converted commercial lofts, city halls, and even large houses.

It is important that a potential structure be carefully analyzed before any decision to reuse it is made. Among the questions to be asked are the following:

- Does the building allow for an efficient layout of program spaces, both current and projected?
- Is the structural system capable of supporting book stacks, typically designed to carry 150 pounds per square foot, or compact shelving, which can weigh up to 300 pounds per square foot?
- Will the structure readily accept conduits for wiring?
- What is the condition of the existing heating, ventilating, and air-conditioning (HVAC) system? If it needs to be replaced, are ceiling heights sufficient to add supply and return ductwork?
- Are electrical, plumbing, telecommunications, and other services adequate, or will they need to be upgraded?
- What is the condition of the building shell? Will significant restoration or replacement be required?
- Are there any potential environmental problems on the site such as asbestos, PCBs, mold, or other hazards that will require potentially expensive remediation?
- Is there sufficient area for parking?
- Is the building in a secure neighborhood that will be viable in the long term?

Even if substantial rework must be done to an existing structure, it may still be more economically and environmentally beneficial than building a new building. Also, many older buildings are in central, desirable locations, close to public transportation and other amenities.

Demolition and Recycling of Existing Buildings

Even if it is not appropriate to save an existing building on a proposed library site, environmental and economic benefits can be derived by recycling and reusing as much of the old building as possible, as opposed to carting the entire building off to a landfill. Many parts of a building can be recycled, including steel, aluminum, glass, and certain forms of asphalt, bricks, and stone. There is a developed secondary market for architectural ornamentation, hardware, fixtures, and fittings. Rather than hand these potentially valuable items over to a demolition contractor, owners may wish to work directly or through a broker with recyclers and resellers.

Site Planning and Landscape Design

Once a building site has been selected, the orientation and shape of the building must be determined. Proper orientation toward the sun and prevailing winds can have a significant impact on energy usage over the life of the building.

In a rectangular building, it is preferable for the long axis to run in an east-west direction. This is because it is more difficult to control east light in the morning and west light in the afternoon than to control north and south light, which trace symmetrical arcs through the day.

In cool and moderate climates, southern sunlight can help to heat the building during the colder months but is undesirable during the warmer months. Because the sun is lower in the sky in the winter than in the summer, sunscreens can be designed that allow low winter sunlight to enter the building but reflect summer sunlight (see fig. 3.1). In hot climates, direct solar heat gain into buildings is rarely beneficial, so limiting the amount of south- and west-facing glass and screening windows with porches, verandas, or awnings is desirable. In hot climates, making a building more compact will lessen the amount of surface area through which heat will penetrate. Direct penetration of sunlight onto collections can also lead to deterioration caused by ultraviolet radiation.

Site microclimate can be adversely affected by the creation of large, unshaded heated surfaces, or heat islands. Heat islands raise ambient air temperature. Heat-absorbing surfaces include large expanses of flat roofing and asphalt roads and parking lots. Large surfaces of asphalt, concrete, and other impermeable materials also disrupt natural site drainage and can require expensive engineering solutions to channel water away from the library. Trees should be used to shade parking lots. Permeable materials such as gravel should be considered as an alternative to asphalt. Parking lots should be broken down into manageable areas, and site drainage should be allowed to follow natural courses.

Prevailing wind direction also affects building energy usage. Unshielded winter winds infiltrate buildings and increase winter heating requirements, but in the summer months, operable windows can take advantage of cooling breezes, thus lowering summer cooling loads. Orienting buildings to capture prevailing breezes in temperate and hot climates can lower mechanical cooling loads.

If possible, the site should connect to a system of walking or biking routes separated from automobile traffic. A bike rack should be placed near the main library entrance, and biking to the library should be encouraged as one of the most environmentally sustainable forms of transportation.

Library landscaping should be designed to minimize the need for artificial irrigation. In hot and dry climates, drought-tolerant plant materials should be used. Designers should specify native materials that have evolved along with the regional climate and require less care and upkeep. The landscape design should consider the preservation and even reconstruction of animal habitats. There is

Figure 3.1. Sunscreen.

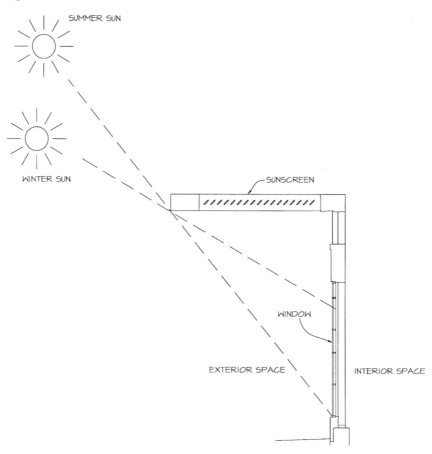

growing interest in the design of constructed wetlands in place of traditional retention basins. Though more complex to design and construct, these wetlands
can function as viable ecosystems with genuine biological diversity. Such elements can also help to support the educational mission of the library.

BUILDING DESIGN

It is interesting to compare the floor plans of nineteenth-century libraries, designed before the advent of modern air-conditioning, with contemporary library
designs. In the Boston Public Library, completed in 1895 (see fig. 3.2) and the
New York Public Library, completed in 1911 (see fig. 3.3), the rooms of the libraries are organized around light courts; which, in the case of the Boston Public,
is also a usable courtyard. Light courts have the effect of bringing light and fresh
air deep within the building, especially when combined with operable windows.

Figure 3.2. Boston Public Library: second-floor plan.

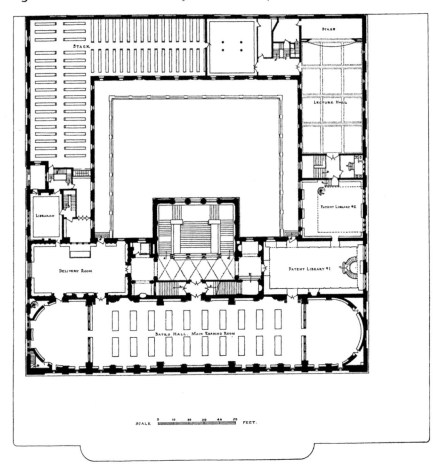

Interior spaces are relatively narrow in width and take advantage of natural daylight and the circulation of fresh air.

By contrast, the recently completed main libraries in Chicago (see fig. 3.4) and Phoenix (see fig. 3.5) are clearly designed with artificial environmental controls in mind. They have large, rectangular floor plates, with many interior spaces greater than 100 feet from any exterior building wall. These buildings rely almost completely on artificial lighting and sophisticated air-conditioning systems to function, with the concomitant high-maintenance costs. The large box remains the favored plan for new libraries due to the flexibility it allows in the layout of collections. From an environmental perspective, such buildings are inflexible, because they lock their owners into a future of high-energy usage to control a wholly artificial environment. In planning library buildings, as in many other building types, it is both cost-effective and beneficial to lay out spaces so that

Figure 3.3. New York Public Library: ground-floor plan.

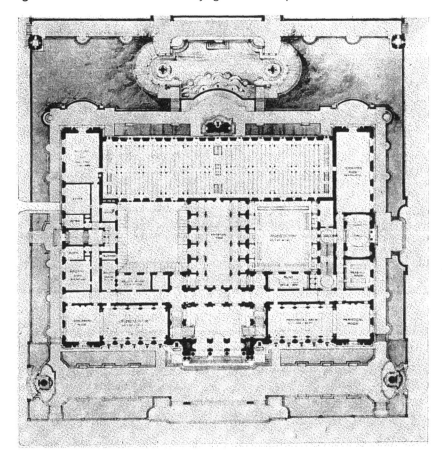

they are no more than 40 to 50 feet from the building exterior. The goal of sustainable libraries is to lessen the requirements on air-conditioning and other engineered systems.

Design of the building enclosure, the walls, and the roof have important effects on the environmental quality of a library. Because massive materials absorb and store heat, the building envelope can act as a large thermal damper, equalizing the temperature within the building as it oscillates through a twenty-four-hour cycle (see fig. 3.6).

Materials of construction and wall assemblies are given thermal transmission values, or U-values, which are a measurement of how resistant they are to the conduction of heat. As an example, most windows (which are not thermally resistive) have high U-values, whereas insulating materials have low U-values. Passive building design relies on the careful use of appropriately resistive materials in combination with the temperature-damping effects of thermal mass. On

Figure 3.4. Chicago Public Library: typical upper-floor plan.

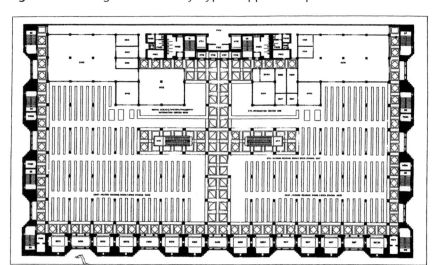

the south-facing side of a building, solar radiation is converted to heat that is stored during the day in the exterior walls or in exposed floors or ceilings; then, as the interior spaces cool at night, heat stored within the structure is transmitted to the spaces, warming them. In the summer, excess heat may be absorbed by exposed floor and wall surfaces during the day and then radiated out to the night sky.

Air movement within buildings plays an important and complimentary role to heat transmission. In modern libraries, the required ventilation and replacement of air is carried out as part of the HVAC system. In a sustainable design, the building design itself can be used to induce air currents that can in large measure naturally ventilate buildings, diminishing the size and cost of mechanical ventilation systems.

Under temperate conditions, cool air enters the building near ground level or through underground tunnels. Warm air is exhausted at the top of the building (see fig. 3.7). Negative pressure will induce airflow within the building, creating natural ventilation. This airflow exhausts excess heat and lowers the amount of artificial cooling required.

In a building with large expanses of flat roof, a big fraction of heat gain in the building is through the roof. There has been widespread interest in "green roofs," primarily in Europe, where they are increasingly common, and to a lesser extent in the United States. Bushes and other plants are placed on grids on the roof or integrated into the roof design. Several benefits can occur: Heat gain in the building is reduced, the heat island effect is diminished, and water runoff is reduced as plants and ground cover absorb moisture (which in turn reduces storm drainage requirements). A pleasant amenity is also created. It is important

Figure 3.5. Phoenix Public Library: fourth-floor plan.

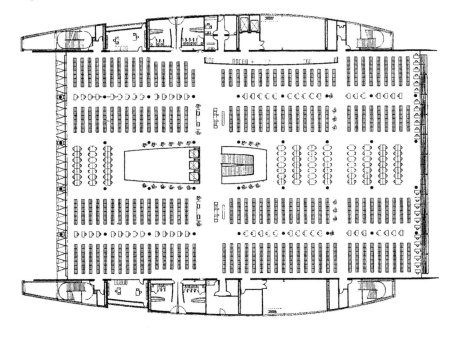

Figure 3.6. Temperature variations in buildings through the day.

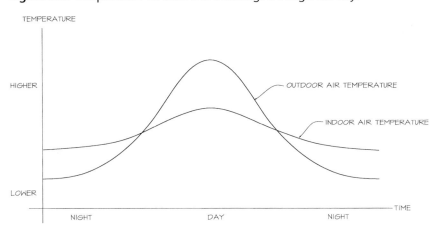

to note that green roofs require more maintenance than traditional roofs and should only be considered if the manufacturer provides a warranty.

Several methods for taking advantage of solar radiation to help meet building energy requirements are available. Two that should be analyzed for their economic payback are the use of parabolic or flat-plate solar collectors for piped hot

Figure 3.7. Natural ventilation diagram.

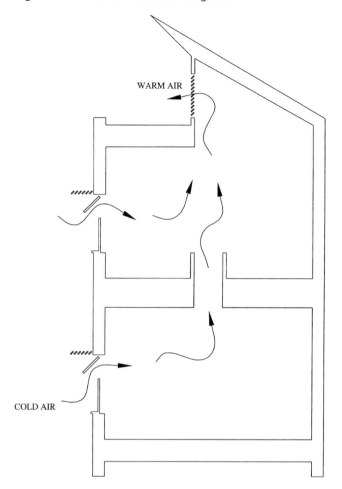

water heating and photovoltaic cells for direct conversion of sunlight to electricity. Photovoltaics have historically been significantly more expensive to purchase and install per kilowatt than electricity from the power grid but may recoup this high cost over the life of the installation, especially if incentive programs are available or if the cost for electricity from the grid increases. Locally generated electricity, either from photovoltaic or other sources, can be used to lower peak demand.

There are many options available for the specification of window glass that has significant effects on energy usage. Coatings applied to glass reflect and transmit varying amounts of light, at selected frequencies. Coatings can selectively screen ultraviolet radiation yet allow visible light to pass through.

INTERIOR DESIGN

The building interior has a significant impact on the sustainability of the overall design. Important considerations include layout, choice of materials, and the selection of furniture, fixtures, and equipment. The design of lighting, air-conditioning, and other engineering systems is also of great importance and will be discussed in the next section.

Libraries should be adaptable to changes in use that may not be foreseen when the building is designed. Spaces must be flexible enough to adapt to a variety of potential uses without costly renovation and retrofit. This does not mean that all areas should be uniform and undefined. Rather, there should be a variety of places in the library; places of solitude, contemplation, and study; places for groups to meet; teaching and learning places. Like the rooms of a house, each place can have a variety of uses over time. The services infrastructure should be robust enough to allow for expansion. Areas in the library should be separated into heavily wired areas that support a significant level of computer and telecommunications use and lightly wired areas that contain traditional library services. Heavily wired areas may justify the use of raised computer flooring.

Building Materials

Materials should be specified that are durable, long-lasting, and require little maintenance. Over the life of the library, maintenance and replacement costs will exceed initial building costs.

In response to rising concern about the destruction of tropical rain forests, clear cutting, and other forest-product-industry practices, there has been significant recent interest in the certification of wood products. Several organizations, most notably the Forest Stewardship Council (FSC), have developed guidelines that include a commitment to best practices and responsible forest management and the protection of land and worker rights. FSC-rated woods are now becoming widely available, both through contractors and outlets like Home Depot.

Materials with recycled content are available in a wide range that includes steel, aluminum, fly-ash concrete, carpet, acoustical treatments, and paints. Post-consumer recyclables include glass, plastics, aluminum, and newsprint; post-industrial recyclables are made from the by-products of industrial processes. Recycled materials offer the benefits of reducing the amount of waste going into landfills, reducing the quantity of material that must be extracted from the environment, and requiring less energy to manufacture than new materials.

Although it is sometimes difficult to determine the level of recycled content in a material, manufacturers are becoming attuned to recycling, and this information is becoming readily available. Carpet manufacturers, in particular, are recycling their products. Some companies now offer the option of leasing carpet to building owners, then removing and recycling it while providing the owners with replacement carpet.

There is also a growing interest in using plant materials such as bamboo, straw, and wheat grass that grow more quickly and densely and require less effort to replace than trees and other renewable materials. Organic materials currently treated as agricultural waste could have uses in buildings.

If a material is quarried or manufactured close to where it is used, transportation costs and environmental impact are reduced. Local plant materials are more appropriate to use because they are attuned to the local climate. There is a benefit in the creation of a regional design approach, which grows from the local conditions, materials, and climate characteristics of the region. Traditional buildings used both locally available materials such as clay (for bricks) and easily grown plants such as straw.

Indoor Environmental Quality

The widespread use of materials containing asbestos fibers after World War II and the resulting costs associated with Legionnaire's Disease, Sick Building Syndrome, and asbestos replacement have led to the desire for a high degree of indoor environmental quality. The average person spends 90 percent of his or her time indoors. Buildings have become ever more tightly sealed, making indoor air quality dependent upon the mechanical ventilation system. Proper ventilation is an important public health issue, as is the release of potentially harmful, even toxic substances from construction materials. The development of mold inside buildings is a common and potentially hazardous condition.

Building product manufacturers, especially paint and carpet companies, have begun to address these concerns. One example is restricting the use of materials with volatile organic compounds (VOCs) that react with sunlight and atmospheric nitrogen to create ground-level ozone, which is detrimental to both air quality and health. Standards for allowable VOC limits for many common building products and processes are being developed.

Carbon dioxide (CO_2) buildup is also common in buildings, especially in the afternoons, when offices and other spaces have been occupied for several hours. High levels of CO_2 can lower productivity. CO_2 levels can be monitored, and increasing the effectiveness of the ventilation system can lower them.

ENGINEERING SYSTEMS

Despite every effort at proper siting, layout, and planning, modern libraries are highly dependent on engineered mechanical, electrical, plumbing, water, and telecommunications systems. These systems account for up to 50 percent of the cost of construction of a library and also for a large portion of ongoing maintenance costs and user complaints.

Over the last century, engineered systems have gone from relatively simple heating systems, with some mechanical ventilation and a small amount of electric incandescent light, to complex systems creating a totally controlled environment. One of the greatest potential benefits of a sustainable approach to library design is lessened dependence on these systems and their high-energy, high-cost strictures. The sustainable building interacts in concert with the climate. To achieve this end, it may be necessary to relax temperature and humidity restrictions that are written into building programs. In the case of one recently completed main library, the relative humidity range allowed was so restrictive that both the heating and cooling systems were required to run year-round to achieve the required humidity levels. Restrictive lighting requirements significantly drive up both construction and operating costs. Recommended illumination levels in libraries have increased significantly over the last 75 years. Although adequate levels of temperature, humidity, and lighting control must be maintained, thoughtful consideration should be given to what is truly needed and what it will ultimately cost to maintain the systems in a regime of high energy and associated costs.

Lighting

Proper lighting is crucial for libraries. Lighting design begins with an understanding that different uses in a building have different lighting needs. Stack lights, lighting for book reading, lighting for computer use, auditorium lights, and task lighting for work areas all have unique characteristics and requirements. There is nothing more pleasant than daylight for reading and writing; the glare of direct sunlight can present problems for computer users, however, and unfiltered sunlight can be detrimental to paper collections. High-efficiency T-5 or T-8 fluorescent lights represent the most efficient appropriate fixtures for libraries. High-intensity-discharge lamps, which are sometimes specified as energy-efficient, are inappropriate for library use due to the harsh and unwelcoming quality of light they provide. Indirect sources of light, which provide ceilings and walls with an even level of illumination, can be very effective in large open areas. Low-level task lighting, such as traditional reading lamps, is most appropriate for work and reading areas, as well as in creating a warm and inviting sense of place.

Lighting controls can help to make systems more efficient. Light control by photoelectric sensors causes the artificial lighting to automatically switch off when the light level from natural daylight is above a specified threshold. Sensors can also be integrated with dimmers so that there is a smooth gradation between natural daylight and artificial light. Lighting should be controlled to automatically shut off at times when the library is not occupied, except as required for safety.

Energy Use and HVAC Systems

There are three main ways to increase the energy efficiency of a library. The first method is to decrease the demand for energy, the second is to meet the demand with energy sources available on-site, and the third is to improve the efficiency of systems requiring external inputs of fuel. Careful consideration of lighting requirements, temperature, and humidity ranges in the building can lower energy use. Proper orientation of the building and use of light courts and other methods that reduce the amount of artificial lighting will result in decreased energy use, as will the damping of temperature swings by using the thermal mass of construction materials. Geothermal exchange and precooling of intake ventilation take advantage of the fact that the earth's temperature remains constant, by using it to heat or cool the water that circulates through mechanical systems. Solar and wind energy, used either to generate electricity or to heat air and water, can reduce energy requirements. Wind can also be used to naturally ventilate libraries. In hot, arid climates, desiccant cooling occurs when hot intake air is sprayed with a fine water mist, which in turn is used to cool and humidify interior spaces. Mechanical systems are incrementally being improved to create higher resource efficiencies; high-performance motors, fans, and heat exchangers should be specified. Control systems that monitor temperature and humidity at many points in the building, coupled with variable-speed fans and remotely adjustable volume dampers, vary the output of the air-conditioning system to meet user requirements while minimizing energy consumption.

Many office buildings have recently been built with under-floor mechanical distribution rather than the more standard distribution in a ceiling plenum. The advantage of this approach is that air travels at slower speed through the system, and large fans are not required to blow cool air down from the ceiling. The cool air is distributed at floor level, where people are working, then slowly rises as it warms in the space. In an office environment, the raised floor offers flexibility, because under-floor utilities can be reconfigured should the interior layout change. One concern in adapting this system to libraries is the weight of library shelving above raised floors; the system has been used successfully at the Vancouver Public Library, however. Low-velocity air systems reduce frictional drag on air moving through the duct wall, as does the use of spiral or cylindrical ductwork.

Proper testing and balancing of systems is of crucial importance, because mechanical systems often do not perform correctly when first installed. One method now acquiring wide support is the hiring of an independent commissioning agent. The commissioning agent may be hired during the design phase to check the engineers' performance, criteria, and design methods. The agent is then retained to rigorously test the mechanical system installed by the contractor to verify that it satisfies the design criteria. These reviews are more thorough than those that have traditionally been provided by design engineers, who check the work for general conformance to the design intent.

Training of the owner's staff in the use of the mechanical equipment is also crucial, as is the provision of a full set of maintenance manuals and warranties. The owner's representatives should be involved throughout the design and construction of the project.

Water Conservation

Water use is an increasing concern in libraries and other buildings. Polluted runoff into storm-water systems and eventually into watersheds is regulated in many areas. Plants and a reduction in the quantity of nonpermeable surfaces reduce runoff, as does the construction of artificial wetlands, which use biological methods to purify groundwater. Rainwater can be harvested in cisterns for a variety of nonpotable uses, as can recycled groundwater. The use of sprinklers to irrigate library sites is unsustainable and should be discouraged or replaced by drip irrigation. In dry areas, drought-tolerant plants should be specified.

Inside the library, low-flow toilet fixtures should be specified. Some builders have gone further, specifying composting toilets, which significantly lower both water use and wastewater treatment requirements. Localized wastewater treatment, either through constructed wetlands or other methods, should be investigated.

CONCLUSION: A VARIETY OF APPROACHES

A sustainable approach to the design and maintenance of library buildings does not involve a simple grand strategy, applicable to all situations in all places. Rather, it represents a commonsense approach to design that is a response to local environmental and economic conditions, one that seeks to create a built environment that is sympathetic and in tune with the natural world. Sustainable design affects all aspects of the building process, from the selection of an appropriate site to determining the best building shape and orientation, using appropriate materials and methods of construction, and designing efficient mechanical and lighting systems. Design decisions can have significant, long-term impacts on the cost of maintaining a library, as well as its durability. A truly sustainable library building requires an understanding of time-tested traditional approaches, an analytical outlook, and an openness to exploring new technologies. As a publicly funded project that reflects a community's highest aspirations, a public library in the new century should be a sustainable building that anticipates the resource needs of future generations of readers.

4 AN OUNCE OF PREVENTION: LIBRARY DIRECTORS AND THE DESIGNING OF PUBLIC LIBRARIES

Valerie L. Meyer

Who better to design a library than a librarian? Yes, you can design a library, especially when you consider your experience combined with your fact-finding and professional organizing abilities and your excellent customer service skills. All of this translates into a body of knowledge and a set of credentials that put you in the perfect position for hands-on participation in the planning and design of your library. The expertise of architects who specialize in library design and space planning will complement the knowledge you bring to the table, and it is vitally important that a librarian participate in the design and planning process as a full-fledged member of the design team.

CHILDREN'S DEPARTMENTS

When designing a children's department, there are a number of important factors to consider. How large is your community's youth population? What percentage of your library's circulation is in juvenile materials? What is the desired collection size? What is the status of school libraries in your community? What is your staffing level? What types of programs does your library offer? Do you want to provide study and reading space? What are the computer/technology needs? What are your storage/workroom needs?

Library staff can provide information to address and answer these questions. In turn, this information can be incorporated into the building program. It may also be necessary to prioritize those features of your children's department that are considered most important. For example, if your community has a large youth population and a high percentage of circulation is in juvenile materials, then the design of the children's department should reflect that in its allocation of square footage. If local school library collections are minimal, it is a given that students will be using the public library collection. Speaking of collections, juvenile collections include many formats, from picture books to multimedia kits. It is wise to investigate the various types of shelving units for each, and their versatility. If your children's department staffing level will not increase, it is very important to consider efficient placement of the public service desk so that the entire dedicated space can be served and observed, including any public-access computers with Internet connections. If story-time programs are an integral component of your service plan, will there be adequate space with comfortable seating (floor or bench)? Or will these programs be presented in another venue, such as a community or multipurpose room? What about space for strollers? Is it important that your library provide quiet study and reading space for after-school programs? Is storage space adequate for books, puppets, program props, and reading-program supplies?

YOUNG ADULT SERVICES

As a librarian, there is nothing more gratifying and satisfying than seeing young adults using the library. Will it be possible to dedicate space for a young adult area? If your library has a teen advisory board or council, can you solicit their input? You may receive the following recommendations: space to display art; comfortable furniture; study space in which noise is tolerated and welcomed; computer workstations with Internet access; and separate magazine, CD, video, and DVD collections. Again, it may be necessary to prioritize design features, but if at all possible, providing dedicated space for young adult study and collaboration will encourage and be appreciated by teen patrons.

MULTIMEDIA COLLECTIONS

Libraries aren't just for books anymore. Alas, many patrons don't seem to think this way, perhaps because they don't know that libraries now have videos, DVDs, CDs, books on CDs and audiotapes, and ebooks. Don't overlook making the large print collection very accessible for older patrons, who may have some visual impairment and find large type comfortable reading. Be certain also to use tilted lower shelves so the call numbers and wording on the spines can be read easily. How can these multimedia collections be incorporated into the design of a new library and thus become more visible and accepted? One way is to locate them together in a very accessible area of the library, close to the entrance or checkout area. These multimedia collections also require their own types of shelving and display, which can be used to your advantage for promotion.

POPULAR MATERIALS

"Where are the new books?" This is probably the second most-asked question in libraries. (The first will be discussed later in this chapter.) New books are popular. Isn't it the first thing you look for when you visit a library? Your patrons are no different. If possible, a new-book collection, circulating or rental, should be easily identified and conveniently located, whether that be near the checkout desk, near the entrance, or near the first point of contact with library staff. Also, size is not the most important consideration; a large new-book collection can invite complacency, meaning that the space should be dedicated to new materials. Your library defines that, however.

LOCAL HISTORY

If the provision of a local-history area is indicated in your building program, it is possible that a local-history collection has already been established in your library. If so, what are the challenges you have faced with this collection? Accessibility? Storage? Security? Display? Who owns the collection, the library or an outside stakeholder group? Will the area be staffed? Ideal features of a local-history collection include locking display shelves for materials and exhibits; locking lateral files large enough to house clippings, pamphlets, and maps; and locking cabinets for scrapbooks, manuscripts, and other ephemera. Is there adequate space to view these materials and to conduct research? Are there special equipment needs such as microform readers and printers? Do staff have a clear view of the area?

GENEALOGY

A genealogy collection may not be included in your library's building program, but if one is, here are some facts to consider. Is this collection owned by the library or an outside stakeholder group? Now would be a good opportunity to mention the benefits of working with stakeholder groups in the library (and there are benefits). These groups can provide an invaluable service as volunteers who are extremely knowledgeable about their respective subject matter. In order to work effectively together and so that there is a clear understanding of the responsibilities of each party, a memorandum of understanding (MOU) should be drafted and signed by the library and the stakeholder group. Defined in the MOU should be issues such as the amount of allocated space the group will have, technology needs and who pays for or provides what, how the collection will be managed (acquired, cataloged, processed, and made accessible), and who will be responsible for providing assistance to the public.

FICTION AND NONFICTION COLLECTIONS

How your fiction collection is organized is a matter of patron and staff preference. Fiction collections lend themselves to browsing. Options to consider are genre collections or intershelving all materials, including paperbacks, classics, and short-story collections. If your library has a foreign language or international language collection, consider its placement. Is it easily identifiable, and are all materials, books, magazines, and newspapers located together?

Nonfiction collections, on the other hand, often need staff interpretation. The closer the collection is located to a public service desk, the more efficient it is for staff to accompany patrons to the shelves to explain the collection and show them the materials.

REFERENCE/INFORMATION COLLECTIONS

Reference collections located conveniently close to the reference/information desk are efficient for staff and patrons alike. How libraries organize their reference collections can be related to how their patrons use the collections. Some libraries separate subject collections such as business, health, and consumer education. If your library collects public documents or maintains a vertical file, consider these space needs as well.

Once the location and designation of the library's collections are determined, what about all the other features that are found in libraries today? Decisions about what shall and shall not be incorporated into your library are determined by your building program, but how do you make those decisions? The following is a discussion of those features and how they have become an integral part of today's modern public library.

DONOR-RECOGNITION AREAS

This area may not be optional but instead may be politically directed. There are a number of ways that donors (past, present, and future) can be recognized, from the traditional nameplates, donor books on a donor shelf, donor tree, donor bricks, to donor names etched on a fossil wall panel. A donor-recognition area should be in a visible location, and there should be some protocol in place that indicates who is responsible for keeping the donor information up to date and consistent.

ART GALLERY AND DISPLAY AREAS

What about art? "Good art maketh glad the heart of man" (Krewson 2003). The library as a public venue for the display of art is not a new concept, but the planning of space for art is. If gallery or display space is included in your building program, planning for this should be accompanied by a policy defining what can and cannot be displayed and who will be responsible for the displays. Display cases should be locking and lighted, and, again, a policy that defines what can and cannot be displayed should be in place. Managing art displays can be time-consuming, yet it can also be a very popular and well-received feature of your library.

QUIET/STUDY SPACE

Today's public libraries are working libraries. When confronted by patrons who want to know why the library is so noisy, I respond with this statement. I also mention that there is a certain amount of collaboration between patron and librarian, patron and patron, and librarian and librarian. Nevertheless, libraries need to offer the public some designated quiet/study space, which can range from a small seating area identified with discreet table signs to actual study or conference rooms. A study room or rooms will be in high demand by your patrons, and you may wish to consider wiring these rooms for technology. Also consider adequate windows and whiteboards.

COMMUNITY/MULTIPURPOSE ROOMS

In many communities, meeting-room space is at a premium and is in demand by nonprofit and commercial entities alike. If a community room can be included in the library's design, it will be a frequently used and popular feature. When considering the size of the community/multipurpose room, it is helpful to know what other public meeting spaces are available in the community and what are their restrictions or limitations in terms of size. Can your library's space be larger? Also to be considered is how the public will access the community room. Will the room have its own separate entrance, with a security system, that enables the room to be used when the library is closed? Other design features to consider are restrooms and adequate storage space for tables, chairs, and equipment. Lighting for different types of events taking place during the day and evening is also important. If the room will offer audiovisual capabilities, consider the necessary cabling for technology, including Internet access and videoconferencing. Other design features to consider are projection screens, whiteboards, fabric wall coverings for displays, and durable floor coverings. Kitchens should include such design features as garbage disposals, dishwashers, and serving windows. Locking cabinets, deep enough for large serving trays and coffee urns, are also a good idea.

ENTREPRENEURIAL SPACE

This may be the first time the term *entrepreneurial space* has been used in writing, but it is a term I use when describing bookstores, rental collections, coffee bars, and locations for that most recent and innovative activity: passport acceptance service. More and more libraries are looking for ways to enhance revenues, and if this trend is sanctioned and appropriate for your community, space for it should be included in the library design. Passport acceptance service does involve some degree of privacy, and people will need a place to sit and wait with an opportunity to read, on a bulletin board, about the application process. Bookstores, usually operated by library Friends groups, can be very popular and bring nonlibrary users into the library. The size of a bookstore should be relative to the size of the library and, once again, there should be some type of formal agreement between the library and the organization that will operate it. Clearly understood should be the designation of storage space, maintenance, cleaning, and staffing. Location of a bookstore within a library will determine its level of visibility and foot traffic: The closer it is located to the library's entrance, the more activity it will see. Another popular feature of bookstores is coffee service; can space be created for coffee sales? Rental collections (usually books, videos, DVDs, and CDs) also perform well when they are located in high-visibility, heavy traffic areas, near circulation desks and entryways.

WORKROOMS

Workrooms are more than just rooms to work in; they are places where staff and volunteers meet and collaborate. Workrooms are also storerooms and storage rooms, and more often than not, they house photocopiers, printers, folding and laminating machines, recycle paper bins, safes, lockers, coat racks, and videotape cleaners. They also serve as book-return areas and space as needed for cart storage, shelving, resensitizing, mending, and book repair. Workroom space, as nonpublic space, is hard to sell, meaning that it must be in proportion to the size of the library. It is important to plan how the workroom will be designed for the library. Will workroom spaces each have only a single function (technical services, circulation, office space), or will one large space be divided for these different functions? Consider the existing library's space deficiencies and plan accordingly. Some considerations might be these: Does your library outsource its acquisitions, cataloging, and processing? Does your library use volunteers? Will the workroom also serve as office space for librarians? If so, it is important to create adequately sized workstations to house computers, printers, and filing space, as well as room for privacy. If the workroom will be used as an area for materials check-in, is there a safe efficient path for materials to move from terminals to resensitizing, to carts or sorting shelves? Are aisles and passageways wide enough for book carts? Is there designated space for cart storage? Are countertops the correct height for their specific functions? Also consider the type of materials used—the more durable the better, such as stainless steel or molded countertop. Libraries receive many deliveries, and it is very convenient—for staff and the delivery service—to have a receiving door in the workroom, with convenient and safe loading-zone parking outside. Also to be considered is convenient access to the site's refuse disposal bins (including recycling receptacles), ideally located just outside the building's workroom and receiving area.

Another component of nonpublic workspace is the staff/volunteer lounge. The lounge should be large enough to accommodate a couch, table, chairs, refrigerator, and perhaps soft drink and/or snack machines (with appropriate anchoring and electrical connections). Depending on the size of the library and the number of employees and volunteers, separate staff restrooms compliant with the Americans with Disabilities Act are necessary and preferred.

REFERENCE

Krewson, Jeff. 2003. www.jeffkrewson.com (accessed February 2003).

PART II
RALLYING SUPPORT

5 COMMUNITY INVOLVEMENT IN THE LIBRARY CONSTRUCTION PROCESS

Carol Speicher

INTRODUCTION

At some point, someone will come up with the idea that a new or remodeled library is what the community needs. That person will begin to share the thought with others. Eventually, the library director may be brought into the discussion. Congratulations! Look forward to this day and *be prepared for it*.

Because you are reading this book, you have probably already begun thinking about why a new or remodeled library facility is needed. If you haven't already done so, take the time to jot down all those reasons. Add to them whenever you experience an "If only we had the space for . . ." moment.

Once you fill a few pages with the many reasons why, type them so that they are brief yet understandable. Be prepared to make additions to the list and many copies of what will become an easy-to-read handout as the months and perhaps years go by. You will need to share this with the supporters of the library project as well as the naysayers.

When determining that a new or remodeled library facility is needed, you are looking toward the future of the community. You are basing the library's needs on the facts: Statistics show the library is currently being well used, there has been a constant increase in use, and you expect that trend to continue. The library also has programs and services in place or in the planning stages that will bring in more patrons and require additional space. Demands for increased technology have outpaced the current facility both in terms of patron use and building infrastructure. Jot down all of the issues that you feel are both today's and tomorrow's needs for a new library.

To gage whether or not the community as a whole supports the idea of a new or remodeled library, a survey of the community can be undertaken, either in conjunction with other needs surveys that the city might be working on or as a standalone questionnaire prepared and disseminated through a variety of methods. There are many books available on survey design, focus-group makeup, and best methods of obtaining community input. The local chamber of commerce and other civic groups may also have survey expertise that they are willing to share. If you have a regional library system or a state library, search for the person with a background in library construction. Call on him or her frequently for advice and assistance.

Remember, you're not alone. There are many other librarians in your state or region who have been through this process before. Contact them often with questions, as well as for reassurance. They will be happy to share horror stories with you and also examples of success. These are the people who understand the value of libraries.

If there is available funding, it may be worthwhile to research the possibility of hiring a qualified library building consultant. The expertise brought to the project by a consultant who is an expert in the field can alleviate many concerns, helping the local building committee to make the best decisions with a minimum of mistakes. Lists of library building consultants are available through your regional library system, the state library, or from the American Library Association. Also check with other librarians in communities that have recently completed library-construction projects.

As you read through this chapter, you will be reminded again and again that communication on every level and at every turn is the key to a successful library building or remodeling project. Communication will be important in working with the local media to help them understand current and proposed library programming and facility needs. Community input is valuable when designing and disseminating needs surveys and in sharing the survey results, in providing a constant flow of information to the members of the various committees who will eventually be involved in the library fund-raising and building process. Communication with the public from beginning to end of the construction project will pay off in enthusiasm and long-term library support.

THE LIBRARY DIRECTOR AS KEY PLAYER

You as the library director will want to take a leadership role in the entire building or remodeling process. This does not mean that you will chair the myriad committees, or that your name will be at the top of the list when accolades are handed out. It does mean that you want to be involved in guiding others concerned with the project, helping them to make educated decisions in the best interests of the new library facility. To quote twentieth-century diplomat Daniele Vare, "Diplomacy is the art of getting what we want" (Vare 1938, 24).

As insiders, you and the staff are in the best position to *know libraries*. As the library director, you should be an authority. This is a situation where you may not want to wait to be asked your opinion because you may never be consulted. Be prepared to speak in support of the best interests of the new library facility. A case in point is the report of an architect who was hired by a library foundation to do a feasibility study of the current library facility in a small but growing community. He concluded that the building could be remodeled and detailed the process that the remodeling should take.

But building renovation will not change the fact that current on-street parking is woefully inadequate, compounded by the volume of people visiting the senior center across the street from the library. The number of users at both the senior center and at a remodeled library will predictably increase, greatly exacerbating the problem. The architect mentioned only the parking issue in his report, however.

Because they experience the parking problem themselves and hear about it in the form of patron complaints, the library staff are well aware of the situation. The library director needs to bring this important issue to the attention of the library foundation for discussion early in the process.

Most architects, contractors, and other building professionals simply do not have the librarians' knowledge regarding library operations. Even building committee members who are frequent library users cannot be expected to understand the day-to-day operation of the library. All of the books, articles, videos, and experienced librarians will tell you not to assume that someone else understands better than you do what the needs of a new facility might be. Once you make it through the construction process, you and the library staff may be "living" in this new facility for years to come.

COMMITTEE FORMATION

Eventually the library board and foundation, Friends of the Library, and community members decide that it is time to begin to make this dream of a new or remodeled facility a reality. A few people may meet informally to review the "reasons why" list prepared by the library staff and to add a few reasons of their own, as well as to discuss the feasibility of embarking on the project at this time. It is wise to also meet early in the process with the library's main funding body— the town or city council, county commissioners, and so on. Members of these groups will want to know early in the process what is being considered and why. They may have questions, may point out other community projects that are being undertaken, or may have valuable suggestions. Their support is often a prerequisite to any further action. Again, communication is the key.

In the majority of communities with which I have worked, a library foundation serves as the umbrella organization responsible for holding the majority of funds raised for library construction. These foundations have IRS 501(c)3 nonprofit designation. Often, the foundation holds title to the property until completion of the project, at which time it is formally turned over to the city.

It is important to make certain that everyone understands which entity has the legal decision-making responsibility for the construction project in the event that disagreements arise. In many cases, that responsibility falls to the library foundation, ideally with input and support from the library board and a building committee. State statutes and local city ordinances may determine this. It may be wise to obtain an attorney's advice, because the issue needs to be clarified very early in the process.

Discussion has now progressed to the stage in which someone suggests that a building committee be formed, along with a publicity committee and a fund-raising committee. Depending on the size of the project, these committees can be one and the same. You need to think about helpful people in the community and call them.

GROUND RULES

Usually the foundation and the library board are well represented on the building committee and any other committees that may be formed, but they should not be the only members. This is the community's library, and as such, it should include additional area residents. Bringing together community members with diverse backgrounds and interests, yet who can successfully form a cohesive working unit, is very important to the success of any project. No one person should be saddled with the responsibility of coming up with the names of those most capable for nomination to these committees.

The formation of an ad hoc nominating committee, some of whom might ultimately be included for consideration on the other committees, may be the best method for coming up with recommendations. Members of the nominating committee should plan to attend meetings of the library board, Friends group, and the foundation, asking for their suggestions. The library staff also need to provide input.

Meeting minutes must be taken by every committee involved and at every stage of the project. They should be kept current, made available for public review, and shared with all who ask. These minutes should help to substantiate the fact that all committees are working for the good of the community, which may be difficult to prove if concerns arise later and no record of meeting proceedings were kept. Written minutes from the previous meeting should be reviewed at each committee meeting, as they will help to refresh earlier discussions, reduce backtracking on issues that were resolved, and help the members to focus on current meeting topics.

MAKEUP OF COMMITTEES

What kinds of expertise are we looking for? People with business acumen, accounting and construction backgrounds; people with grant-writing and fund-raising expertise; respected community leaders with a knack for diplomacy, consensus building, project management, and organization. Let's not forget library patrons, members of the Friends, members of the library foundation, and certainly members of the board of trustees. Don't overlook community members who would be perfect for this project but are currently involved in many other activities. They may be quite adept at handling several tasks at once.

Do not bypass someone who might make a significant contribution to the project because of the possibility of conflict of interest. First discuss conflict-of-interest issues with an attorney who can advise you on the best route to take.

My experience has been that, when asking people to serve on committees, common sense is one of the most necessary assets. It will come into play time and time again as various issues are discussed and argued. Do not overlook people who may not have any noteworthy background other than the use of common sense in getting things accomplished. All should know that the library director will attend every meeting of every committee. As with every successful committee, ground rules need to be discussed and accepted during the first meetings. Even with an able chairperson skilled at reaching group consensus, seldom will the group agree on every issue that comes before the committee. Revisiting the ground rules from time to time will help the group over the rough spots. A primary goal of the committees involved in this project is to work cooperatively in the best interests of the community's library. Representatives from all committees will want to meet together on a regular basis to keep abreast of each others' activities. The design of an overall activity/timeline that is kept up to date and shared by all is a key to successful communication.

For purposes of simplicity, I will briefly describe the general responsibilities of three types of committees that may be responsible for a library construction or remodeling project.

BUILDING COMMITTEE

The building committee usually has the overall responsibility of seeing the entire project through to completion. They are the big-picture people who must also be aware of the need for accuracy in details. Vision, leadership, and cooperation are assets that cannot be overemphasized.

Once the members of the building committee have been chosen, the library director can help the members to better understand the inner workings of library operations by giving them a tour of the current facility. Plan your tour stops well beforehand (the areas of importance that you want to stress to the building committee). Include a brief handout highlighting these same points. Plan a dress rehearsal by giving the same tour to library staff. Their input during this trial run will help you add key points to the final presentation to the committee.

Don't expect that all committee members will realize that you want two exits from behind the circulation desk, why a computer lab should not be located next to a wall of windows, or why the quiet reading area should be placed somewhere other than next to the children's section. Your tour will point out the need for the inclusion of many of the same areas in a new or remodeled facility as in the current library. (Yes, the library still needs a staff workroom, book drop, and space for such patron use equipment as copy machines, microfilm reader/printers, and patron access to automated catalogs.) The tour will also explain the need for new or expanded spaces.

Ask a member of the library board to share with the building committee the board's goals for future library services and programs, and to describe how a new facility will help to meet those goals. This is the ideal time to point out, in the form of another handout, how much library floor space is actually needed. Do the math ahead of time. There are several books available that provide guidelines for library space planning. In my fourteen years as a library consultant, the lack of allowance for adequate space to meet the needs of the next generation of library users has been a major concern. Many newer facilities are already inadequate.

It is not possible for all of the building committee members to initially be aware of every one of these issues without an introduction to the library, its operation, and proposed additions in services. Although this information gathering may be seen as time-consuming for those who just want to dive in, the knowledge gained from this process will pay big dividends in the coming months as the committee members begin their work.

The building committee may have the luxury of hiring a project manager who works to oversee their interests. In many cases, the library director becomes the unofficial project manager. This committee will meet with architects, choose an architectural plan, oversee the letting of bids, and work closely with contractors and perhaps interior designers.

This committee has the monumental task of conveying to the architect its vision of the perfect library at a reasonable cost. How do the members develop this vision? One way is to look at other communities' visions. This requires travel, and it helps if there is a travel allowance available to encourage members to find out more about buildings in general and library construction in particular. There really is no substitute for this, as it can change the way that committee members think about libraries.

For those who feel that they simply cannot get away, the members who do travel should bring back interior and exterior photos of buildings that they have visited, sharing with the other committee members those points that they felt were worth noting. Librarians and those who have completed construction projects are usually eager to tell their stories of what worked and what didn't. They want to share successes as well as any mistakes that happened along the way. It may fall to the library director and one or two building committee members to make these trips, but they will be well worth the time and effort. There are books available that list what to look for in new construction, and a review of these prior to visiting libraries and other buildings should help the group to focus on certain concepts that may add to or detract from a building.

After the building committee members have had the opportunity to discuss their own experiences with similar projects, make site visits, talk to people who have been there, and perhaps invite experts to speak to the group (such as regional or state library consultants, librarians and building committee members from other cities), they will want to assimilate all of this information. Now is the time to form these ideas and suggestions into a cohesive program of wants and don't-wants for the new facility. They should be copied, dated, and shared at every meeting, with changes incorporated along the way. This list will become very important when the building committee begins to meet with architects.

PUBLICITY AND PROMOTION COMMITTEE

Communication about the library building or remodeling project, or lack of it, can make or break the entire endeavor. Informing the public about the proposed project needs to be handled professionally. This is the responsibility of the publicity committee. One person, often the chair or another person who feels comfortable with the job, serves as the contact through which all information is distributed. The concept of having only one contact person cannot be over-stressed, as it will decrease the amount of misinformation that goes to the public concerning the project.

Communicate early and often. From the official announcement of the possi-bility of a library project to the building dedication or open house to celebrate the remodeling or addition, a weekly undertaking should be press releases, news-paper columns, photo opportunities and radio interviews. The more successful this communication is, the better accepted the project will be and the easier and more successful the actual fund-raising will become. This is true no matter what the size of the community. Don't assume that "we're a small town; everyone al-ready knows what's happening." What they do know may be incorrect, thus se-verely hampering progress.

In order to provide accurate, up-to-date information, one or more members of the publicity committee must attend all meetings of the other committees. Internal as well as external communication is vital to a successful building proj-ect. The publicity committee has the task of preparing a packet of information that will be shared with the local media. This information can be used again and again in many different settings and changed as needed.

A brief history of the library is often included. A brochure listing the needs of the library and showing (perhaps with the aid of photographs) why the cur-rent facility cannot meet those needs is also standard. Including several photo-graphs of patrons (with their permission) enjoying the library's services is also appropriate. List additional programs and services that a new or expanded facil-ity might provide.

Library statistics are very helpful for media purposes. Include circulation numbers and use statistics for computers, meeting rooms, open hours, everything that shows increased library use over the years. List the current square footage of the present facility compared to recommended space needs.

After an architect has been chosen, the packet should contain the architec-tural rendering depicting both the outside and inside of the proposed library fa-cility. Any factual information regarding construction that the committee deems of value should be included. Cost estimates are important, along with plans as to how the proposed funding will be obtained.

Members of all the committees should have copies of these packets to share with others, and they need to become very familiar with the information contained therein. It will pay off in accurate communication about the building project and will increase project support. No matter what size the community, many worthwhile projects are doomed by inaccurate information shared at the coffee shop, hairdresser's, barber's, and so on. No one knows how such rumors start, but it takes a lot of work to stop them once they are in circulation.

Example: Jim says to Oscar, in the coffee shop, "I hear that new library is going to cost us an arm and a leg, and we'll never be able to afford the utility bills. Why do we need a new building anyway? No one uses libraries anymore."

Oscar replies, "Well, you know Jim, I'm serving on the building committee, and I've heard the same rumors. Let me give you some facts. In this packet I'm carrying is a wealth of information refuting these fallacies. Based on similar types of architecture, the new building is going to be very cost effective, both in construction and in maintenance. Here are some of the features to control utility expenses. It will have new thermal glass windows to reduce the loss of heat or cooling, in season. Lighting will be much better and less costly because of improved light bulbs and fluorescent tubes. The building will be placed on the site so more natural light will enter through the windows, saving more electric power. As for use of the library, it has increased every year for the past ten years. Look at this report of service statistics. Last year circulation of the collections was double that of five years ago. Reference questions tripled in number in the same time period. We need this new building, and Jim, you'll be happy, too, when you see it and use it. Please remember this information when you talk to our neighbors about the new library."

Multiply many times over this scenario of speaking knowledgeably and positively about the library project, and support for the endeavor can be appreciably increased. Fund-raising Committee members who call on people to ask for donations will take presentation packets with them and leave them with donors and potential donors. In addition to including the kinds of information already discussed, these packets may also contain suggested donation levels, if this is a method the committee has chosen, as well as information on additional giving opportunities such as engraved bricks and furnishings and the opportunity to name the building, rooms, or specific areas within the building. Everything should be in writing for the prospective donor to review, which is why these presentation packets are so worthwhile.

If there is no publicity committee, then the fund-raising committee often shoulders these responsibilities, but the duties still remain important.

FUND-RAISING COMMITTEE

This group has the daunting task of making certain that enough funds are acquired to pay for the entire project. In all but a few of the communities I have worked with, the people responsible for raising funds worked the hardest and lost the most sleep. Burnout of members of this committee is often quite high.

Only in a perfect world will everything fall into place and the necessary funds be acquired with a minimum of effort.

Committee members must be goodwill ambassadors of the library construction project. They must, in effect, do everything right in order to obtain the needed dollars in a minimum of time, whether through donations, grants, bond issues, city dollars, a variety of fund-raising projects, or a combination of one or more of these.

The responsibilities of fund-raising committees are not for the faint of heart. I have seen rapid turnover once members realized just what was expected of them. Raising money, whether a few thousand dollars for a small remodeling or several million for a new facility, can be a challenging job that not everyone can or should accept. It is important that members of this committee be informed early in the project exactly what they will be asked to accomplish, along with suggestions as to how they can accomplish it. Members must have access to all of the information: funds on hand and their sources, expected revenue and exactly where it will come from, and a breakdown of planned expenses. No rose-colored glasses here.

For instance, the majority of construction dollars may have to come from individual donations. If so, every member of the fund-raising committee should be given the opportunity to attend a fund-raising workshop that covers the nuts and bolts of how to ask for money. Often the facilitators will walk the participants through the steps of asking for donations. Even so, it is a skill that not everyone can acquire, and I have seen few people born with this admirable ability. There are many books and videos available on fund-raising and how to make requests for major donations. These can be very helpful. Regional and state library consultants may also be able to share their expertise in this area.

After the books and videos are reviewed and experiences shared, nothing beats continuous practice. Even in the best situations, it can be very difficult to ask for money. But it must be done, and in a way that makes the donor feel good about doing it, perhaps even willing to encourage friends and relatives to do the same.

Not everyone on the committee must be able to sit down one-on-one with a prospective donor and successfully ask for money. On the other hand, someone will probably have to be responsible for this aspect of fund-raising. In my experience, this is the only way to obtain sizable personal donations.

Success seems to beget success. It certainly increases self-confidence on the part of the fund-raisers. Again, communication with both current and former members of the community is of utmost importance. Unless people believe that a new or remodeled library is needed and that it will become a reality, they are often reluctant to support the project.

Some library foundations have hired the services of professional fund-raisers to bring in the money needed for new or remodeled libraries. The communities I have worked with have not had particular success with this method. Nothing seems to surpass the simple plan of meeting personally with individual friends, neighbors, and relatives to ask for donations to better the hometown.

Inexperienced fund-raisers often believe that charitable foundations are the best source of large grants. Although there are several foundations that are interested in making donations for library construction or remodeling, most of them have specific criteria that must be met. For example, the organization may require that 50 to 75 percent of the funds be raised locally before the grant application will be considered. Other stipulations might be that the parent organization does business in that community or that the library will be named after the foundation. The foundation's annual allotment of funds may be expended for the current year, or the entity's focus of giving may have changed. I urge fund-raisers not to put all of their eggs into one basket when it comes to grants but instead to try to determine the correct mix of contributions for the project.

The committee may devise several methods of increasing public awareness and may undertake many projects to raise funds. The types of programs that can be used as fund-raisers are numerous, and several books are available on how to successfully undertake everything from raffles to silent auctions, from gala dinners to fund-raising on the Web. As someone who had personal experience raising money for a library addition once told me, "Soup suppers won't do it." Although these projects can be time-consuming and may not garner a great deal of money, they do serve to publicize the fact that funds are needed for the new facility in a way that a simple newspaper article cannot. They also allow community members to come together in a show of support and enthusiasm for the project.

Throughout the fund-raising process, information on the status of the project needs to be *publicized*. How much has been raised so far and where did it come from? Some donors may prefer to remain anonymous, but who in the community is willing to come forward to talk about his or her donation and to encourage others to do their part? No one should be overlooked. Major contributions may come from those whom you least expect to make a donation if they are given the personal opportunity.

CONCLUSION

This very brief overview of community involvement in the construction project should help you to build not only a new or remodeled facility but also a foundation for long-term library use and support. Throughout the process, there will be good days and bad days, times of exuberance and feelings of defeat. The entire project may take much longer than you expected. You will be working with people from diverse backgrounds and dealing with a wide range of issues. There will be nights of seemingly endless meetings and occasions when you will wish for expertise in human relations, accounting, or construction rather than skills in referencing or cataloging.

When you begin to doubt that all of the effort will be worthwhile, rely on colleagues in the library profession who have been through similar building projects. They will be the first to tell you inspiring stories of strengthened community pride and a very noticeable increase in library use. Once the project is complete, you will be trading worries about where construction money will come from for concerns about meeting-room scheduling demands and the increased need for popular fiction. And that's just the way it should be. Enjoy!

REFERENCE

Vare, Daniele. 1938. *The Laughing Diplomat*. New York: Doubleday.

SELECTED BIBLIOGRAPHY

Clow, Faye. *Forming and Funding Public Library Foundations*. Chicago: American Library Association, 1993.

Dolnick, Sandy, ed. *Friends of Libraries Sourcebook*. Chicago: American Library Association, 1996.

Grassroots Fundraising: The Kim Klein Video Series. Oakland, CA: Grassroots Institute for Fundraising Training, 1995. Available from Headwaters Fund, 122 West Franklin Avenue, Minneapolis, MN 55404.

McCarthy, Richard C. *Designing Better Libraries: Selecting and Working with Building Professionals*. 2nd ed. Fort Atkinson, WI: Highsmith Press, 1999.

Sannwald, William W. *Checklist of Library Building Design Considerations*. 3rd. ed. Chicago: American Library Association, 1997.

Woodward, Jeannette. *Countdown to a New Library: Managing the Building Project*. Chicago: American Library Association, 2000.

6 GETTING TO YES: THE PUBLIC LIBRARY BUILDING PROCESS IN HENRICO COUNTY, VIRGINIA

Janet C. Woody

Henrico County's 244 square miles lie to the east, west, and north of the city of Richmond, Virginia. According to Census 2000 figures, the current population is 262,300, and the median household income is $50,348. Henrico has a highly regarded school system and a healthy business and development climate, which attract a steady flow of new residents and businesses. The public library system comprises three area libraries, six branch libraries, a municipal law library, and a bookmobile. The newest branch (2001) is a 15,000 square-foot replacement building for a 1,700 square-foot "temporary" fabricated building that served for sixteen years. Henrico has a county manager system of government, with five elected supervisors representing five districts. A library advisory board, one for each district and appointed by the supervisor, provides guidance to the director of libraries, who reports to a deputy county manager.

What can be more exciting than the prospect of embarking on a new library building project? All the best in the American way of life, where free and open access to information and the right to know are cornerstones of democracy, are embodied in a public library building. And, just as important, people like to be entertained, informed, and amused, all incentives for a trip to the public library. So how could anyone hesitate to give an enthusiastic yes to funding for a new public library? Politics can turn a library project into a tempest of conflicting needs and emotions, however. In worst-case scenarios, politicians may engage in a kind of parochialism that may limit their ability to evaluate impartially projects that do not directly benefit the citizens in their home districts, as discussed by Michael D. Shear in his article, "Fairfax Board's Structure Criticized" (*Washington*

Post, August 26, 2001). Shear describes some of the pitfalls of district versus at-large elected officials and the effect on decision making, as does Woodward (2000): "Every library is enmeshed in some sort of political environment. . . . In some libraries they may become such an overriding concern that they jeopardize the success of the project" (p. 6). This chapter describes the experiences of one county's library system and suggests some ways to be prepared for the unexpected in planning for a new building.

Keeping statistics on library use is a normal part of operations and is ex-tremely valuable to a building project. How a building or buildings in a library system are used tells much about how the community views the library and about how the community may react to a proposed building project. As a matter of course, it should be easy to get a report on the use of a building, with all the standard numbers such as circulation, volume count, and visitors each year. Be-yond these standard numbers, it is wise to have on hand a fact sheet for a public library building that is updated at least yearly and includes the following: total square footage with detailed breakdown of square footage for each part of the operation, number of parking places, and any changes or modifications to the building, with the dates and cost of each. The importance of demographics can-not be overstated, and the wise librarian will keep an eye on how the neighbor-hood is or is not changing, as well as looking for any new factors that might change use of the library in the future. These would include ages and demo-graphics of user populations, anticipated changes in school population or school construction, commercial and residential development influencing library use, and ethnic diversity of the area. Some localities require annually updated capital improvement plans, which are the logical vehicle for detailing and presenting needs for library construction. It may be useful to have all of this information readily available, in whatever format is required by a particular jurisdiction, be-cause the political process can bring background issues to the forefront with little advance notice. And, in addition to hard numbers and facts, it is wise to have on hand narrative descriptions of how libraries add to the quality of life of a community, a topic that received much coverage in the library press during 2001. Citizens respond well to reminders that libraries are places of "civic en-gagement" (Preer 2001), and politicians like to hear that tax dollars are well spent in supporting and enhancing the quality of life for their constituents (Al-banese 2001; Vaillancourt and Hughes 2001).

In this case study, an aging, undersized building of 32,000 square feet and a newly elected county supervisor made the right combination for progress to-wards a new, larger facility. As is often the case, a newly elected official brought in new ideas and vision and wanted to respond to those who helped make the election possible. This politician heard many times that the well-used and much-loved library was too small and that parking was terrible. As often occurs, when such complaints are heard often, things began to happen. Also looming large was the need for this building to meet the minimum standards for access required by the Americans with Disabilities Act (ADA). The building originally opened in 1971, with an addition added in 1975; refitting it to meet ADA standards was an expensive and problematic prospect. Parking and usable space would be lost to add an elevator and wheelchair-accessible restrooms. A hard choice had to be made before committing to ADA improvements to this building. The choice turned out to be foregoing ADA improvements, at an approximate cost of $500,000, in favor of constructing a new building. This solution was found to be more practical, as it would address long-standing space issues that ADA improvements would have exacerbated in the existing building.

The location of a new library often can be controversial and fraught with emotion. In this example, that was not the case. Parcels of a usable size were scarce in this magisterial district, and several parcels were purchased near the current library location. The condition of the land and covenants on the use of the land would become issues later, but the choice of the location didn't set off any noticeable public controversies. In fact, the surrounding community was excited about the library being placed on this site. The proposed size of the building, however, was a sticking point and, over time, was scaled back to a size that all concerned could support. Originally, a size of 100,000 gross square feet was proposed, in a county where the largest library building was 32,000 square feet. Such a large new building was understandably a hard sell, and when the time for a bond referendum rolled around, a more reasonable 50,000-square-foot building was presented to the voters, along with a phase two expansion of 25,000 square feet.

The November 2000 bond referendum placed library funding and several other projects on the ballot. To educate and inform voters, several teams of bond speakers were formed, each team composed of representatives from each agency with projects on the ballot: schools, fire, roads, parks, and libraries. These teams were available to speak before civic, business, and community groups or associations. Each agency representative had several minutes to present project details describing what the voters had to consider. The issue for public libraries was the willingness of voters to commit the county to a debt in the multimillions of dollars for two library construction projects. One of these was the building discussed here, and the other a new building in a fast-growing section of the county without nearby library service. Each agency's projects were grouped together for a separate vote. In other words, voters could vote yes or no for all or none of the projects or make a combination yes/no vote. All projects passed, with the libraries receiving a 66-percent-approval rating.

When the bond referendum was completed, an experienced library building consultant was selected using the bid process, and a series of data-gathering events was executed to learn what users wanted from this building. County executives and the board of supervisors were interviewed, as well as library advisory board members. Several small focus-group sessions were held with representatives from different user populations, such as seniors, parents of young children, local business representatives, and teenagers. Library staff were also given opportunities to voice their opinions, and two general public meetings were held, one at night and one on a Saturday morning. Attendance was small at the general public meetings, and one citizen told a staff member not to worry about that, that it only meant "people know the librarians will do it right."

All collected data were assembled into a proposed building program. It was apparent that 63,000 gross square feet were needed to house all the services and collections identified by the public and staff. More of everything seemed to be the desire of those surveyed, with the addition of Sunday hours being the number-one issue. It was apparent from listening to every group that a traditional book- and audio/visual-filled library with all the latest technology would please them. The library as a place for education and self-improvement was a recurring theme in all of the focus groups. It was interesting that some were strongly in favor of a café space, whereas others thought that this was a terrible idea—after all, libraries are for serious business, not drinking coffee!

The dilemma now was to scale back our wish list to fit into the approved 50,000 gross square feet. It was understood that those services and features promised in the bond referendum presentations would have priority and could not be cut or diminished without risk of public ire. The café, computer lab, abundant parking, computers, public meeting rooms, quiet reading room, group-study rooms, and children's area separate from the adult area all had to have their space, as well as allowing space for all those books, magazines, and audiovisual materials that the public wanted. The current building was noted and well used for its large children's area occupying its own floor, separate from other users. To appear to reduce that particular space commitment would be folly.

A scalpel was needed to delicately trim away excess, or nonessential, features without shortchanging any service area or operation. A hard look was taken at shelving needs, particularly for print reference materials and nonfiction. Although it was not difficult to picture a less generous print reference collection, it was more troubling to accept that print nonfiction would have to be a no-growth area, if all of the services mentioned were to be accommodated. It was disappointing to realize that the overcrowded conditions of the past two decades would not be alleviated in phase one, but the phase two expansion would address space needs well. According to the American Library Association (ALA 1995), "Doubling existing space may not provide for growth or for change in service deliveries. If further expansion is suggested but not affordable, then review the needs of the customers and staff and modify the library mission and revise the program to include planning for a second phase of expansion" (p. 3). A somewhat different version of this cautionary statement appears in ALA's Building Blocks for Planning Functional Library Space (2001, 1). Since future expansion was part of our plan, we reviewed the immediate needs and trimmed shelving, storage, and staff workspace (even the restrooms) wherever possible to reach a compromise that would serve immediate needs. This unenviable task completed, the latest square footage estimate stands at about 52,141 gross square feet of building area. It remains to be seen if, once design begins, we can meet all of our ambitious goals for services and collections and not exceed the 50,000 square foot size that was approved by the county board.

Adding to the space challenge, several property concerns were raised during the development of the building program. The water table on the chosen site is very high, there is a need for a water retention area, and there are height restrictions on any construction, placed there by covenant with the neighbors many years ago. A portion at the edge of one parcel has a 25-foot restriction, and the remaining land has a 35-foot height restriction. A post office access road needs to be moved to free some of the land for library development. Because of the odd shape of the parcels, parking may have to be split between two or more areas, thus causing what many will perceive as too long a walk to the building entrance. These conditions, on top of the space challenge, will make the design process very challenging. None of the conditions listed are unsolvable when creative design and compromise are employed. Political review will come into the picture again, as is desirable on a public building project.

REFERENCES

Albanese, Andrew Richard. 2001. "Libraries as Equity Building Blocks." *Library Journal* 126 (9): 40–43.

American Library Association, Library Administration and Management Association, Buildings and Equipment Section, Functional Space Requirements Committee. 1995. *Building Blocks for Library Space*. Lanham, MD: Scarecrow Press.

———. 2001. *Building Blocks for Planning Functional Library Space*. Lanham, MD: Scarecrow Press.

Preer, Jean. 2001. "Where Are Libraries in Bowling Alone?" *American Libraries* 32 (8): 60–62.

Vaillancourt, Renee, and Kathleen Hughes, eds. 2001. Public Libraries Build Sustainable Communities [Special issue]. *Public Libraries* 40 (1).

Woodward, Jeannette. 2000. *Countdown to a New Library: Managing the Building Project*. Chicago: American Library Association.

PART III
KEY ISSUES FOR PLANNING

7 RETAIL TECHNOLOGY APPLICATIONS AND THEIR ROLE IN THE MODERN LIBRARY

John Stanley

Why is a retail consultant involved in a book about libraries? It is because I believe libraries are one category in the world of retailing, and what works in retail stores works in libraries. When I first introduced this concept to librarians, they often found the thought concerning and demeaning, but it's a fact of life. Librarians need to be aware of retail trends and to adapt the relevant aspects into their libraries.

My definition of retailing is a situation in which an organization has a transaction with a consumer. The only difference between Barnes and Noble and the local library is that the library has a wider range of transactions, more return customers, and very little money changes hands (but even that is changing).

To illustrate how retail skills can enhance your library service I will illustrate the concepts in this chapter by using a case study, the Brisbane City Library Service in Queensland, Australia.

Brisbane City Council had a vision. That vision was to create the most livable city in the Asia-Pacific region within a ten-year strategic plan. As far as residents of Brisbane are concerned, the biggest exposure they have to the council is via their local libraries. Therefore, there was a need for the libraries to be seen as innovative facilities, using best practices and, especially important, becoming the ideal community hub in the eyes of the local residents.

Just as a leading edge retailer would have social interactive skills, excellent product knowledge, a desired physical image, merchandise effectively, and build displays with flair within corporate guidelines, so should a library. In 2002, Brisbane City Library Services are doing this exceptionally well; having implemented the best practices of retail technology, they now excel.

Libraries are now an integral part of the retail mix, and Toowong Library is situated in a shopping center.

This chapter will take you through the logical sequence I went through in training the library staff. My objective is to help you go through the same sequence in your own library.

CONSUMER DATA ARE CRITICAL

First, don't change anything because you think it's a good idea. Change should take place to enhance the consumer's experience. You therefore need to talk to your consumers and local residents and get their views.

In Brisbane, data were amassed over a number of years; consumers were telling the library service that their libraries were considered difficult to navigate. Customers were unaware of the services and range of products available and were not being inspired to borrow or request more books than they had initially planned.

Brisbane had a challenge, customers had needs and wants that had to be addressed, and the council had a limited budget. The key was to increase customer awareness while maximizing value for the expenditure of public funds. The answer was a clear and defined retail strategy.

External graphics must attract nonlibrary and library users to grow the market.

PLAY THE IMAGE GAME

Every business plays the image game; libraries are no exception. The second strategy, after listening to your customers, is to ensure that the library image is acceptable to existing customers and attracts new customers. Customers make an image decision in ten seconds. You have to make those ten seconds, or moments of truth, count in a positive way.

In Brisbane, within the first ten seconds of entering the library, customers were confronted by confusing product messages, half-dead plants, negative and irrelevant signs and cellophane tape on the walls and counters.

All this had to change. A consistent image checklist was drawn up by the library staff to ensure that the customer always has a positive moment of truth. In new libraries, the designers were instructed to see that the entrance signage was exciting, customer friendly, and clearly communicated products and services. The key to success is to use a written checklist of items for which staff members are responsible (see table 7.1).

USING MERCHANDISING KEYS IN THE LIBRARY

The objective of a retailer is to increase the average sale per customer, whereas the aim of a library is to spread the joy of reading and use of information.

Table 7.1
Image Checklist

	STANDARD	TEAM LEADERS	TICK	OTHERS	TIPS
First Impressions	1. Power display at your entrance	Blitz Agenda Item Library Ground Rule	☐☐☐		•Pause CKI Trolleys at displays restock them
Aiming for a welcoming transition zone	2. Acknowledge customers as they enter (when you can)	Agenda Item Ground Rule	☐☐		
	3. A clean entrance	Discuss with cleaner. Monitor	☐		•If problems persist T/L contact - contract manager (by GroupWise)
	4. Checklist	Integrate into daily roster	☐		
	5. Plants (keep fresh)	Monitor	☐		•If problems persist as above

COUNTERS - AIMING FOR EFFICIENT LOOK & UNCLUTTERED

STANDARD	TEAM LEADERS	TICK	OTHERS	TIPS
Sticky Tape Free	Blitz Agenda Item Ground Rule	☐☐☐		•Use Blu-Tack or Sellotape rings to affix items
Brochures in stands •Don't need to display all, but •Display all BCCs	Blitz Agenda Item Ground Rule	☐☐☐		•Use perspex holders •Store extra brochures out of view (or discard) •Never leave brochures flat
A4/A5 Free standing poster folders: •Max 3 on view at counter •None flat on counter	Blitz Agenda Item Ground Rule	☐☐☐	•BST to supply paper to use	
Storage behind counter: •No lost property, drink bottles, personal items & other grunge on view •Box everything neatly Cleanliness No staff info notices on view	Blitz Agenda Ground Rule	☐☐☐		•Request order

This can be measured by the number of loans made. Merchandising and display principles are the same for both aims. Alas, many libraries miss these opportunities, and their customer's lives aren't as enriched as they should be. We therefore need to review these principles and discuss how they are applied to libraries.

One objective is to get 100 percent of patrons to see 100 percent of books. To do this, you need to get the customer flow correct. The guru on customer flow is Paco Underhill, and his 1999 book *Why We Buy, The Science of Shopping* should be essential reading for all designers of libraries.

In Australia, the United Kingdom, New Zealand, India, and South Africa, consumers prefer to enter a public building on the left and travel in a clockwise direction. In the United States, Canada, and mainland Europe the reverse applies. Therefore, the layout of a library is crucial in order to expose patrons to the greatest number of books and services and to maximize the use of public space in the building.

In Brisbane, our case study, we needed to work closely with architects to redesign libraries to maximize the use of space. Not only do you want patrons to flow in the right direction, but you also want them to linger longer. Therefore, the ambience of the library is also a critical factor. Public space in libraries is critical to the success of the library, and you need to pay attention to the following areas.

BUTT BRUSH

It is not the space allocated to books that is critical; it is the space allocated to people. Customer comfort will determine how many books are borrowed and how long customers will stay in your library.

Generally, only 40 percent of floor space should be dedicated to bookshelf fittings and information tables, with the remaining 60 percent allocated to browsing patrons. Some items such as CDs, newspapers, and magazines require more space to ensure that customers' personal space is not compromised. Paco Underhill (1999) uses the term *butt brush* when patrons feel their space is being threatened—the result is that they will leave the restricted environment as quickly as possible. Ambience can also be improved by the use of aroma. This was introduced into Brisbane City Libraries, by using natural aromatherapy products (with great success).

Historically, patrons looked on libraries as austere environments where silence was the rule of the game. Now they look on libraries as places to relax, and background music is being considered. In Brisbane the music of Enya has proved to be popular. The key is to provide relaxation music as a faint background experience to remove the complete silence.

Probably the most contentious issue we had to grasp at Brisbane was the issue of food and drink. Traditionally, library books and refreshments did not mix. But now consumers respect coffee shops in bookstores such as Barnes and Noble and Borders. Therefore, they expect the same in libraries.

Coffee is an important ingredient. The local coffee shop networks with the library to provide this essential ingredient for library users' enjoyment.

Main city libraries may form partnerships with fully established coffee shop chains, and smaller regional libraries may find that vending machines suffice. The key is that refreshments are now an integral part of the social book-browsing experience. More and more libraries are now building refreshments into their consumer profile.

POWER SPOTS INCREASE LENDING RATES

Power spots are those positions in a library or retail store where you are guaranteed that 100 percent of patrons see a display of available materials. In these locations, research shows that turnover can increase by at least 540 percent over the rate produced by standard shelving. Critical success factors to ensure this increase in book lending include the following:

- *Location.* Power spots are normally located at least 12 feet into the library. Customers must pass through a transition zone first (an area where they get used to a new environment and don't look at products). A power spot may also occur as they move toward the checkout counter.
- Products topical to patrons on the display. Here are some examples:

  - Books relating to popular new movies (such as Tolkien's *Lord of the Rings* books when each film is released)
  - Books related to current world events
  - Books related to local events

- *Pyramid shape.* Consumers prefer to select products from a pyramidal display. This has been the case since we first started trading along the Euphrates River in Mesopotamia in 5000 B.C., and it is still true today. The construction and height of the display is critical to its success (see fig. 7.1).
- *KISS (Keep It Simple Sells).* This has always been the golden rule in retailing, and it is true of pyramidal displays. Displays should be themed with a simple message in the eyes of the consumer. Keep to one message; that is, one author or one category theme.
- *Make it look touchable.* Don't make the display look so perfect that consumers won't want to touch it. Consumers must feel that if they take a book from the display, they won't be spoiling the arrangement. Perfection may make you feel good, but it won't do anything for your book lending rates.
- *Use clear signs.* Displays should be promoted using clear, distinctive signage. Sonja Larson's book *Signs that Sell* is a great tool for learning how to write effective signs. Remember, your patrons are exposed to thousands of signs every day of their lives. People don't read all the signs they see, but you have to write signs that encourage them to read yours. To get people to read your signs, use lowercase serif style (as on this page). The most effective signs are constructed as shown in figure 7.2.

Power displays should be changed regularly, a minimum of once per month, but should be consistent in their professionalism in the eyes of the customer.

END-CAPS

End-caps are the ends of bookshelves. Displays in these locations can increase lending rates by at least 240 percent. Libraries should design custom-made shop fittings to display books on these ends, and they should constantly be refreshed with new books.

SHELF MERCHANDISING

Not all books need to be placed on the shelf spine to spine. Facing the occasional book (e.g., every 4 feet) provides an eye break for the browser, as well as

Figure 7.1. Pyramid-shaped displays make very effective power displays.

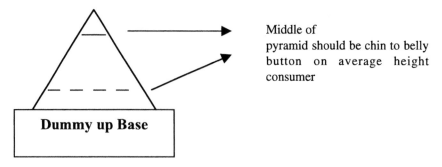

Middle of pyramid should be chin to belly button on average height consumer

Dummy up Base

Figure 7.2. Creating an effective sign.

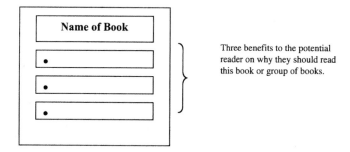

Name of Book

Three benefits to the potential reader on why they should read this book or group of books.

promoting specific books. Remember that the position on a shelf affects the lending rate. Vertical merchandising of books affects the lending rate dramatically. In retailing, the following principle applies, as shown in figure 7.3: Highest sales rates occur when customers can view merchandise vertically between their belly button and chin. As the figure shows, sales rates decrease somewhat when the merchandise is above a customer's chin level, but drop steeply as the display falls below the belly button. I have never seen research in libraries to compare the retail statistics shown in figure 7.3 with book lending in libraries, but I suspect that a similar pattern exists.

One important practice is the trend to design fixtures that allow librarians and customers to look over the tops of the shelves. This helps with the ambience of the library.

CREATING ROOMS WITHIN ROOMS

A library should not be just one room; it should be a series of different environments created to appeal to different target groups of consumers. Children's

End-caps to bookshelves are essential. Custom-made end-caps ensure that Brisbane Library's lending rate per capita is one of the highest in the world.

zones should use primary colors and be very theatrical zones. Easy chairs, cushions, murals, and theatrical book shelving should all be incorporated in this zone.

A youth zone for teenagers should be located at the opposite end of the library from the children's zone; these two don't mix. In our experience, youths should be involved in the design. This should be a zone that nobody else has an inclination to enter.

The newspaper area should attract browsers. Round tables will encourage them to linger longer, and the zone should be decorated in a more serious color zone. Chairs should be comfortable, and this may be an ideal location for your coffee facility.

Finally, you may wish to allocate a zone for older patrons, an area where senior citizens can meet and relax.

Figure 7.3. Vertical shelving affects borrowing.

Stretch Shelf	**75 Sales**	
Sight and Take Shelves	**100 Sales**	Chin to Belly button
Top Shelves	**55 Sales**	
Bottom Shelf	**20 Sales**	

BUILDING SUCCESS INTO YOUR LIBRARY

It is all very well to bring in a retail consultant to improve your library, but for successful implementation of the design, staff members need to take ownership. This was a key to the success at Brisbane. The first phase was an analysis of improvements, and the second phase was a training session on implementation. A date was chosen for this session, and some local retailers were invited to help by discussing some merchandising techniques and answering questions. Senior library managers were asked to participate. Staff were divided into teams, each with a leader empowered to speak for the others.

The training day, I believe, is crucial to the success of the project for the following reasons:

- Senior management members need to attend to raise interest, understanding, and to ensure support in implementation.
- Team leaders can air their concerns and talk through possible hurdles and potential problems.
- Retail principles are seen in action, and team members have the opportunity to talk to retailers about the concepts.
- Training in retail techniques signals a cultural shift to a more businesslike and customer-focused attitude.
- Training for improved service to customers transfers ownership to the team.

IMPLEMENTATION STRATEGIES

Changes in libraries toward a more customer-friendly, retail-oriented environment should be introduced using a three-pronged approach:

1. Macro design
2. Learning strategy
3. Operationalizing

MACRO DESIGN STRATEGY

To maximize the opportunities, a team composed of a retail consultant, architect, asset manager, and librarian should be brought together to develop new libraries. In the past, too many libraries have fallen short of their full potential due to the lack of retail input. In these days of more demanding consumers and tighter budgets, you need maximum return on your dollar input.

In Brisbane, Toowong Library became the showcase. It incorporates clear signage, neon light boxes, modern signage, open floor space, comfortable furnishings, retail-designed bookshelves, a clockwise racetrack layout, a café and vending machines, and boutique-themed areas for targeted consumer groups. It is a center for the consumers of a new millennium; social interaction is part of the overall package.

LEARNING STRATEGIES

Success is about consistency. For Brisbane, I produced a staff handbook describing and illustrating the techniques and sample checklists to be used by team members. Team seminars have been designed and delivered explaining the rationale of the project. Participants are taken to various retail precincts (streets and districts where traffic is excluded) and shopping malls to spot power displays, pyramids, and interesting use of props, images, and layout. They visit another library and walk through, noting good practice and areas where improvement is needed.

OPERATIONALIZING

At Brisbane, the real challenge and opportunity was to get the team to implement the plan. The manager (head librarian) was behind the project and gave the team a two-month window of opportunity to implement the program. After the agreed-on period, the executive head of the state retail association was invited to judge the most improved displays in each of the libraries. The team that had implemented the most ideas were given prizes and certificates.

To maintain standards, a group of champions was chosen to draw up standards. These standards included the following:

- A smile for every patron
- A power display in every library
- A new book display in every library
- All brochures to be displayed in perspex stands
- Displays to be kept 70 percent full at all times with attractive stock
- Implementation of presentation checklists (see table 7.2)

In the future, I believe that libraries will become community hubs. They will need to be sleek, attractive, and aligned with what consumers expect when they venture into retail areas. I see no reason why libraries cannot become partners with florists, coffee shops, bookstores or other retail establishments. The interaction with

New books should be promoted on custom-made stands in prime locations.

patrons will change; self-service outlets will increase to free up frontline team members. Libraries will have the challenge of ebooks and may become host partners with online bookstores.

Consumers have always and will always compare what a library offers them with their retail leisure experiences. The libraries' aim should be to be leaders in these experiences, not followers.

Acknowledgment

I would like to acknowledge the support I have had from Brisbane City Libraries and especially Fiona Emberton, the coordinator of the Brisbane project, in writing this chapter.

REFERENCES

Larson, Sonja. 1991. *Signs That Sell*. Minneapolis, MN: Insignia Systems.

Underhill, Paco. 1999. *Why We Buy: The Science of Shopping*. New York: Simon & Schuster.

SELECTED BIBLIOGRAPHY

Stanley, John. 1999. *Just About Everything a Retail Manager Needs to Know*. Queensland, AUS: Plum Press.

Table 7.2
Presentation Checklist

Standard	Team Leaders	Tick	Others	Tips
Public floor space: 60% free of clutter where possible	• De-clutter • Agenda Item • Library Ground Rule	☐ ☐		
Wheelchair access: 1.5m clearance (minimum)	Blitz Agenda Item Ground Rule	☐☐☐☐		
Furniture & fittings - De-grunge	Blitz	☐		•Send excess to auction

DISPLAYS - AIMING FOR A CLEAN, SLICK IMAGE

	Standard	Team Leaders	Tick	Others	Tips
	•Pyramid shape or conical •Use attractive props	•Monitor quality of props Agenda Ground Rule	☐☐☐☐☐	Prop kits available – see intranet	
	Stock: •Always at least half full - quality stock	Blitz Agenda Ground Rule	☐☐☐		•Make it a CKI room duty •Delegate this task •Make it a priority •Save on shelving effort
Standard	Signage •Use menu holders •coffee coloured paper •Times/Aerial font •Black border	Blitz Agenda Ground Rule	☐☐☐	•CCSL to send out paper •CCLL to send out standard sample	•Order from BST with 2 weeks advance notice if necessary

8 A GUIDE TO SELECTING LIBRARY FURNITURE

Robert W. Fetzer

INTRODUCTION

My intent in writing this chapter is to give you, the librarian or purchaser, an insider's view of library furniture—that is, from the perspective of a manufacturer of library furniture. The outcome I hope for is that you who may not have had previous responsibility for purchasing library furniture will feel increased confidence in making sound purchasing decisions, and that those of you who are veterans in the procedure will come away with new and helpful insights. I need to tell you at this juncture, however, that my particular emphasis—or bias—will be toward furniture that is predominantly of wood construction, as opposed to furniture whose structure is chiefly of metal fabrication. You may also pick up on a distinct preference for *custom-manufactured* over *stock* (or assembly-line) furniture, although I will discuss the important role in the marketplace for both options.

STOCK FURNITURE

Library furniture manufacturers who invest in the creation of a few to several different designs or lines of furniture, with catalogs containing illustrations of the items in each line and corresponding price lists, are known in the industry as stock furniture manufacturers.

Advantages of Purchasing Stock Library Furniture

Cost Manufacturers of stock furniture mass-produce their furniture according to preprogrammed "recipes" for each item in each line they offer. Once the research and development costs for a line have been expended, those costs can be recovered by repeat sales. These are usually one-time costs, and if the line has been in production for a few years, the purchaser is paying very little of the overhead costs that were expended to create it. Also, as the employees of the firm become habituated to the processes for generating that line, their production efficiencies increase, and the manufacturer is able to offer the line to customers at competitive prices. Probably the most significant overhead factor that you, the purchaser, help pay for is the substantial sales and marketing budget that stock manufacturers must cover in generating furniture catalogs and in maintaining nationwide sales forces. Still, if you are a librarian on a tight budget who needs to purchase only a few reading tables and carrels with matching chairs, or if you are a purchaser (still on a tight budget) who must purchase large multiples of these items, you may still be best served by finding a stock manufacturer with a reputation for dependable, durable furniture.

Refinement of the Product Line   Theoretically, stock manufacturers, because they have already done their research and development and have produced runs of their stock lines over and over, can turn their attention to perfecting what they have created—or getting the bugs out. That should certainly be true of the firms committed to excellent customer service and long-term profitability rather than to short-term market domination as low-bid providers. Manufacturers committed to customer service and product quality will learn very quickly what doesn't work about their lines, because their sales representatives will find it out from you, their customers, and will report it to manufacturing. Management will then initiate and follow through on the needed corrections and refinements. Stock manufacturers can perform these refinements in a cost-effective manner because, for the most part, they have only to tweak processes that are already in place. If they are strong, successful firms, they will not have released very many untested Edsels into the marketplace.

Predictability   When you have worked with a stock manufacturer repeatedly, you become familiar with the features (i.e., both the advantages and limitations) of their lines. In the best of circumstances, this is a source of comfort and security for obvious reasons: you have come to know the people you're dealing with and how they operate; you can predict cost, ordering lead times, and product performance—and thus save yourself the time and pain of new research and the risk associated with unfamiliar product features and untried relationships.

Familiarity   There are only a handful of stock library furniture manufacturers in the country. They all maintain a consistent presence at American Library Association (ALA) convention shows, and it does not take long to become familiar with the characteristics of their respective lines.

Disadvantages of Stock Library Furniture

There is a caveat to the advantage of purchasing stock furniture solely on the basis of cost. It has to do with the first disadvantage of stock-manufactured furniture, and I want to elaborate on it here.

Cost of Change   If you have tentatively picked a line of furniture because you like many of its features but at the same time recognize that some don't work for your library and that you need certain features the line does not include, don't expect stock manufacturers to change their recipes for you if the features you need require them to make radical changes in their designs (or even changes you might not consider to be very radical). Their processes for each line are set; these processes extend from purchasing materials, to material and labor flow, to accounting for the labor cost for each step in manufacturing the different furniture items in that line. Ask them to depart from those set formulas and you have thrown a wrench into their well-ordered but relatively inflexible production paradigm. The cost for changing the setup of their machinery and reprogramming their computers is a major one. Those stock manufacturers who are willing to make significant alterations to pervasive features in their lines, or to certain furniture items within a line, will be sure they cover themselves monetarily for the uncertainty and inconvenience of departing from processes for which they have a sure-fire cost-tracking system, and entering into the twilight zone of untested manufacturing procedures. They will do it for what they consider to be a large order, or they will do it if they consider you an important customer or potential customer, but don't expect a stock manufacturer to modify the line for a small order of a few pieces of furniture. Remember also that such manufacturers' strength in the marketplace derives from their having invented workable designs and exploiting them, and certainly not from departing from those designs, which points to the next disadvantage.

Tendency to Perpetuate Flaws   Because stock manufacturers have a very real cost disincentive for altering manufacturing formulas for the lines they have already introduced and are selling, there is an inherent tension between making radical design changes to their existing lines and responding quickly and aggressively to customers' requests for those changes, even if they're warranted. Here is a hypothetical example: A stock manufacturer buys hundreds of *bunks* of plywood for tabletops from a supplier with whom the firm has done business for many years. The manufacturer has come to depend on the supplier because the supplier provides predictable delivery and a product that meets specification criteria at a low price because of the consistently large volume and regularity of the firm's orders. Enter the problem: A potentially important customer wants to enter into a contract for library tables but has had a bad experience in the past with plywood tops. (Plywood can contain internal voids that show up as sunken spots on the table surface.) The stock manufacturer disregards the slightly sunken spots in such tabletops as an inherent characteristic of a natural and therefore unavoidably imperfect material. Because production has been tied for so long to one material and one process so the firm can remain price competitive, the stock manufacturer may not want to break from the paradigm that has served well in the past and risk potential growth by recognizing flaws in present processes and finding better solutions.

Familiarity and Predictability Can Equal Boredom   If you don't particularly mind that the furniture you select for your library is identical to that of many other libraries around the country, apart from relatively minor differences in the color of wood stain or plastic laminate finish, stock furniture can be a fiscally responsible solution. (I say "can be" because the all-important performance criteria for selecting stock library furniture are essentially the same as those for selecting custom furniture, and I cannot emphasize too strongly that they override considerations of purchase price alone. This issue is discussed more fully in the section on furniture construction.) In fact, purchasing from the same stock manufacturer (a firm that offers limited design options but has a proven record for consistently producing dependable furniture) can play into your design intent for a series of branch libraries whose interior finishes you wish to be comfortably and recognizably similar. Contrast that scenario with this one: You are responsible for purchasing furniture for a new or remodeled library for which a major impetus is the preservation of a cherished identity—such as in the case of a Carnegie library—or in the creation of a new one, as in the case of the Denver Public Library addition, designed by the renowned architect, Michael Graves. Most stock library design solutions won't do for a Carnegie library: They are too contemporary. At the Denver Public Library, Michael Graves provided library furniture whose design complemented his interior architecture. In either scenario (and in many others in which the community, school, or university wants to set itself apart with a design motif that is uniquely its own), the stock solution is, by definition, not an option.

CUSTOM FURNITURE

Manufacturers committed to making custom furniture come to their craft from essentially the same premise as that of stock manufacturers—the belief in their ability to problem solve through the art and science of furniture design and manufacture. Beyond that, there is divergence. Stock manufacturers may be driven more by the potential economic rewards of enterprise. They have expended much thought and effort into creating a marketable product. Now the drive is to exploit it—to quickly get, and then perpetuate, a healthy return on that investment of energy and capital. Custom manufacturers, though they must show profits in the real world alongside their stock-manufacturer counterparts, may be driven less by practical economic considerations than by an artist's or inventor's quest: The process of creation is, in itself, a more fulfilling end than the realization of monetary gain from that creation alone. True custom manufacturers are caught up in a perpetual process of invention and reinvention. There are no stock lines in their catalogs. In fact, there are no catalogs in the sense of those produced by stock manufacturers, only a portfolio of past projects in which the creative process was reinitiated with little reference to the previous project, except for pervasive and time-honored principles governing the selection of materials and of construction.

Advantages of Purchasing Custom Library Furniture

Flexibility and Innovation   By definition, custom furniture manufacturers are free of many of the constraints that limit stock manufacturers. Their lifeblood is design flexibility and creativity, and with that comes a fascination with new and different materials options. Instead of studying to narrow material choices and production methods to an efficient few, custom manufacturers operate from a broad familiarity with a vast array of materials and methods. This gives them an advantage in the domain of problem solving. Instead of having to impose a stock furniture design onto a project that resists a stock solution, the custom manufacturer comes to your furniture problem with few preconceived ideas and with the attitude of wanting to discern your unique needs. They then design furniture to answer those needs in every important particular, constrained only by the real-world limitations of material costs and dimensions, economies of production volume, and the skill level of their craftspeople—their single most valuable resource. The skill and expertise of their workforce, probably more than the sophistication of their machinery, is what sets the best custom manufacturers apart from stock manufacturers.

Aesthetics   Equally motivating as the unrestrained freedom to problem-solve is custom furniture manufacturers' obsession with making tangible objects of intrinsic beauty. They are as concerned with art as they are with function. They will also adhere to a strict standard of craftsmanship even if that means sacrificing a degree of price competitiveness. Their primary motivation never has been nor ever will be to come in as low bidders for the sole motivation of being able to offer the cheapest prices. The goal of the best custom manufacturers is to produce and sell value, where value is defined as the optimal convergence of quality and price. (The very important concept of quality is discussed in a later section.)

Interface with the Architectural/Design Community   Custom library furniture manufacturers are ideally suited to fruitful collaborations with architects and designers whose mandate is to create signature designs for their clients. An excellent case in point is the recently completed Nashville Main Library, designed by Robert A. M. Stern of New York City. The architecture, both exterior and interior, is classical. The architect for the interior also designed the library furniture, adopting and incorporating meticulously researched motifs of classical Greek furniture into the lines of the Nashville reading tables and carrels. The custom furniture manufacturer's responsibility and opportunity in this collaboration was to bring to bear the very best solutions for ergonomics and construction, as well as the level of craftsmanship and finishing that the richness of the design legacy warranted. This is a lofty example and an exception, in terms of cost and scope, to most library projects, but the principles apply to any project for which the driving motivation is to create—even to create within a limited budget, which leads to an assertion you might not expect.

Value Engineering for Cost   Because custom manufacturers operate from a mindset of flexibility and innovation, they can approach cost in the same way they would address your need for a custom-designed circulation desk: They can design your furniture to fall within a targeted budget figure. *Value engineering* is a term often misused in the construction industry. In the worst sense, it means cutting the quality out of a product in order to get the price down; in the best, it means finding ways to eliminate unnecessary costs in material and labor without sacrificing quality. Admittedly, even value engineering has its limitations. If you need an unconventional solution for one service desk or three computer tables for a small library, you want the services of a small custom manufacturer. Such firms carry a much smaller overhead burden than large custom manufacturers, and their price to you will be less. The big manufacturers may come up with solutions for you that are just as good, but they cannot, even by employing all their expertise and imagination, value-engineer a custom service desk at as low a dollar figure as a small shop can. Conversely, the small shop cannot, in all likelihood, pass on to you the economies of scale for large output that a large company can, nor can they manufacture in nearly as short a time frame. This may seem too obvious to mention, but intelligent people often don't realize that small shops do small jobs; large shops do large jobs. This, by the way, is a characteristic of custom manufacturers much more often than it is of stock manufacturers. Custom furniture manufacturers can range from large to small family-run businesses. Stock furniture manufacturers are almost always large enterprises with several million dollars in yearly sales, and nationwide, if not worldwide, distribution. Another tip: You may be as well served by going to a custom woodwork house for your circulation and service desks as to a manufacturer of strictly library furniture. Across the country are custom woodwork manufacturers who are members of the national association of U.S. woodworkers called the Architectural Woodwork Institute (AWI). AWI has established quality standards that have been adopted by the nation's woodwork and construction industries as well as by the American Institute of Architects (AIA). Among these AWI member firms are those with a particular reputation for producing fine custom woodwork, and even if many of them do not regularly manufacture library furniture, they would be capable of fabricating most of the pieces that stock manufacturers typically do not provide.

Disadvantages of Custom Library Furniture

In fairness to stock manufacturers, *quality* stock manufacturing has a potential advantage over the custom manufacturing process. Stock manufacturers get to rework and refine their furniture designs before they go on the market; custom manufacturers get only one shot. This means, in practical terms, that the architect or designer who conceives your furniture on paper must be knowledgeable in the appropriate use of materials and must be a good furniture engineer— aware of the stresses on the parts of a chair or table and versed in the ergonomics of the human body, not just a wonderful and creative aesthetician. If that is not completely the case, you still have a safety net: the expert custom manufacturer. The expert custom furniture maker thrives on taking a good aesthetic (but not wholly practical) design and making it structurally and ergonomically sound while preserving the architect's design intent—and making it affordable. One obscure but very competent library furniture maker I know graduated second in his class from the Art Center College of Design in Pasadena, California, a college long revered as a mecca for the nation's best and brightest in the field of interior, industrial, retail, and furniture design. This man has gone on to design one-of-a-kind treasures, from the 50-foot-high by 80-foot-long organ case (the woodwork that encloses the organ pipes) for one of the largest performing arts halls in the world, to the classically beautiful walnut boxes that housed each Olympic medal awarded in the 2002 Winter Olympic Games. In addition, his skills as a library furniture designer and craftsman make him an invaluable resource to any gifted but practically inexperienced design professional.

I can think of no real disadvantages of the quality custom solution except in the case in which price has to be the controlling factor in the purchase decision. Time and again, it has been borne out that purchase decisions based on price alone are poor decisions, and that the low-price purchase must, as often as not, be replaced at a higher cost than that of the original purchase, resulting in a net cost of more than double the original expenditure. You might want to argue that the stock manufacturer has the advantage over the custom manufacturer in the event of the need for a reorder or a replacement order. That sounds reasonable until you understand that stock manufacturers do not, as a rule, keep large inventories of their stock lines. There is no more incentive for them to maintain large inventories of furniture in their warehouses waiting to be sold on speculation than there is for custom manufacturers to do so. Stock and custom manufacturers alike fabricate on an order-by-order basis.

DECISIONS ABOUT FURNITURE MATERIALS

Given that my background is in wood furniture, I will not address metal components of library furniture such as tubular steel table legs, metal aprons, or metal chairs, most of which are mass-produced catalog solutions. I want instead to give you insight into the decisions that manufacturers, both stock and custom, make regarding the materials they use to build their wood furniture.

Wood

Most library furniture manufacturers use all three major wood materials in their furniture: *solid wood* (lumber), *plywood* (wood panel products made of compressed laminations of thin sheets of wood), and *particleboard* or *fiberboard* (flat wood panels made of wood chips, coarse or fine, pressed and glued together to make large sheets of uniform thickness).

Solid wood, or lumber, is the ideal material for structural parts of tables, carrels, chairs, or any surface that must withstand intense wear or abuse. Some woods are much better suited to serve as structural elements or wear surfaces than others. The following are all appropriate for these purposes, and this is by no means an exhaustive list:

maple	walnut
birch	cherry
oak (red and white)	beech
ash	mahogany
hickory	makore
pecan	

All of the above are considered *hardwoods,* or woods from deciduous trees, which shed their leaves each year; and though the name usually applies, some hardwoods, such as mahogany, aren't much harder than the hardest *softwoods* (the wood of evergreens, or *conifers*). Mahogany is easily the softest wood listed above—you can make an indentation in its surface with your fingernail, yet almost everyone knows what an elegant choice it is for fine furniture.

In the United States, we are used to thinking in terms of only a few species of wood, whether for furniture or kitchen cabinets. In the 1950s and 1960s, a dominant wood was birch. Birch is essentially a blond wood, difficult for most people to distinguish from maple. Like maple, it is very hard and closed grained, but the birch we most often see tends to have a slightly more distinct and a slightly wilder grain pattern. It can also be pinto-colored—blond and brown, with the blond wood being the color toward the outside of the log, closest to the bark, called *sapwood,* and brown coming from the center of the log, or the *heartwood.* Much of the birch you see you would not recognize as birch, because it is an ideal wood for painted moldings and doors. It is relatively inexpensive, resistant to abuse, and, because it is tight-grained, birch holds paint on its surface well rather than absorbing the finish, as open-grained woods will do. It is also an excellent structural wood for unexposed or painted furniture parts (see fig. 8.1).

Oak has been and continues to be the workhorse wood of America. It is, like the apple, a symbol of our heritage. Oak (as we know it in furniture, doors, and cabinetry) is usually one of two subspecies: red oak, the more common of the two, which is really amber-colored, and white oak, which is certainly not white, but usually comes off as gray-brown, often with greenish undertones. (That may sound ugly, but white oak, when *quarter cut,* can be one of the most elegant of woods.) This nation has become so programmed on oak that it has been the all-but-automatic choice for "real wood" cabinets and moldings over the past several decades. To Americans, wood equals oak. In reaction to that mindset, the architectural and design community has veered very determinedly away from the eternal oak-ad-nauseam trend, attempting to awaken us to the realization that oak is merely one of at least twenty wood species that are beautiful, affordable, and readily available for furniture applications. You may have become aware of this influence in the emergence of American cherry (not a new species option, by any means), a wood rich in color and character that has, in its quiet and refined way, taken a back seat to the brawnier oak.

Figure 8.1. Illustration of log cross section. Reprinted with permission from the 7th edition of *Quality Standards Illustrated,* Architectural Woodwork Institute, Reston, Virginia.

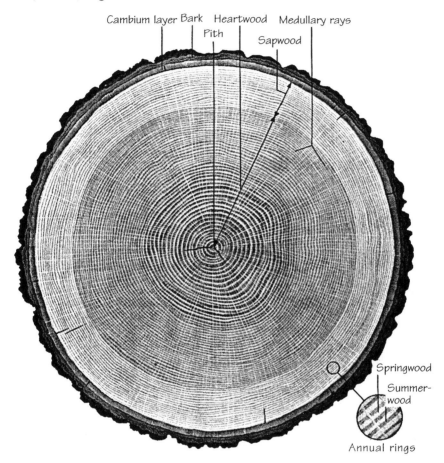

Concurrently with cherry—and more emphatically in the northwest and north central states—maple is the staple. Maple, as already mentioned, is hard, heavy, and closed grained. It is also slightly less expensive than cherry and comparable in cost to oak. Like oak, it is a durable, dependable wood, excellently suited to furniture parts such as legs, table edges, stretchers, and aprons. Specified in the form of clear-white maple, it is consistently light blond, with an indistinct grain that makes it monochromatic but not boring. Maple is not a diffident wood: it makes its own strong statement—subtle but substantial, imparting a cheerful lightness to any environment in which it is used.

An affordable and eminently useful wood that can be even lighter in color than maple (yet is often mistaken for oak), ash is also one of the most overlooked species options for furniture. Many of us think we have oak kitchen cabinets when in actuality they are made of ash. The ash we mistake for oak tends to be stained yellow-brown. Like oak, it is coarse-grained; its grain patterns are very pronounced—alternately tight and open, manifesting in irregular, alternating ribs of light and dark. Like oak and maple, ash is hard, heavy, and durable. Ash is an excellent choice for furniture, and if, as in the case of maple, it is specified as white (coming from the sapwood), ash can be lighter in color than any wood but the albino English sycamore, the European cousin of maple. Another bonus: ash is every bit as affordable as oak.

I can't leave the subject of solid wood without giving you some important information regarding the selection of your species. Solid wood—wood that comes in the form of boards—is essentially cut in two ways, and understanding the difference is fundamental to making sound aesthetic and cost decisions. The terms the industry uses are *plain-sawn* and *quartered*. Plain-sawn wood is solid wood, or boards, sawn parallel to the diameter of the log. This method of sawing results in boards that manifest the grain patterns you would typically associate with wood but probably have never consciously considered. I can best describe this pattern as coming from roughly parallel bands of grain that bend together at the top in a kind of peak. Each plain-sawn board tends to have peaks within peaks from top to bottom (see fig. 8.2).

The other method of cutting solid wood from logs is *quarter sawing*. Quarter-sawn boards are cut from logs that have first been cut longitudinally like four equal pieces of a pie. Each pie-wedge of the log is then sawn into boards with the saw cuts running parallel with the point of the wedge. This method of cutting yields boards, usually narrower that plain-sawn boards, with straight, parallel grain lines running uniformly the length of the board. When oak is cut this way, it yields a unique characteristic called *flake*, which runs transverse to the grain lines, and shows as shiny flecks, bands, or ribbons distinct from the grain. (The flake characteristic shows the truncated *medullary rays* of the tree.) Many people consider flake a beautiful accent feature in oak, whereas others feel that it detracts from the regularity of the uniformly parallel grain pattern of the quarter-cut wood. If, when you see quartered oak, you find the flake a distraction, you can specify *rift-cut* oak, which is a variation on quarter-cutting, and which magically eliminates the flake. Remember that the term *rift–cut* applies only to oak, and to no other wood species.

All the woods in the list show off beautifully finished. Some, however, tend to go blotchy when stained (maple and cherry being the prime examples). Only true experts in wood finishing are skilled in the idiosyncrasies of staining cherry and maple, especially if the stain is dark. Why stain maple dark in the first place? It is a blond wood and is beautiful being itself. If you want a dark finish, pick a dark wood from the available natural palette: dark brown—walnut, dark reddish brown—*sapele* (identified further on). Birch is usually painted instead of stained because of its indifferent appearance under a transparent clear or stained finish. Beech can take a stain better than maple, but, like maple, it shows off best with a clear finish. Walnut, oak, ash, and especially mahogany stain well. Be aware

Figure 8.2. Illustration of plain, quartered, and rift sawing. Reprinted with permission from the 7th edition of *Quality Standards Illustrated,* Architectural Woodwork Institute, Reston, Virginia.

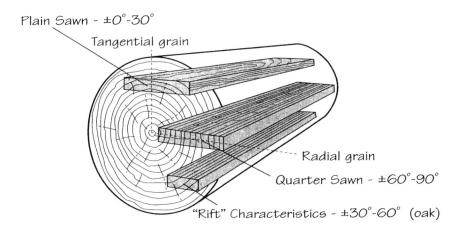

Plain Sawn - ±0°-30°
Tangential grain
Radial grain
Quarter Sawn - ±60°-90°
"Rift" Characteristics - ±30°-60° (oak)

that mahogany, oak, and ash are open-grained woods—that is, the pores in the grain are large. Tabletops made from oak and ash make somewhat rough writing surfaces unless their surface pores are filled with a wood filler or finish.

There is a growing trend in the architectural woodwork industry—that is, among the custom manufacturers who work closely with architects and designers—to look for and offer a palette of wood species most people in the world have never heard of: woods such as *makore* (pronounced ma'kor ray), *anegre* (a'neh gray), *sapele* (sa pee' ly), *bosse* (bah say'), and Australian eucalyptus, to name a few. With the exception of the obvious—Australian eucalyptus—most of these "new" woods are from Africa, Central and South America, and Southeast Asia, including Malaysia. Some are formal-looking, pricey, and available only in veneer form; but others—and *makore* is a wonderful example—are available as both veneer and lumber, can be more economical than American cherry, and are easily as rich looking when finished.

Another advantage to many of these woods is that they are absolutely beautiful with only a clear finish. Many of them actually defy staining, possessing a uniqueness of natural color and an inherent iridescent quality under a transparent lacquer that would be lost if they were stained. In veneer form, most of these species owe their visual richness to a naturally occurring characteristic in the wood called *figure*. I will describe figure as tight and regular or broad and broken undulations in the wood surface that give the wood (when clear-coated), a virtual 3D appearance. A tabletop surfaced in such a veneer actually appears kaleidoscopic, because light reflecting and refracting from the wood surface causes it to shimmer alternately light and dark as you walk around it. You may think this furniture maker has been breathing too many lacquer fumes and that, at the very least, such furniture would be visually distracting and over-the-top expensive; but I can promise you that what I am describing is a subtle beauty that, with a little forethought, can be designed and specified for moderately priced furniture, both stock and custom. A notable example is the furniture in the Mountain View Public Library, a 10,000-square-foot facility near San Francisco completed in 1998. It was conceived by the San Francisco architecture firm, SMWM, highly regarded for furniture design as well as architecture, whose architects chose Australian eucalyptus veneer and maple solids in their design of the elegant circulation and service desks, the round and rectangular reading tables, and the study carrels.

I have used the term *wood veneer* in passing, but it warrants clearer definition. As I mentioned, *veneers* are thin slices of solid wood. The only difference between boards and veneers is their thickness. Where boards—or lumber—are *sawn* in nominal thicknesses of 1 to 3 inches, veneers are *sliced* from the log $\frac{1}{10}$ to $\frac{1}{40}$ of an inch thick, by means of a very large and very sharp steel blade. Like "particleboard," "veneer" has come to mean cheap or fake to many people, because, like particleboard, it has been incorrectly used. In truth, real wood veneer can impart stunning beauty and value to fine woodwork and furniture. Expensive and rare woods with unusual grain characteristics yield vastly more usable surface area cut as veneer than they would as lumber, and in any case, their harvesting is restricted by international sanctions. Certain logs of many species are harvested expressly for the beauty of their veneer. The veneer, as it is sliced from the log, peels off in sheets called *leaves*. The leaves are bundled in numerical sequence according to the way they came off the log. The skilled furniture maker can trim and glue these veneer leaves edge to edge in matched, symmetrical patterns and apply them to panels to make tabletops, stack ends, and fronts of circulation and service desks, to give a few examples. The most common method of matching is called a *book match*, in which every other veneer leaf is turned over, creating a pleasing repeating design. A round tabletop lends itself to having a pattern of veneer leaves trimmed into tapered, pie-shaped wedges, creating a *starburst* effect. This technology, involving the creation of design patterns in veneer, is sophisticated woodworking. In this correct application, the veneers are always protected by solid wood borders and hard, durable finishes (see fig. 8.3).

The term *wood panel products* refers to processed wood such as plywood and particleboard, which are commonly used in the woodwork industry for the core material in countertops and the sides, backs, bottoms, tops, and shelves of cabinets. Particleboard is made of coarse to fine wood chips combined with resins and then molded into large, flat panels under heat and pressure. A close sibling of particleboard is fiberboard, often referred to as MDF (medium-density fiberboard). Instead of wood chips, fine wood fibers (almost of the consistency of those that go into making paper) are soaked in resins and pressed into panels. This product is about thirty cents per square foot more expensive than particleboard, heavier, and has superior finishing and screw-holding properties. We're

Figure 8.3. Veneer illustration showing book match and sunburst. Reprinted with permission from the 7th edition of *Quality Standards Illustrated,* Architectural Woodwork Institute, Reston, Virginia.

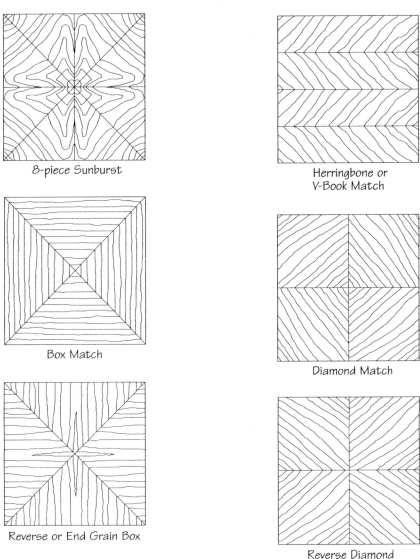

8-piece Sunburst

Herringbone or
V-Book Match

Box Match

Diamond Match

Reverse or End Grain Box

Reverse Diamond

all familiar with particleboard, or pressboard, and many of us have come to disdain it because we know from personal experience that the particleboard bookcases, desks, and other inexpensive furniture we bought at home center stores tended to be flimsy and quick to disintegrate. We are inclined to think of particleboard as cheap or imitation, and solid wood as real, strong, and inherently valuable. This is an important perception, and I address it in the section on furniture construction, which lists and elucidates keys for judging quality.

Plywood, the other important panel product, is made from three to several layers of thick wood veneer, *crossbanded*, that is, having each veneer layer glued perpendicular to the previous layer. When you think of plywood, you may think of the coarse-grained panel product made of fir that is used extensively in house construction for roof sheathing or subflooring. The plywood used for furniture is usually of a higher grade: its veneers have fewer knots and voids, and, in the case of drawer material, table tops, and "bentwood" furniture, the veneer laminations are not made of fir, but of birch or maple. In some design circles, the exposed edges of the alternating layers or *plies* of wood are considered an aesthetic feature. The form of plywood from which library tabletops are usually constructed is a particleboard or a denser fiberboard core panel ¾-inch thick, to which wood veneer is glued on both surfaces. The top surface receives the *face veneer* (the thin layer of wood sliced directly from a solid wood log). Every face must have its corresponding *backer* (a sheet of veneer of the same or compatible species as the face veneer) glued directly to the underneath surface of the panel; otherwise, the panel core, thick as it is, will warp (see fig. 8.4).

I should mention here that the woodwork industry is always inventing variations on the standard products. For example, in lieu of particleboard made from wood chips, there is an even "greener" option available now, made of very renewable wheat straw. Other innovations take the form of hybrid panel products that combine laminations of particleboard or MDF alternating with veneer plies.

Plastic laminate is the generic name for a product you may know better as Formica, which is probably the most prominent brand name for what amounts to laminated sheets of paper impregnated with resins and surfaced with a thin layer of melamine (which gives it color, texture, and surface durability), then compressed under heat to a thickness usually of about ¹⁄₁₆ inch. Plastic laminate makes a durable work and writing surface. Its drawbacks in your mind may be that it is too hard a writing surface. More important, it sometimes delaminates from its substrate and will not adhere very well when glue is reapplied. It also tends to "clam-shell" or chip where it receives impact at its exposed edges. These chipped edges are usually not repairable, and because it is very difficult to remove the entire laminate sheet cleanly, the entire panel usually has to be replaced.

Solid surface material is a substantially more expensive alternative to using plastic laminate for a service desk worktop, for example, and vastly more durable. You probably know it as a brand name: Corian, Avonite, or Fountainhead. It is a less expensive substitute for a marble or granite top—but at about fifty dollars per square foot, still a serious purchase decision.

Linoleum is a brand name for vinyl tile material used (like *Formica*) incorrectly but universally as a generic term. It has gained some proponents in the last few years because it provides a softer writing surface than laminate and has a look similar to leather, which is still used to cover expensive desktops. Its drawbacks are obvious: it can be easily scored with a knife or other sharp object, and it is certainly easier to scratch than plastic laminate, though most scratches can

Figure 8.4. Plywood types showing make-up. Reprinted with permission from the 7th edition of *Quality Standards Illustrated,* Architectural Woodwork Institute, Reston, Virginia.

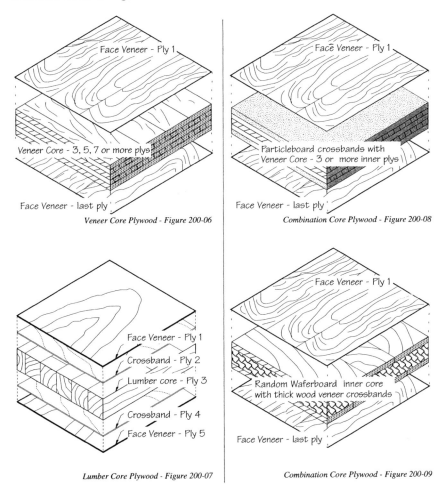

Veneer Core Plywood - Figure 200-06

Combination Core Plywood - Figure 200-08

Lumber Core Plywood - Figure 200-07

Combination Core Plywood - Figure 200-09

be repaired. It is not a suitable material for a table edge and must be captured by a protective wood or metal border.

Wood finish may be the most important ingredient in the aesthetics and durability of library furniture. In the furniture industry, the various steps and material components that make up the finish process are called finish systems. The systems include the steps of final sanding of the wood to be finished, application of a primer or sealer coat, sometimes application of a stain that is applied before or after the clear sealer coat, and then finishing or topcoating with a clear lacquer or varnish product that has properties including hardness, chip- and wear-resistance, and imperviousness to water and chemicals. Certainly a good wood finish can bring out the beauty in the wood surface to which it is applied and preserve that surface—which is usually a wood veneer—for decades.

FURNITURE CONSTRUCTION: KEYS TO JUDGING QUALITY

What you don't know—and what you don't see—*can* hurt you in the selection of library furniture.

Library furniture manufacturing and sales are as price driven as most other consumer markets, because the typical purchaser, as you can so well attest, is on a tight budget. That said, however, one of the most frequent laments I have heard from school librarians as well as librarians from public and private colleges and universities is that, driven by limited budgets, they purchased the low-bid offerings only to discover, in as little as two years, that they were faced with replacing it all because it was failing. And this is the result of normal use. One facilities manager for the public school system in a borough of New York City asked me if we might come up with a line of prison-grade indestructible furniture. Nothing was holding up under the level of not just use, but abuse, that in his world was regrettably the norm.

I realize that trying to define quality is a tricky endeavor, because its definition is tied to your needs, and your needs are in some ways unique. Also, our individual backgrounds and experiences foster biases from which we all make automatic, almost unconscious, judgments. Having said that, I am going to share an insider's view of quality and leave you to form or reform your own convictions.

I measure quality in furniture—in this case, library furniture—in terms of these criteria:

1. Structural integrity
2. Durability
3. User-friendliness and ergonomics
4. Craftsmanship and aesthetics

Structural Integrity

Structural integrity is a component of quality that you can verify in part by examining the furniture and then by cross examining the furniture maker. Here are some hypothetical but true-to-life examples of furniture that possesses, and furniture that lacks, structural integrity:

A year ago you purchased reading tables that have been repositioned or relocated several times. Because they are heavy and you are short of staff, the easiest way to move them is to drag them across the carpet. After the fourth or fifth move, you notice that the table legs have begun to wobble, and you detect gaps between what were once tight joints between the tops of the legs and the table *aprons* (the shallow wood stretchers just underneath and usually set back from the table top, that span between and butt to the tops of the legs). You stoop to examine the problem. Underneath the table at the inside corner, you discover no evident fastening of the top of the leg to the underside of the tabletop. Then you see light between the apron and the top of the leg, broken, possibly, by two narrow shadows, which are the dowels that held the leg to the apron. They have come loose from the holes in the legs: the glue has failed under the pull created by the friction of the carpet on the legs as the table was dragged repeatedly across it. The table legs *are* attached to the tabletop. You just can't see the screw that was inserted into the top of the leg through the top or sub top, but it is doing little to prevent the table leg from racking. Then you notice something else. What you assumed was a solid wood apron turns out to be a $3/4$-inch-thick slat of particleboard, faced in veneer. Until you were willing to compromise your dignity by getting under the table, you did not see the familiar granular bottom edge that translates to "cheap" and "insubstantial."

I have seen a similar problem on a massive scale in the main library of a large Midwestern university, but involving chairs instead of tables. As you know and have probably experienced, library patrons of all ages like to lean back on their chairs so that all their body weight is concentrated on the rear legs. That, in itself, constitutes a good stress test on a chair, but your patrons will invariably administer the coup de grace by rocking back and forth repeatedly on those two rear legs. In this instance, virtually every reading chair on four floors of that library was coming apart where the rear legs attached to the seat and apron. At over one hundred chairs per floor at a cost of more than two hundred dollars apiece, that library administration faced a significant replacement expense, and regrettably, one that could have been avoided.

The methods by which furniture parts are attached to each other constitute what we in the industry refer to as *joinery*. The joinery of a piece of library furniture is especially critical because no other furniture undergoes more stress in frequency, magnitude, or variation, than do the tables and chairs in your library. I want to rewind the example of the library table and re-record it. You have now had the tables for over twenty years. Aside from dings and surface scratches and the stalactites of hard chewing gum under the table edges, there is no evidence of wear. If you're still limber enough to get underneath the table, study the inside corner where the table leg attaches vertically to the subtop and laterally to the aprons. You notice that the top of the leg is tight against a heavy-gauge steel plate that fills the corner where the leg and two aprons come together. The steel plate is attached to the subtop with large-diameter wood screws or even bolts screwed into threaded steel inserts (which you can't see) in the subtop. The aprons may be doweled into the top of the leg, or they may be *mortised* and *tenoned* (see illustration). But that's not all. A W-shaped corner block of solid hardwood has been mortised or screwed and glued where the aprons meet the leg. In twenty years of dragging those tables around the library, you have not been able to loosen that joinery. And by the way, don't forget to notice that the aprons are solid oak (or maple, or cherry, or walnut), just like the table legs and edges. Now examine the chairs you purchased to go with those reading tables. If you tip one upside down, you will see, besides the gum, a joinery solution at the juncture of the aprons with the legs that is very similar to that used in the table, except that the blocking may extend even higher up the apron and consist of multiple mortise and tenon joints. Again, despite your patrons' best efforts, the rear legs are still tightly married to their side aprons (see fig. 8.5).

Durability

Durability, *reliability*, and *longevity* are all synonyms that are a function of

1. sound joinery,
2. the correct use of materials, and
3. appropriate wood finishes.

We've touched on joinery in the foregoing examples. I want to explain how a legitimate furniture craftsperson combines the materials I discussed in the previous section to preserve integrity and achieve long-term dependability.

The most inexpensive table has a ¾-inch particleboard core top laminated to a thin *melamine* wear surface (a plastic-like film, and the surface material of all plastic laminates). The raw particleboard outside edge is covered with a vinyl T molding or with a thin band of PVC (polyvinyl chloride—the material white plumbing pipe is made of). This solution is in no way suitable for library furniture. One step above this is a table with a particleboard core tabletop surfaced in a vg (vertical grade) laminate, the thinnest plastic laminate commercially available, which is about ⅟₃₂-inch thick and intended for vertical, low-wear surfaces such as cabinet doors. This also is a quality shortcut and will not endure. The only acceptable plastic laminate for a tabletop is ⁵⁄₁₀₀-inch thick. This is standard for a horizontal wear surface. For just under three dollars per square foot (standard laminate is about one dollar per square foot), you can get twice the wear out of your plastic laminate tabletop by specifying that the grade of laminate be the same required for laboratory work surfaces. Each of the three major brands of plastic laminate (Formica, Wilsonart, and Nevamar) has its own name for this product. Essentially, this upgrade consists of additional surface laminations of melamine bonded with chemical- and mar-resistant resins.

Plastic laminate, especially that which has been upgraded for wear, can be a dependable, long-life solution for library tabletops. How you have the tables edged, though, is important. Earlier, I mentioned PVC as an edge material. It is available as thin as wood veneer, but it can also be three millimeters thick. For an inexpensive but durable edge to a plastic laminate table- or carrel top, PVC at least two millimeters thick is a good choice.

If you want plastic laminate tabletops but want to dress them up, ask for a solid wood edge from ¼ to 2 inches in width. The University of California at Berkeley Haas Graduate School of Business Library combined a matte green

Figure 8.5. Table leg attachment.

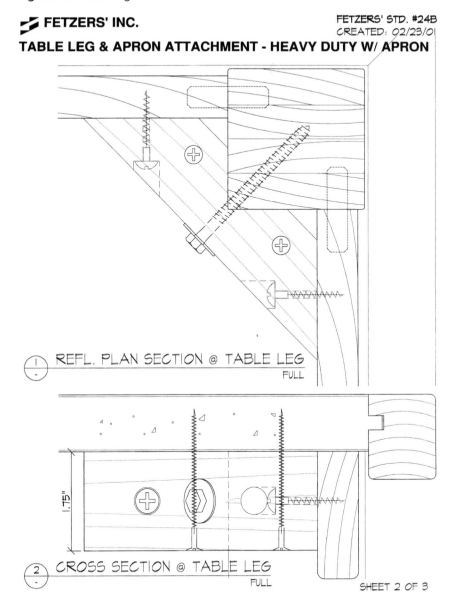

FETZERS' INC.

FETZERS' STD. #24B
CREATED: 02/23/01

TABLE LEG & APRON ATTACHMENT - HEAVY DUTY W/ APRON

REFL. PLAN SECTION @ TABLE LEG

FULL

1.75"

CROSS SECTION @ TABLE LEG

FULL

SHEET 2 OF 3

laminate top with a custom profile cherry wood edge for a refined look and good durability.

You might think that if cost were not an issue, the top-of-the-line solution for a library tabletop would be solid wood. Such a table is what you would surely see in Tudor banquet halls, having withstood for centuries the slamming down of pewter flagons and the weight of dancing drunken revelers. Think of such tables, built up of 2-inch-thick oak planks, burnished to a dull luster with countless rubbings of fine furniture oil, still as magnificent and indestructible as when they were crafted so long ago by artisans whose secrets went with them to their graves. This is a satisfying and romantic notion with a distinctly melancholy savor to it. The reality is that such furniture can be and still is made, which isn't as romantic as the previous notion; and yes, it can be expensive, which is even less romantic. One outstanding custom library furniture maker you may have heard of makes only solid wood furniture. That firm's design is its own. Its craftsmen cater to no architect or designer: They are indeed artists in wood, and no one does what they do better than they. The price of their furniture is high, not because they take unfair advantage, but because it reflects both the value of their art and the labor hours they are committed to expend to achieve the finesse their consciences as craftspeople and artists require. I have just described the Lexus of library furniture. If you prefer a BMW, consider this approach: library furniture constructed of a combination of beautiful solid wood and wood veneers of the same and complementary species, employing *marquetry* (the artistic piecing of pieces of wood veneer to create a pleasing design or match) and joinery solutions that have been employed successfully for centuries and have not died with ancient artisans but have mysteriously endured. There are many crossover skills employed in the creation of both types of furniture. They are merely choices between two legitimate furniture-making methods and philosophies.

Here are some trade-offs to consider. A solid wood tabletop may be hard to wear out. After all, how easily can a determined adolescent carve through 2-inch-thick oak or maple? On the other hand, wood, especially solid hardwood, is an eternally dynamic material. Even the centuries-old Tudor banquet tables are forever shrinking and swelling in reaction to changes in temperature and humidity—even inside a room. This accounts for splits and separations in the solid wood planks that are glued together to make such tabletops. Wood veneer, although its finished thickness may be only that of construction paper, is much more dimensionally stable when hot-pressed to an inert core such as MDF, and when sealed and finished with state-of-the-art polyurethane or polyester finishes. Institutional furniture—especially library furniture—needs more than several coatings of wax or oil to protect it, unless those hand-applied and temporary finishes are regularly and religiously reapplied. Oiled furniture picks up dirt from fingers and body oils, leaving black smudges that must be continually scrubbed off.

Several years ago a case in point was an order of oak carrels for the library of a prominent West Coast university. The administration insisted on an oil finish, because, as they are reputed to have said, they "didn't want anything to come between them and the wood." Within a year, the golden tones of the red oak carrels were hidden under a patina of body oil oxidized and blackened with dirt. All the carrels were shipped back to the manufacturer, sanded down and refinished, this time with a closed-pore catalyzed lacquer finish that still separated the owner from the wood by only a fraction of a millimeter but preserved the beauty of the wood with virtually no upkeep.

User-Friendliness and Ergonomics

Quality library furniture just has to be comfortable to use. When we sit at a reading table, our minds are not on the furniture but on the books in our hands. Yet we know (both as library furniture makers and library patrons) that when we lean our forearms against the table or carrel edge as we read, if the edge is abrupt, our arms may go numb; and if the porous oak wood grain of the tabletop has not been filled, our writing will be a little erratic as the pen's tip bumps across the uneven surface. User-friendliness is in large part a matter of good ergonomics. Library furniture should be adapted to the reach, sit, and lean of the human body. Granted, institutional furniture cannot adapt optimally to every possible body size, build, and conformation—and that is certainly the reality of the library world. The best that manufacturers can do for you is to build to a norm that accommodates as wide as possible a range of body shapes and sizes. For example, we build lumbar support into every chair we design. When we set a prototype library chair out at a recent ALA show, dozens of individuals tested the chair, and their assessment of the height, depth, and curvature of the lumbar design varied—just as we expected it would. That being said, some basic rules still apply: The standard height of a reading table is 29 inches, but the range for reading table height can fall comfortably between 28 and 31 inches. Chair seats are typically 17 inches from the floor at their front edges. That height still leaves short individuals with their feet dangling and basketball centers with their knees in the air.

A problem related as much to sociology as to ergonomics is that of the four-person reading table. Many librarians swear that there is no such thing. Unless a library is so crowded that patrons have no other option, four people will never opt to sit together at one table. That same obscure but astute library furniture maker designed a reading table with a wood veneer top with a white oak field and two intersecting bands of English brown oak, creating four equal rectangles or "domains" on the tabletop. Because all of us are by nature territorial, particularly when we don't know one another, each person seated at that table had his or her own workspace. Enhancing the privacy of each space was an integral light fixture at the center of the table, which ran almost the length of the table and was designed to sit at a height that effectively blocked all possibility of eye contact between patrons seated opposite each other—a real stroke of genius.

POWER AND DATA SOLUTIONS

There can be no discussion of library furniture without addressing the very real need to make accommodation for the ubiquitous laptop computer. The problem has been and continues to be where and how to place the electrical and data outlets.

I have found, through observation and discussion with many librarians, that power and data ports in reading tables and carrels should be easily accessible but as simple as possible. The fewer the moving parts (such as pop-up columns—which are usually made of plastic—or tilt-up or pivoting trap doors, which become gum and wrapper receptacles), the better. We have found that the cleanest and simplest presentation of the power and data boxes is in the end-table aprons or in a corner column on the carrel walls. Raceways must separate the power and data wires, and those raceways can be conveniently mounted to the insides of the table keels and then run down a center pedestal underneath the tabletop, or down the inside of one table leg into a floor-mounted junction box. The concealed raceway must be accessible by means of an easily removable panel.

THE CASE FOR VALUE *AND* PREQUALIFICATION

In conclusion, I want to offer a definition of value as it pertains to library furniture—or almost anything else, for that matter. Value is the optimal intersection of cost and quality. It is your "money's worth." This definition should make the purchasing decision between short-term savings with the probability of imminent, high repair and replacement costs, versus higher purchase cost with the assurance of long-term savings, a relatively easy one. The painful reality is that you may be constrained by law or policy to go with the low-bid provider, which almost inevitably means you will get the lowest quality product. Really. The solution to this dilemma, many buyers have found, lies in the process of *prequalification*.

If this chapter and other information sources have helped you establish essential criteria for your library furniture, these can be incorporated into a questionnaire by which prospective furniture makers are prequalified for admission to an *approved bidders list*. Only those manufacturers who demonstrate their ability to meet or exceed the prequalification criteria are invited to bid. The strongest prequalification procedures add a foolproof component: the request for a mock-up. The design professional you retain takes all the important criteria for your furniture—aesthetic and practical—and incorporates them into a drawing of a single furniture item or portion of that item. It then becomes the responsibility of the prospective furniture makers to actually demonstrate their competence by submitting the finished mock-up with the written questionnaire. Only those furniture makers who pass *both* portions of the prequalification are admitted to the bidders list. Then, you, as the library furniture buyer, can have reasonable assurance that even the lowest bidder will perform to expectation. This may sound like a complicated and time-consuming effort, but many professionals in the design and construction industry routinely use prequalification to find worthy suppliers and contractors. Issuing a prequalification request is analogous to distributing a take-home test: once the teacher has formulated it, the work rests with the students. And a good prequalification procedure can be used over and over again.

This treatise on library furniture from an insider's viewpoint—in addition to imparting information—may also have raised new questions. I will be pleased to refer you to sources of additional information.

9 LANDSCAPE DESIGN, ESTABLISHMENT, AND MAINTENANCE

James J. Flott and Merri A. Hartse

INTRODUCTION

Landscaping is a prominent feature of the urban infrastructure and is as essential to a site as the building. Trees, shrubs, and herbaceous perennials have been a part of the earth for a very long time and are a source of oxygen, food, fuel, and building materials. In addition to these functional uses, they also add much to the aesthetic appearance of the built environment.

The first impressions of a library are important and lasting. Customers' initial perceptions are often formed from the appearance of the landscape. These first impressions frequently stay with customers and may set the tone of their library experience, as well as how they interact with staff and how they treat the facility and its contents. The landscape is often treated as an afterthought to the design process, however, and is the capital item often reduced or cut entirely from the project budget despite its potential for adding 7 to 20 percent to the value of the site (Harris, Clark, and Matheny 1999). Even Andrew Carnegie did not include funds or plans for landscaping in his gift of library buildings to over 2,800 communities.

Significant attention should be given to decisions concerning the design, retention, and maintenance of landscapes on library sites, given the high value often placed on landscaping proximate to buildings. It is equally important for managers to consider the exterior as much a part of the infrastructure of the library as the interior, to meet the requirements of a facility. The first impression begins with a well-designed landscape and maintenance program to ensure that the quality of the design is lasting and meets the needs of the site. A well-designed and properly maintained landscape is an essential component in providing a productive environment for staff and a pleasant experience for users.

The focus of the grant-funded partnership between the American Library Association and Global Learning, Incorporated, has been to create library programs, services, and collections that help to build sustainable communities. The challenge, as pointed out by Boyden and Weiner (2001), is to take the sustainability concept and apply it to library building projects and operations, not just programs. "The library building itself can express a community's pressing need to take local responsibility for processes that have global impact" (p. 45). Sustainability embraces three principles: economy, ecology, and equity. Economy implies how resources are managed and used to meet community needs. Equity demonstrates how community members' interests are shared and balanced through the design process, and how everyone in the community then shares in the project's benefits. Ecology is the relationship between living organisms and their environment. Sustainable design is "understood to be a part of a long-term life cycle of investment, use, and renewal" (Boyden and Weiner 2001, 45). These principles will be emphasized as this chapter demonstrates how to apply the sustainability concept to the landscape of a new library building or renovation of an existing facility.

ECOLOGICAL DESIGN

All human changes to the environment involve design. The natural world has been forged in evolution over a period of four billion years. The human world of cities, roads, farms, and other artifacts that people have been designing for themselves have existed over the last few millennia. Today, much of design is influenced only by necessity, short-term economy, or greed. The designed mess made of neighborhoods, cities, and ecosystems owes much to a lack of a coherent philosophy, vision, and practice of design grounded in an understanding of ecology and sustainability. In a landscape, the lack of ecological design leads to the degradation of resources, living systems, ecosystem services, and human life (Van Der Ryn and Cowan 1996).

In contrast, ecological design integrates conservation, regeneration, and stewardship to achieve sustainability. Ecological design is a way of integrating human purpose with nature's own flows, cycles, and patterns. It proposes a form of design that is able to translate the vision of sustainability into the buildings and landscapes around us. It suggests a new set of questions and themes to order the design process.

Ecological design begins with an intimate knowledge of the site. It is small-scale, direct, and responsive to both the local conditions and local people. It is a sense of place attuned to the particular history, culture, and knowledge of region. It will take endless forms, the very diversity of design possibilities helping to ensure a sustainability that is suited to the particularities of the site. Design solutions grow from a local knowledge of place.

Ecological design cuts through the insularity of the various design professions. The conventional design approach begins with an engineer, architect, or landscape architect developing a plan without the contribution of the community, the occupants using the building, or the staff maintaining the landscape.

The design process is fragmented into dozens of technical disciplines, each with its own specialized language and tools. Eventually, all of the contributing specialists' recommendations are integrated. In contrast, ecological design suggests a deeply participatory and equitable process in which technical disciplinary languages and barriers are exchanged for a shared understanding of the design problem. One of the best ways to ensure that a highly interactive design process occurs is to have the architects, engineers, landscapers, builders, board members, occupants, maintenance staff, and others with a stake in the building and landscape develop the design together. Ecological design suggests that sustainability is a cultural process rather than an expert one, and that we should all acquire a basic competence in the shaping of our environment.

DESIGN CONSIDERATIONS

Plant Placement and Selection

A well-designed landscape that includes trees, shrubs, and perennials is not only beautiful, but an asset to the property. The placement and selection of plants determines whether the manager considers it a dream landscape or a maintenance nightmare, however. The tenet among green industry professionals is the "right plant in the right place" (Fazio 1989). This concept is critical to an ecological design and a comprehensive low-maintenance program.

Plants are one of the most important landscape features, and their placement and selection affect the design and maintenance program. They provide many benefits throughout the year with their variety of forms, flowers, fruits, and leaf colors. They deflect noise and wind, screen unwanted views, reduce pollution and erosion, cool buildings and parking lots, provide pedestrian and traffic control, and, most important, provide oxygen. These benefits are usually a result of careful placement and selection. In fact, if a plant is not properly matched to the landscape site, the plant can become more a liability than an asset. Choosing the right plant for the right place is one of the most important decisions to ensure an ecological design, low maintenance, and long-term benefits.

The first consideration must be what the plant needs, or in other words, what environmental conditions limit the ability of a particular plant to thrive. Every plant has certain cultural requirements, including temperature, light, water, and soil. Each landscape site has unique environmental characteristics such as temperature extremes, available growing space, and light levels that can limit which plants will thrive. Additionally, plants are chosen to fulfill a particular function in the landscape. It is important to choose a particular plant that is capable of growing in the environmental and cultural conditions at the site and meets the desired landscape function. The highest priorities are those that will affect the survival of the plant. In some instances, the functional requirements cannot be met entirely because of site limitations that will cause the plant to fail.

Many site conditions must be taken into consideration in plant selection. Climate factors such as temperature, rainfall, sunlight, and wind direction must be considered. The proximity to buildings, pavement, other plants, and overhead and underground utilities affect the choice of plant. For example, tall-growing trees should never be planted beneath utility lines. Trees without sufficient growing space can interfere with sidewalks, curbs, electrical transmission lines, and building entries. Soil pH, fertility, and volume are important when selecting the type of plant to use in a particular site. The level of maintenance to be provided is an important part of the site characteristics that will affect the plant's ability to thrive.

Once the site characteristics have been determined, landscape functions can be considered. These may include such considerations as controlling pedestrian traffic, hiding unsightly features, acting as wind screens, or shading parking lots. Ornamental features such as fall leaf color or flowers may be a desired landscape function.

Urban sites present a harsh environment for plants. Besides site conditions, the plant characteristics must be considered in plant selection. The plant's ability to survive low and high temperatures and its growth habit, mature height, and spread are characteristics affecting the selection. Ornamental attributes such as flowers, foliage, fall color, bark color, and fruit may make a plant more desirable or may preclude the use of certain plants. Resistance to insects and diseases, drought tolerance, water and light requirements, and root zone requirements are other plant characteristics to consider when selecting for a given site. The careful placement and selection of plants should protect and enhance the library's landscape investment.

Safety and Security

The mitigation of liability is a critical concern in the design and construction of grounds and landscapes for public use. As society becomes increasingly litigious, crime, vandalism, and injuries will add immense strains on budgets of libraries and other public agencies. Staff and customer safety and security in public open spaces can be directly traced to the design of the landscape, implementation of grounds management standards, and staff knowledge and training, as well as to the personnel, supervisors, and governing boards responsible for them. Libraries are public facilities. Therefore, library planners must design safety and security into their sites and employ strategies to maintain facilities that are safe for staff and customers.

The amount of money allocated to safety is an indication of safety's priority in the organization. To make the most of funds provided for safety and security, however, library managers need to first examine the landscape design to determine in what patterns vegetation should be planted to minimize risk and maximize the ecological and social benefits vegetation provides. In his book, *Defensible Space*, Newman (1972) suggested that design plays a key role in reducing crime and vandalism while maintaining an aesthetic landscape. It is possible to design and maintain a safe and secure landscape by employing plant selection, plant placement, and proper maintenance.

This chapter emphasizes plant selection as a critical component of sustainable and ecological design. Plant selection is also important to the safety and security of a site. In public places, the design should increase open views, reduce concealment, and eliminate places of entrapment. Plant selection should consider the height and width of plants at maturity to avoid obstructing windows, walks, and doors. It may be necessary to remove overgrown plants in the renovation of existing landscapes and to start over with smaller varieties. The use of defensive plants under windows and around doors and areas that are not well lit will deter contact and access to these areas. Plants such as barberry, pyracantha, and quince are thorny, spiny, and not inviting. Choose plants that are less vigorous varieties to minimize pruning and avoid blocking windows, doors, and sidewalks at any stage of growth and maturity. Avoid plants that hide the view and can provide concealment for burglars or attackers along pathways.

Plant placement and location are other elements to keep in mind when designing and maintaining a landscape. Plant positioning defines property lines and creates physical and psychological barriers that direct or deter access. For example, a low-growing thorny hedge along the bottom of a fence deters intruders from jumping the fence. Similarly, a line of plants along a walk will encourage pedestrians to stay on the sidewalk. Use of lighting to accent plants will aid security, enhance the design, and provide good sight lines after dark.

Proper maintenance is necessary to sustain the quality of the landscape and is also important for improving safety and security of the facility. Proper pruning of plant material can enhance the safety and security of your facility. Security pruning can be done at the same time as routine maintenance pruning. Shrubs should be pruned 12 to 18 inches away from and 8 to 10 inches below windows and doorways to allow better visibility and easier detection of offenders by staff, customers, neighbors, and authorities. Tree branches should be elevated to 8 feet above the ground for clearance and visibility. Local ordinances may exist regarding clearance issues for trees and shrubs located at street entrances and along sidewalks. Regular pruning and inspections of trees by an International Society of Arboriculture certified arborist will reduce the liability associated with tree failures and will also lessen the severity of damage to trees from ice storms and other natural events. Prune deadwood and debris from trees to mitigate failure risk, and prune tree branches away from windows and roofs to reduce criminal access.

Other design features to consider for a safe and secure landscape are the structures used in the landscape and the associated nonplant landscape materials. Structures such as fences should not be over 3 feet high unless they are visually permeable. Taller fences may provide privacy and a sense of security for the site, but they are easy to climb and actually provide concealment for offenders as they gain access into a building. Nonplant landscape materials such as mulch may seem rather mundane, but an incorrect choice of material can create opportunities for falls or vandalism. Consider wood chips as a mulch versus landscape rock mulch. Wood chips stay in place, are not easily dislodged by foot traffic, are inexpensive, and provide a beneficial environment for plant growth. Landscape rock mulch does enhance plant growth somewhat, but it does not stay in place, is easily kicked out of a landscape bed, and is expensive. When landscape rock litters sidewalks, it becomes a fall hazard much like a bag of marbles spilled on the sidewalk. Additionally, landscape rock mulch can be used as projectiles to break building or vehicle windows.

Public perception of libraries as safe places can be partially validated by designing safer landscapes and public areas with proper selection of plants; well-conceived placement of structures, plants, and lighting; and proper maintenance. Constant awareness of safety and security by everyone involved—from policymakers to maintenance workers—is necessary to minimize potential liability in public facilities.

Water Conservation

Water is one of the nation's most critical natural resources. Booming populations have increased the demand on the country's finite supply of high-quality water. In addition, seasonal fluctuations and periodic droughts impact water availability. Parks, gardens, and landscapes need water chiefly in midsummer, when it's scarcest and costliest to provide. They often account for two-fifths to four-fifths of urban water use (Hawken, Lovins, and Lovins 1999). Much of the water is used to maintain traditional landscapes that demand large amounts of moisture, or it is simply inefficiently applied. For example, a study of the Irvine Ranch Water District in California revealed that landscapers overwatered by 25 to 250 percent (Gangloff 1995).

Ecological design using the concept of xeriscaping produces quality landscaping that conserves water and protects the environment. This is a comprehensive approach to landscaping for water conservation. Xeriscape landscaping is not only beautiful but can also provide natural cooling, fire protection, and wildlife habitat. It also saves such inputs as labor, fertilizer, herbicides, and fuel, plus it reduces chemical runoff. Xeriscape landscaping is not turning lawns into cactus gardens; it is green landscapes full of beautiful plants maintained with water-efficient practices. The traditional green landscapes to which we are accustomed can be achieved and still conserve water by following the principles of xeriscaping.

A water-efficient landscape begins with an ecological design. In creating the design, you should group plants based on the amount of water they need. This will prevent overwatering the drought-tolerant plants and underwatering those that need more water. If possible, use permeable surfaces that allow water to soak into the soil.

Most building sites have very poor soil. During construction, most of the topsoil is removed, soil compaction increases, and construction debris is buried. Soil improvement is the best insurance for increasing plant health and conserving water. Reducing compaction and adding organic matter increases the soil's ability to absorb and store water in a form available to plants.

Select trees, shrubs, perennials, and grasses based on their adaptability to the region's soil and climate. Each region of the United States has an abundance of native plants naturally adapted to the site. Most of these have lower water demands, fewer pest problems, and less fertilizer requirements than many of the nonadapted exotic plants. Many nonnative plants are well adapted to each region and, in combination with natives, provide a beautiful, interesting landscape that conserves water. Consult a nursery or county extension agent for sources of healthy, high-quality plants, and plant them correctly to get a landscape off to a good start.

The type of watering system selected can make a big difference in water conservation. The goal of any irrigation system is to give plants a sufficient amount of water without waste. An irrigation system design should create zones to water grass areas separately and more frequently than other plant material. Sprinkler irrigation is the most commonly used method of watering grass, but it is much less efficient for plants and often applies water where it is not needed. Trees, shrubs, and other plant material are most effectively irrigated with drip or trickle systems. Drip irrigation increases irrigation efficiency and plant performance. Irrigating properly incorporates both systems to achieve water conservation. Seeking professional irrigation advice ensures choosing the correct system to meet landscape water needs efficiently.

Applying the right amount of water, at the right time, and in the right way is important for water conservation. Automated sprinkler systems are especially prone to encouraging waste. The convenience of an automated system makes it easy to overwater, because less attention is paid to the landscape. Trees, shrubs, perennials, and grasses have different water needs. Adjust the irrigation system to meet the needs of the plants. Consult with the local extension office for specific water requirements for plants in the region. Watering infrequently and deeply promotes deep root systems and helps plants endure drought better. It is especially important to maintain the irrigation system. Check systems weekly for broken nozzles or heads, ensure that the timing clock and rain sensors are working, and adjust the days and times as needed to avoid excessive watering. Water at night, as close as possible to the early morning hours, to avoid water loss from evaporation and to allow leaf surfaces to dry more quickly (to avoid disease problems).

Landscape water loss typically occurs from water applied too rapidly that runs off the site rather than soaking into the soil, or water that is applied to bare soil surfaces and evaporates. Water is lost when it evaporates from exposed soil. Mulch, a layer of material covering the soil surface around plants, conserves moisture by reducing evaporation from the soil. It can be organic material such as bark, wood chips, compost, or inorganic material such as rock or landscape fabric. Use it whenever possible. Mulch also reduces weed populations, prevents soil erosion and compaction, and moderates soil temperatures.

No landscape is maintenance free. Appropriate maintenance preserves the landscape and conserves water. Proper pruning, mowing, weeding, fertilization, pest control, and irrigation system maintenance all conserve water.

Parking Lot Design

Parking lots, parking, and cars are a part of everyday life and impose a particular set of design restrictions on the library and grounds. Large asphalt and concrete parking lots are often unsightly, but with a good design they can provide a useful space in which to plant trees while accommodating the prerequisite number of parking spaces. The design should strive to create both beauty and functionality.

The design must first consider safety. The parking lot is where vehicles and pedestrians intersect. Pedestrians should have a clear idea where it is safe to walk, and a clear traffic flow is important so drivers follow a planned pattern as they search for parking spaces. Often the roadway for cars is also the pedestrian walkway. This is analogous to combining oil and water—the two do not mix. Therefore, safe sidewalks that lead the pedestrian to the building entrance are important. Plants can soften the harshness of parking lots and provide useful pedestrian and traffic control that guides, directs and slows, reduces pollution, and cools both people and their automobiles.

The difficulty experienced in establishing trees or groups of plants in large areas of unrelieved hard surfacing is often due to dry and hot conditions, soil compaction, light intensity, and poor air quality. Simply dropping a few trees in the ground to add some greenery creates a disjointed landscape and fails to provide a clear flow or function to the parking lot design. Additionally, it is important to understand the needs of the plants. Ecological design should be used in the development of parking lots. Critical to the issue of trees and other plants thriving in parking lots is dedicating more space for plant material. This is a difficult problem for landscaping where parking space is at a premium. Local zoning regulations, the number of spaces required by a facility, and handicap accessibility will impact the design. Nevertheless, if parking lots are to be more aesthetically pleasing and functional, it is essential to provide more space for plant material.

In selecting plant material, many of the same principles outlined earlier apply to parking lots. But the microclimate of a parking lot is also of major importance. Plants are subjected to much harsher conditions such as heat, soil compaction, limited planting space, snow piles, ice melters, petroleum runoff, and vehicle contact that results in damage. Plant compositions that include trees, shrubs, and groundcovers (not turfgrass) in a relatively large bed create a better environment for plant growth than the scenario of a single tree in a small hole surrounded by asphalt or concrete. Plant trees such as columnar beech or hornbeam with upright growing branches to avoid interfering with traffic and obscuring pedestrian and motorist visibility.

Similarly, shrubs and groundcovers used in parking lots should be low growing, with a maximum size of 3 feet at maturity. In situations that require a clear line of sight, use low groundcovers rather than shrubs. Avoid using trees that produce fruit or litter twigs. For example, oaks are excellent trees, but acorns on sidewalks can cause falls and injury to pedestrians; falling acorns also pelt cars. Tree species that are weak-wooded and known to fail, such as cottonwood, should not be used in the landscape. Select deciduous trees to provide shade in the summer and to allow warming sun rays to filter through in the winter to melt ice and snow. Mature trees in parking lots will lengthen the life expectancy of asphalt, because the surface stays cooler and the aggregate remains bonded in the asphalt. Trees also reduce pollution emissions from parked cars.

Perennials are also attractive additions to any parking lot. The location and size of the planting bed should be large enough to be noticed but without distracting the driver looking for a parking space. Sidewalks should be wide enough for pedestrian traffic and to avoid conflicts with vehicles. Plan the pedestrian walkway system closest to the route people want to walk. Then add plants to these walks for pedestrian and traffic control and to make the walks more interesting and attractive. Planting trees along sidewalks also provides necessary shade for pedestrians.

The maintenance of parking lots with trees, shrubs, and perennials goes well beyond sweeping, striping lines, and cleaning the lot. The landscaping in a parking lot is an investment, and the more sophisticated the planting, the more horticultural knowledge is required to keep the parking lot looking good. As a manager, consider the level of resources and maintenance expertise available to the site, and match the complexity of the landscape to a realistic level of maintenance.

Snow and ice removal is an important part of parking lot maintenance. Designing the parking lot to provide holding areas for snow will avoid loss of parking spaces and reduce the need for hauling snow off-site. If it is necessary to haul snow off-site, allowances for the entrance and exit of large snow removal equipment is required. Chemicals used to melt ice and snow are harmful to plant material. Keep these chemicals away from plants or use salt-tolerant plants such as sea buckthorn.

Heavy rains and melting snows should be considered in the design. Traditional design practices consider surface water as something to be eliminated. Meanwhile, water shortages and drought are frequent problems in many communities. A valuable resource is sent down the river whenever a site grade directs surface runoff into the storm-water system. Aquifer recharge and underground water tables depend on absorption of surface water for replenishment. Landscape buffer systems can assist this process by using ponds, irrigation catchments, or bog gardens to collect water and purify it naturally before it enters the aquifer. Trees are an excellent aid in increasing rainfall absorption. Leaves catch and hold rainwater while slowing its descent to the ground, allowing for a slower and more complete absorption rate. Annoying parking lot experiences caused by a failure to plan for surface water runoff include being splashed by cars driving through standing water and having to step into a puddle of water before reaching higher ground. These problems should be addressed in the design.

Material used for parking lot surfaces also affects the sustainability of the site. For example, consider replacing dark-colored asphalt with a lighter, less heat-absorbing color that will reduce heat generation during summer months.

Parking lots are a design challenge and need to be considered for the safety of all, both employees and customers, who will be using the library. If the walk to the library entrance is a safe and pleasant experience, the parking lot will provide extra appeal to attract customers to the facility. It is an investment in a quality environment.

MAINTENANCE MANAGEMENT PROGRAM

Grounds maintenance is one of the most costly expenses that property and facility managers face. Maintenance costs for landscaping will exceed the initial design and installation costs in just a few years. Consequently, the design must reflect serious consideration of long-term maintenance and associated costs, and positive steps need to be taken to minimize these costs. The landscape can be a source of maintenance problems if it is not designed with maintenance in mind. Ecological design decisions can control current and future landscape and grounds maintenance costs and minimize the need for maintenance in this area. This does not mean that ecological designs are maintenance free and can be left to natural processes with no human guidance. What ecological design does mean is that landscapes incorporating native and adapted plant materials that thrive in local environments will require less time, money, and energy for upkeep than designs in which plants are selected and placed for ornamental effect alone. Such designs require less watering, mowing, pruning, fertilizing, and other cultural treatments. An ecological design reduces the use of pesticides and other chemical treatments. Ecological design aims not only to reduce these negative effects, but also to make a positive contribution to the surrounding environment. Ecologically designed landscapes can also become functioning ecosystems capable of providing food and shelter for animals and insects to sustain biological diversity in your region. By employing specific guidelines, low maintenance with an ecologically sound, naturally beautiful landscape can be achieved.

Maintenance Guidelines

1. Cultivate an appreciation of the beauty in the region's ecological zone. There is a responsibility to contribute to the community and a sense of place to the larger landscape. Random informality often passes for ecological design, when in reality, nature is highly ordered and anything but random. Understanding this order and using it in a design is the key to making ecological design work. A planned landscape interacts with the surrounding landscape, both natural and constructed.

2. Select plants with few cultural or physical requirements. Choose those that are appropriately sized for the available space. It is not wise to select plants that require regular pruning or ornamentals that are weak-wooded. Reconsider before using plants that require specific soil conditions or are very susceptible to diseases and insect pests. Avoid plants with high water requirements, and use mulches to conserve water and reduce weeds. Eliminate or greatly reduce the amount of turfgrass especially on steep slopes. Great amounts of water, fertilizer, pesticides, labor and fuel are expended for lawn upkeep, and the amount of pol-

lution from small engine exhaust is well documented. There are many alternative groundcovers that require less maintenance and cost less to maintain.

3. Plant placement requires careful thinking. The location of plants in a landscape influences its maintenance needs nearly as much as the plants themselves. Be aware of trees' and shrubs' mature sizes in relation to other landscape elements, sidewalks, and buildings to avoid creating additional regular maintenance. For instance, do not plant trees with weeping habits next to walkways, streets, or parking lots where branches could interfere with traffic. Allow enough space for the plant to achieve its natural form, but not so much open space that weeds also become established. Consider other infrastructure maintenance when placing plants, such as painting and snow removal.

4. Determine whether to use a private contractor for maintenance or trained staff. Landscape maintenance and establishment, tree care, and irrigation maintenance are technical professions that require academic training, work experience, and in some cases professional licenses. Far too often, great designs are turned into disasters by using unskilled staff such as custodians or building engineers to perform maintenance. The potential risk of damage or destruction to the infrastructure and the potential for staff accidents are very high when the staff person is not qualified for the task. Quality maintenance programs begin with skilled staff performing the maintenance. A staff person trained in horticulture or arboriculture will protect your landscape investment and ensure that it remains an asset. The goal of any infrastructure maintenance is to protect and enhance the investment.

Consideration of the level of maintenance and the funds available for staffing must be tailored to meet the needs of the facility. An equitable view of the cost of maintaining a landscape should compare the cost of staff professional(s) versus hiring contract professionals. Staff wages, benefit costs, and administrative costs should be compared to the cost of hiring a contractor. The cost of having a custodian perform part-time landscape maintenance versus the cost of contract professionals could prove to be too high when all relevant costs are considered. Additionally, there is a higher risk of injury to the staff person or damage to the landscape that is rarely figured in the cost of maintenance. The cost of maintenance equipment for all landscape tasks should also be considered in the choice between in-house maintenance workers and private contractors.

5. Establish maintenance standards for staff or private contractors. In order to achieve and maintain the desired level of quality in landscape maintenance, standards must be developed. This is the basis for determining what maintenance activities are to be performed, how frequently they are to be performed, and the average time required to perform a given task under normal operating conditions. There are standards and specifications written for landscapes that provide examples of annual maintenance activities, frequencies, and completion times. These standards are applicable for in-house staff or for use as contract specifications when hiring contractors. They are quite helpful to the director for

scheduling maintenance and in the preparation of budgets. High, moderate, or low levels of maintenance for grounds, trees, shrubs, perennials, and turfgrass may be required, depending on the site and the goals of the organization. Standards and specifications provide consistent maintenance levels that meet the goals of the facility, regardless of who performs the work or changes in administration or staff.

CONCLUSION

The library landscape design is as important to the success of a building project as the building itself. The landscape can become a safety threat, contribute to the depletion of the earth's natural resources, and bear a high cost to the community if planning is left to the last minute, or if its budget is limited or omitted. The landscape serves a functional purpose and adds to the aesthetic quality of the built environment. In this aspect, the landscape becomes part of the infrastructure of the library and should be treated as such in terms of planning, construction, and ongoing maintenance. Landscaping is the only infrastructure item that increases in value in an urban environment. All other infrastructure items, such as buildings and interiors, decrease in value as they age. A library manager who understands ecological design concepts will construct a sustainable building and landscape that conserves resources for future generations.

This chapter emphasizes the use of ecological design and the integration of human purpose with natural patterns while promoting the key concepts of sustainability. This design process is economical, ecological, and brings everyone together in the planning phase for the benefit of society and the environment.

Ecological design involves several considerations. Plant placement and selection are emphasized. In choosing the right plants and putting them in the right spaces, the ecological design goals are met and maintenance costs are reduced. Participation of community members is important in the design process, but the design should be a collaboration of all who have a stake in the facility. For additional expertise, look to county or state horticulture extension agents, certified arborists, conservation districts, and state departments of ecology or natural resources. Xeriscaping will help to ensure that the library is doing its part for water conservation while (again) reducing maintenance costs. Xeriscaping involves not only choosing plants that require less water, but also carefully selecting the type of irrigation system to provide the right amount of water at the right time without waste.

Parking lots play a significant role in the library's exterior design. They also produce unique challenges. Placing and selecting the right trees, shrubs and groundcovers will aid in controlling the harsh microclimates of parking lots. Plants and design can do much to mitigate the effects of heat islands, pollutants from cars, water runoff, and snow removal. Careful design will also ensure the library customer's safe passage from parking lot to building.

Design elements such as careful selection and placement of plant material require a level of maintenance expertise to match the landscape. The maintenance components of a landscape design are critical to meeting the sustainability components of the plan. No landscape is maintenance free, but ecological design provides an opportunity to reduce maintenance and maintenance costs. Library managers must consider the resources and staff available for maintenance. Gardener positions should be considered integral staff positions, to ensure that the landscape remains an asset to the facility.

Current trends toward reducing chemical use, pollutants, water consumption, maintenance, and other environmental issues make the case for ecological design even stronger. The opportunity and responsibility to treat the land as a living entity and a source of human life are available to everyone. In order to capitalize on this opportunity, we need to develop reliable strategies for landscape design and combine these with horticultural management based on ecological principles.

REFERENCES

Boyden, Lynn, and James Weiner. 2001. "For the Public Good: Sustainability Demonstration in Public Library Building Projects." *Public Libraries* 40 (1): 44–46.

Fazio, James R., ed. 1989. *The Right Tree for the Right Place*. Tree City USA Bulletin 4. Nebraska City, NE: National Arbor Day Foundation.

Gangloff, Deborah. 1995. "The Sustainable City." *American Forests* May/June: 30–34, 38.

Harris, Richard W., James R. Clark, and Nelda P. Matheny. 1999. *Arboriculture: Integrated Management of Landscape, Trees, Shrubs, and Vines*. Upper Saddle River, NJ: Prentice Hall.

Hawken, Paul, Amory Lovins, and L. Hunter Lovins. 1999. *Natural Capitalism: Creating the Next Industrial Revolution*. New York: Little, Brown.

Newman, Oscar. 1972. *Defensible Space: Crime Prevention Through Urban Design*. New York: Macmillan.

Van Der Ryn, Sim, and Stuart Cowan. 1996. *Ecological Design*. Washington, DC: Island Press.

SELECTED BIBLIOGRAPHY

Chengrian, Dan. "Analyze Landscape Sites." *Grounds Maintenance*, March 1995, 50–56.

Clark, James R., Nelda P. Matheney, Cross, Genni, and Victoria Wake "A Model of Urban Forest Sustainability." *Journal of Arboriculture*, January 1997: 17–30.

"Denver Water." Xeriscape Plant Guide. Golden, CO: Fulcrum Publishing, 1996.

Ferguson, Nicola. *Right Plant, Right Place*. New York: Summit Books, 1984.

Lueder, Dianne C., and Sally Webb. *Administrator's Guide to Library Building Maintenance*. Chicago: American Library Association, 1992.

Melby, Pete. "Plantings Can Provide Pedestrian and Traffic Control." *Grounds Maintenance*, May 1997, C6-C10.

Metcalfe, Audrey. "Landscaping for Security." *American Nurseryman*, February 1993, 90–93.

Michael, Sean E., and R. Bruce Hull IV. "Effects of Vegetation on Crime in Urban Parks." Interim Report. Savoy, IL: International Society of Arboriculture Research Trust, 1994.

Moffatt, Anne Simon, Marc Schiler, and the Staff of Green Living. *Energy-Efficient and Environmental Landscaping*. South NewFane, VT: Appropriate Solutions Press, 1994.

Nasar, Jack L. "Safer Communities by Design." *Grounds Maintenance*, November 1996, 10–14.

Nicolsi, Ralph. "Make Lawn Maintenance Low Maintenance." *Landscape Management*, June 2001, 33–37.

Scott, Klaus I., James R. Simpson, and E. Gregory McPherson. "Effects of Tree Cover on Parking Lot Microclimate and Vehicle Emissions." *Journal of Arboriculture*, May 1999, 129–142.

Trotta, Carmine J., and Marcia Trotta. *The Librarian's Facility Management Handbook*. New York: Neal-Schuman, 2001.

VanDerZanden, A. M. "Conserving Water in the Garden: Designing and Installing a New Landscape." Corvallis: Oregon State University Extension Service. [http://eesc.orst.edu/agcomwebfile/EdMat/html/EC/EC1530/EC1530.html]. May 2001.

Washington State University Cooperative Extension. "Low Maintenance Landscape Demonstration." Handout. Spokane: Washington State University Cooperative Extension, n.d.

Wasowski, Andy, and Sally Wasowski. *Building Inside Nature's Envelope: How New Construction and Land Preservation Can Work Together*. Oxford, UK: Oxford University Press, 2000.

Weaner, Larry. "Ten Elements of Natural Design." *American Nurseryman*, January 1996, 34–41.

Welsh, Douglas F., William C. Welch, and Richard L. Duble. "Landscape Water Conservation … Xeriscape." College Station: Texas Agricultural Extension Service. [http://aggie-horticulture.tamu.edu/extension/xeriscape/xeriscape.html]. Revised October 26, 2000.

PART IV
JOINT-USE LIBRARIES

10 JOINT-USE LIBRARIES: THE ULTIMATE FORM OF COOPERATION

Alan Bundy

INTRODUCTION

A core value of libraries and librarians locally, nationally, and internationally is cooperation, more so than perhaps any other agency and profession. The manifestations of that client-focused cooperation are many, but the ultimate manifestation and challenge is a joint-use, or combined, library. It is not, however, a form of cooperation usually initiated or advocated by the profession. Despite this, interest in the concept continues, and the number and variety of joint-use libraries is increasing worldwide.

DEFINITION

A definition of a joint-use library is a library in which two or more distinct library services providers, usually a school and a public library, serve their client groups in the same building, based on an agreement that specifies the relationship between the providers. Such libraries have existed for nearly a century. From numerous failures of the concept (during the last forty years in particular), lessons have been learned.

Joint-use library variations include libraries for two or more educational institutions, research institutions, government agencies, and even business corporations. This chapter is concerned primarily with the most common type of joint-use library, the school-housed public library or school-community library, less frequent but increasing variations of which are the community college and the university-housed public library.

THE LITERATURE

The published and unpublished literature on joint-use libraries relates mostly to school-community libraries. That literature, as a whole, emphasizes the susceptibility of joint-use libraries to failure or dysfunction. It is substantial but includes few in-depth and evaluative studies. Amey's (1987) review of this literature therefore led him to the conclusion that it "tends to be disjointed, discontinuous, largely descriptive and particularised" (p. vii). Of its largely negative tone, he observed that "it reads like the story of Job ... an endless chronicle of righteous endeavours, undone by unanticipated calamities" (p. vii).

Still the best record of the literature is the 514-item bibliography in Amey's (1987) *Combining Libraries: The Canadian and Australian Experience*. Also of substance is the 330-item bibliography in the California State Library's *Public and School Libraries: Issues and Options of Joint Use Facilities and Cooperative Use Agreements* (Berger 2000). These are complemented by the bibliographies in *School and Public Library Relationships* (Fitzgibbons 2000) and *Combined Libraries: A Bibliography* (American Library Association 2002). The latter covers exclusively U.S. literature from 1984 to 1999, and in particular, items from Colorado.

BACKGROUND

School-housed public libraries date back to at least 1906, with one having operated continuously in New Hampshire since then. Another, in Canada, has operated since 1940. Informally, they have existed even longer, it having often been the practice in rural areas to allow parents and other members of the community to borrow from school libraries where they existed and had acquired books suitable for adults. A first instance of this was recorded in the state of South Australia in 1875.

The negative literature about them began with a 1963 U.S. survey of 154 libraries (White 1963). White herself made no recommendations, but the librarians responding to the survey were very critical of the concept and its reality. Their objections included the following:

- The fact that schools are usually distant from the business and shopping areas frequented by public library clients.
- The differing purposes of school and public libraries—one meeting the specific curriculum needs of the school and the other meeting the broader and more diverse needs of the public.
- The conflicts between the two administrations.
- The unlike demands on the school and public libraries.
- Insufficient specialist training to allow either type of librarian to deal effectively with public and school clients.
- Wasteful duplication in the book collections.
- Lack of real savings.
- Reluctance of the public to use a library in a school.

By 1977, the negative tone of the literature had not shifted much. An international study of joint-use libraries funded by the State Library of Florida concluded, "It is unlikely that a community able to support or now supporting separate types of libraries would offer better school and public library service through a combined program, because the combination of factors required to promote a successful combined library program seldom occurs" (Aaron and Davie 1977, 120).

The Florida study did note that the combined libraries do have a possible place where services are limited or do not exist, but stressed that there was no documentary evidence that economies result. It recommended that

> Communities with limited resources that are considering this approach should not select the combined program to improve library services except under the following circumstances: (1) that implementation of the concept allows the hiring of professional library personnel where such positions previously had not existed; (2) that this alternative provides a means of strengthening resources available in the community; (3) that an adequately planned program of services to meet both public and school needs is developed and implemented; and (4) that a systematic evaluative procedure is used on a regular basis to determine the status of the program and provide for future directions. (Aaron & Davie 1977, 131)

THE CANADIAN EXPERIENCE

The next significant publication was Amey's 1979 book, *The Canadian School-Housed Public Library*. In it, Amey brought together a wealth of information, data, commentary, and analysis of 179 school-community libraries in Canada, 43 percent of them in the Province of Alberta. Most of the libraries were in rural areas, serving communities with an average population of 3,685, about the maximum population to be recommended for school-community libraries in, for example, Australia. The size of the Canadian communities served ranged, however, from less than 100 to city populations of over 50,000. Most of the libraries were created after 1970. Amey's book was a response to the lack of consolidation of material on school-community libraries. His concern was that "as long as the information on the subject remained dispersed and elusive, researchers would have to continue to duplicate each other's efforts in ferreting in out, or make decisions on the basis of insufficient evidence" (Amey 1979, xii).

In reviewing and analyzing the successes and numerous failures of the libraries in Canada, Amey posed the question, "Are school-housed public libraries a good thing?" His response to the question, despite the fact that "the provincial and territorial reports contain a stockpile of ammunition for those who would fight the concept," was that "it would be a mistake ... to conclude that a school-housed public library will never work for any community at any time" (Amey 1979, 5). He urged the need for "the most careful planning" before attempting a school-community library.

Amey's book began with a perceptive prologue by his Canadian colleague Ken Haycock. At the time he was writing, Haycock was coordinator of library services for the Vancouver School Board, which operated four school-community libraries. It was with knowledge of the reality of the libraries that Haycock observed the tendency to overlook past experiences with them

to extend the services to the public and the school while miraculously saving the taxpayers' money at the same time. Interestingly enough, the move for combination quarters tends to come from school trustees and not citizens in a community. Savings to the taxpayer are purported to be found in the avoidance of duplication of expensive materials and overhead expenses such as the building, lighting, heating, and custodial services. However, if reading by the adult or the student is inhibited, there is only a poor return on investment. (Haycock 1979, 7)

Haycock continued by observing that although school and public libraries are educational agencies with broadly similar aims, their specific purposes, approaches, and operational methods are quite different. But he concluded that, despite the different roles of school and public libraries, school-community libraries had real potential where expert, informed planning preceded decision making. Haycock also stressed, as did the 1977 Florida study, the importance of continuous evaluation:

Good management practice means constant evaluation on a formal and informal basis from both perspectives. Too frequently, one partner, usually the school where there has been a strong program, gains in service but public library service suffers because it is evaluated not on the basis of what should and can be, but on the basis of what was—"something is better than nothing." (Haycock 1979, 10)

THE PENNSYLVANIA EXPERIENCE

The first doctoral study on joint-use libraries was Jaffe's 1982 dissertation. This examined past and existing school-community libraries in the state under three sections. The first described the 12 school-community libraries in Pennsylvania which had ceased as joint-use libraries since 1965. Factors identified by Jaffe in their demise were lack of funds (five libraries); vacated facilities (three libraries); dissatisfaction and lack of use (three libraries); and retirement of librarian (one library). He examined the 11 operational school-community libraries in Pennsylvania, which were primarily in sparsely populated areas. Of these libraries, he observed that several were at risk because of financial difficulties and falling school enrollments.

Despite the condition of the school-community libraries in Pennsylvania, Jaffe correctly concluded that:

The combined school-public library controversy will not soon diminish. Shrinking funds and community desires to maximize use of facilities will maintain pressure for its consideration. The underlying observation is that some communities would have no or minimal public library service without this organizational format. (Jaffe 1982, 2)

As local evidence of this conclusion Jaffe noted that, despite the literature generally advising against combined school and public libraries, several communities in Pennsylvania were considering their establishment. He suggested that success was more likely for those proposed libraries if a five-element framework was followed:

- The combined school-public library requires as a minimum, one school librarian and one public librarian working with adequate support personnel in a framework that permits mutual planning and application of goals and services.
- The combined school-public library should be designated in advance of use with adequate space and selected separate areas for school, public, and staff use.
- The combined school-public library must strive to select and acquire a balanced collection for all patrons and establish the most simple and useful means of access to materials.
- The combined school-public library must aggressively develop and participate in formal mechanics for resource sharing (e.g., networks).
- Governing structures and channels of authority in the combined school-public library must be formally established and permit efficient decision making and resolution of conflicts without abandonment by any party of financial support without due and proper notice. (Jaffe 1982, 100)

A MAJOR INTERNATIONAL STUDY

The next major study was Amey's 1987 *Combining Libraries: The Canadian and Australian Experience*. It remains the closest to a definitive text on joint-use libraries.

In his introduction, Amey (1987) relates his contact with public library professionals strongly opposed to joint-use libraries, contact which had led him to conclude that "too much of what has gone before has been tainted by professional jealousy and narrow-mindedness . . . . The information in this book will provide a basis for a cooler, more open and objective appreciation of the subject" (p. xv). The first part of the book is devoted to joint-use libraries in South Australia, which Amey observed "may seem at first glance a rather unlikely location to focus upon. South Australia, however, is *the* laboratory for joint-use exploration. It is the only place in the world in which a state has adopted as official policy a plan of library provision based upon school-community libraries" (p. viii).

This part of the book also contains, in addition to papers on school-community libraries, a paper on joint community college/public libraries. Its second part describes some of the Canadian experience, and the third part focuses on the evaluation of joint-use libraries, described as "a thorny problem for school-community libraries" (Amey 1987, xi). This was because of the deficiencies in standards for school and public libraries and the lack of standards for joint-use libraries, and also because there are special aspects of joint-use libraries not measurable by separate standards.:

> Truly successful school-public libraries are greater than the sum of their parts. They are unique social institutions that merge and cooperate, by means of their integrated collections and services, to offer enhanced community access and involvement. Attempts to cut the school-community library in two and make separate comparisons against two different standards are not sufficient, for they overlook the special concerns and achievement that grow out of the corporate nature of the joint-use library. (Amey 1987, xii)

The fourth part of *Combining Libraries* contains five Canadian and Australian legal agreements for joint-use libraries, it being noted that the South Australian agreement for rural school-community libraries "is the most detailed, well conceived, and thoroughly tested manual available anywhere" (Amey 1987, xiii).

THE SOUTH AUSTRALIA EXPERIENCE

The outcome of a South Australian political mandate to rapidly provide rural communities with public libraries was the creation, beginning in 1977, of 46 school-community libraries serving rural populations of up to 3,600, although a few now serve larger populations. In 2002, all of these—some of them in new or extended buildings—have developed into technologically advanced libraries with a wide range of electronic resources and very rapid access to over three million books and other resources in the state's public library system (Bundy 1997). They are complemented by a number of urban and regional school- and community-college-based public libraries.

THE FLORIDA EXPERIENCE

Shirley Aaron, one of the investigators in the 1977 Florida study, became, with Amey, the best-known international commentator on joint-use libraries. In 1993, she updated her 1977 study, reporting the following:

> The impetus for renewed interest in combined school and public libraries stems from state and local efforts to find more economical ways to offer community services. Combined libraries appear to be a cost-saving device for eliminating needless duplication and making effective use of existing facilities. Further, the "one-stop school" concept advocated by Governor Lawton Chiles supports the centralization of selected community services as the school site. (p. 120)

The pressure for public schools to demonstrate accountability through community access to underused school facilities has undoubtedly been one reason for proposals for joint-use libraries in several countries.

Aaron (1993) undertook a review of the published and unpublished literature from 1985 to 1992. She concluded that much of it reiterated previously stated advantages and disadvantages of school-community libraries.

> Proponents often cite savings from shared facilities, personnel, collections, maintenance services, and utilities; increased hours of operation; addition of professional personnel to a program otherwise unable to afford qualified staff members; availability of information in a broader range of formats; and provision of library services to small communities lacking a sufficient tax base to support an independent public library. Major disadvantages frequently identified include the staffing difficulties associated with attempting to adequately meet the needs of students and community members through one program; the reluctance of adults to use a library located in a school building during school hours; differing site requirements for public libraries and schools; the reluctance of students from other schools to use a public library located at a school site; and the censorship of adult materials considered unsuitable for a school collection. (p. 123)

Among Aaron's observations was that community members and decision makers are often not willing to accept the professional judgment that a joint-use library may not provide adequate services to all client groups. She therefore concluded that there was a need for a kit to assist community members and librarians in determining the potential effectiveness of a joint-use library. This call was responded to well in several jurisdictions, including Wisconsin (Wisconsin Department of Public Instruction 1998), Southern Ontario (Southern Ontario Library Service 1999) and California (Berger 2000). Two other major conclusions were drawn by Aaron. One was the need for an evaluation method, as a refinement of "Amey's ... important approach to evaluation and planning" (Aaron 1993, 126). The other conclusion was that "the unified library approach (rather than two separate programs in one facility) so common in rural sections of Australia and in some parts of the United States merits further investigation to determine its effectiveness" (Aaron 1993, 126).

UNIVERSITY-PUBLIC LIBRARIES

Although school-community libraries numerically dominate the joint-use library scene, since 1990 some major (and sometimes controversial) joint university-public libraries have been developed in countries such as Australia, Finland, Latvia, Sweden, and the United States. These follow the long-standing precedent in European countries, such as Germany, in which some university libraries also function as state public libraries. Germany is also now considering at least two school-community libraries.

The Swedish Experience

In describing such a university-public library development in Sweden, Gómez, Hulthen, and Drehma (1998) stated, "A central location both for the community citizens and for the students was seen as a very important prerequisite if the project was to succeed. . . . In a world characterized by lifelong learning the combined library resources should give citizens, students and researchers a high-quality service" (p. 22). The Härnösand Library, which opened in February 2000, retains separate library directors and is being developed in the context of a Swedish government expectation that research and public libraries should work more closely together.

Another Swedish university and public library, which opened in 2001, is the Almedal Library in Gotland. Unlike Härnösand, it has one director but two employers and two responsible authorities. The director has stated that, for integration to work, "it is important to understand who is your boss. . . . The borderlines are easier to distinguish, and you are more secure in the work of integration" (Rabe 2002, 32). He also has commented that

> When the plans to bring together the university library and the public library were agreed upon, a furious debate broke out in Gotland—a debate which went on for a long time and involved several different levels. It was town against country—old public library tradition of popular enlightenment against a utilitarian "education society." Differences in class and social structures come to light. (Rabe 2002, 32–33)

The U.S. Experience

Contemporaneous with the Swedish developments has been the Nova Southeast University and Broward County joint-use US$45-million library in Florida. This opened in December 2001 and is unusual—if not unique—worldwide because it is a collaboration between an independent university and a public body. A key advantage claimed by the library (as by many other joint-use libraries) is that members of the public have direct access to all materials in the library, which is open more hours each week than many public libraries.

The most controversial joint-use library project in the United States has been the partnership between California's San José State University and the City of San José. The eight-story, 475,000-square-foot library, scheduled to open in 2003, is the largest to be built at one time west of the Mississippi River. The founding concept was to share resources and so increase access to information and improve opportunities for learning. Contrary to the experience described in Florida, this project has generated as much acrimony as the Almedal Library in Sweden, and for similar reasons. Not least of the opposition has been the university's faculty and their SOUL (Save Our University Library) campaign and website. It was a campaign supported by some librarians, one of whom wrote to the convener of the faculty in protest, "By no means is there anywhere near widespread support among librarians for the type of future your University Librarian and City Librarian envision" (Harger 1998).

The initiators of the proposal for the library, the university president and the city mayor, suggested in 1997 a cost of US$40 million. This is now US$177.5 million (including relocation), only a minor saving on the projected US$180-million cost of two separate libraries. This has been justified as "constructing a facility of much higher quality at a reduced total cost" (Freeman 2001, 22).

An Essential Connection

Dr. Patricia Senn Breivik, the dean of the San José University Library, has also highlighted the rare opportunity such a library presents for an accelerated whole-of-community approach to information literacy development—an issue for public libraries (not just schools, community colleges, and universities) to address. In this context, public libraries worldwide typically have at least 30 percent of their clientele in common with educational institution libraries—students and teachers. This emphasizes the challenging common endeavor to develop information-literate young people and convince tomorrow's decision makers, during their formative childhood years, of the value of investing in libraries. In addition to the clientele they have in common, school and public libraries have three shared goals:

- Ensuring that students develop as information-enabled learners
- Providing access to a wide range of analog and digital resources
- Motivating students to benefit from libraries and their professional staff for educational, informational, and recreational purposes

There is a voluminous literature about the very important connection between the school library and the public library. An excellent U.S. reference about this, which includes a substantial contextual section on joint-use libraries, is *School and Public Library Relationships* (Fitzgibbons 2000).

An Australian survey of school and public libraries about their connection in 2000 showed that teacher and public librarians are aware of the importance of their working together. Among the positive responses were those from school-community librarians, such as the following: "Having worked in a school library previously I can see the tremendous benefit derived by students in having a public library on site. The availability and ease of procuring hard-to-find resources is fantastic, and the interaction between the general public and students is good" (Bundy 2001, 152).

The most effective way to make that essential connection between school and public libraries may be a joint-use library. This educational advantage of a joint-use library is given little weight in the literature. As public libraries focus more on their information-literacy role, this should change.

OTHER ADVANTAGES OF JOINT-USE LIBRARIES

Experience in joint-use libraries compared with separate public and other services suggest the following possible advantages. An overriding consideration is the synergy of a joint-use service—the whole is greater than the sum of the parts.

The purported advantages are economic, social, and educational. Joint-use libraries

- represent efficient use of public money (staff costs may be shared between authorities; buildings and facilities may be provided more cost effectively; resource acquisitions may be coordinated to provide savings, e.g., in reference material; there may be savings in operating costs).
- provide a greater quantity and quality of collections, electronic resources, services, and facilities than is possible with separate services and smaller budgets;
- provide access to more staff than in each separate service;
- allow extended opening hours;
- are convenient to clients in providing all services on one site;
- facilitate the collection in one place of archival and local history material of interest to the whole community;
- allow more flexibility in providing and obtaining resources and making innovations;
- provide access to more than one system for support services (e.g., professional development);
- promote greater community interaction by providing a community focal point;
- provide greater access to information on community services;
- increase the community's awareness and understanding of current education practice;
- promote lifelong learning through the educational role of the joint-use library;
- encourage the development of a positive attitude in students toward school;
- provide more avenues for promotion of the service;
- bring different community groups together on the governing board;
- may provide a social-justice outcome for smaller communities that could not support separate services.

These issues and a number of others (such as conflict in philosophies, approaches to censorship, Internet filtering, security, unions, and governance) are discussed by two U.S. library directors in an article entitled "Share and Share Alike" (Flagg, 1999).

KEY SUCCESS FACTORS

The literature has also delineated the key success factors for joint-use libraries:

- A formal agreement endorsed by all cooperating authorities is essential.
- The agreement should include all the essential items but not attempt to cover all policy issues.
- The agreement should provide for dissolution of the joint-use library.

- The level of service provided must be equal to or better than that which could be provided in separate facilities.
- Systemwide support is essential (e.g., for staffing, professional development and advice, and financial support).
- A governing board should participate in the establishment of the service, to develop ongoing broad policy for its operation and to determine goals and budget priorities. A profile must be established for each joint-use library to define the community to be served.
- Provision must be made for any projected growth of the profile community.
- Choice of site is critical (if the site is predetermined and not ideal, an extra effort must be made).
- Very good signage is necessary, in the environs and on the site.
- Opening hours should meet the needs of the profile community.
- Physical facilities should be appropriate to the profile community.
- There should be awareness of the special needs of the profile community.
- Staffing levels should be adequate and the composition of the staff should reflect the requirements of the profile community.
- Staffing should be integrated if possible.
- Support structures should discourage too-rapid fluctuations in staffing numbers.
- The library director should be a professional librarian and have freedom to manage, including having direct control of staff and budget.
- The library director should be represented on the senior decision-making and policy bodies of each constituent institution.
- Direct two-way communication should occur between the director and funding bodies.
- Regular consultation with, and reporting to, all parties concerned should occur.
- Regular internal and external evaluation of the library should take place.

THE IMPORTANCE OF THE AGREEMENT

The literature places considerable emphasis on maintaining a written record of all understandings and commitments leading to the establishment of the library. Similarly emphasized are the content and detail of formal agreements. If these are deficient in five major aspects in particular, the operation of a joint-use library may prove to be extremely demanding and, at worst, very stressful, for its staff. The five areas that should be emphasized in agreements are space, staffing and staff development, information technology, the role of a governing board, and evaluation.

Space

Joint-use libraries in schools often do not present well as public libraries because of lack of space and an institutional ambience. All libraries, particularly because of the demands of information technology, tend to need more space over time. Once joint-use libraries are functioning, it may be very difficult to gain agreement on the need for more space and, more critically, who should pay for it. In Australia, for example, municipal local government, as the public library provider, has proved reluctant to contribute to extensions of libraries on state education department premises and in which it has no legal equity. Agreements should specify how the need for more space will be identified and brought forward, and how it will be paid for.

Staffing

It is for good reason that joint-use library staff should be carefully selected. They need special qualities of advocacy, marketing, organization, diplomacy, and commitment to the concept; it is one of the most challenging and demanding areas of professional employment. The reality, however, is that many joint-use libraries are developments of existing school libraries. This means a change-management process for the staff already involved is desirable, but this is rarely considered. Poor attitudes and service to the public may result.

Work overload and unpaid work to meet dual, sometimes even triple, responsibilities is common, particularly in small joint-use libraries. Inadequate levels of staffing can be particularly conspicuous in school-community and community college–public libraries during student vacations, when the library must continue to function as a public library.

Of even greater moment is the extent of the integration of the staff. Lack of integration can be an industrial, personnel, and public-relations minefield if staff have different managers; operate with different salary schedules, working hours, and other conditions; and do not contribute to meeting the needs of all library clientele. There *are* examples of libraries that appear to function well with staff reporting to different managers and with different conditions of service. They tend to be the larger joint-use libraries. Experience shows that, if it can be achieved, the best approach is for all staff to be employed under the same conditions of service and supervision by one library director. As an example of how this can be done, one joint-use university–community college–public library in the State of Western Australia gave library staff the option of transferring to the most favorable of the employment conditions of the three partners. This proved to be the university's conditions. All staff are now employed by the university, with the community college and the public library effectively contracting their service to it (Hamblin 1998).

Information Technology

Information technology—and how it is to be prioritized, paid for, found space for, and supported—needs to be specified. This is such a critical part of the operation of any library that uncertainty about responsibilities can significantly undermine its effectiveness and staff morale. Of particular importance is a clear understanding of which library management system will be used in a new joint-use library, and how it will be upgraded or replaced in due course.

The Governing Body

The role of a governing board should be defined in the agreement. In many instances, as for the school-community libraries in South Australia, the governing board may consist of teachers, students, the school principal, the library directory, and representatives from the local authority or municipality and the community, with a community member as the chairperson. This broad constituency may be more problematic, however, if a legally constituted public library requires a board of trustees separate from the school board, as is the case in parts of the United States.

Evaluation

Regular in-house and external evaluation of all types of libraries, their operations, and client satisfaction with them is becoming increasingly common. It has particular value for joint-use libraries. Because the objectives of many joint-use libraries are not easily quantifiable, the emphasis in evaluation methods will be qualitative, but this must necessarily be combined with quantitative measures of success. A regular, externally facilitated review of the library, beginning within three years of its establishment, should be specified in the agreement, as well as how that review is to be paid for. Difficulties in joint-use libraries tend to remain hidden from their partners until there is a crisis. Provision of a mechanism for transparent external evaluation will minimize this. Such a mechanism should build an ongoing self-evaluation and assessment of performance as detailed by Amey (1987).

PLANNING A JOINT-USE LIBRARY: A CHECKLIST

The following checklist extends and enhances that developed by Wisconsin's Department of Public Instruction (1998). It is specific to school-community libraries, but much of it can be applied to other combinations such as community college–public libraries and university-public libraries. A negative or equivocal response to a significant number of the items in the list suggests that serious reconsideration of the proposal is necessary.

Planning

Yes	No	
☐	☐	Similarities and differences in the mission statements of the school library and the public library are understood and reconcilable
☐	☐	The school and public library catchment areas are similar
☐	☐	A preliminary feasibility study has been conducted

Yes No

☐   ☐   Relevant groups have examined the complementary roles of school and public libraries and are aware of the services, resources, and access that must be offered to meet the needs of both client groups

☐   ☐   Community groups are involved in, and support, the decision to have a joint-use library

☐   ☐   Teachers and the Student Representative Council are involved in, and support, the decision to have a joint-use library

☐   ☐   The parties that will govern the library will define their responsibilities in a formal agreement

☐   ☐   An evaluation program will be specified in the agreement

☐   ☐   Dissolution of the joint-use library will be provided for in the agreement

☐   ☐   Population growth or decline projected for the catchment area has been considered

Administration and Funding

Yes No

☐   ☐   The operation of the library has been agreed to, including the opening hours, budgeting, access to resources and activities, and authority for daily decision making

☐   ☐   Collection development and access policies consistent with the mission statements have been developed for both the school and public library use

Access to Information, Resources, and Facilities

Yes No

☐   ☐   A policy for access for all age groups and maturity levels has been agreed

☐   ☐   It is accepted that children and teachers from other public and private schools in the community may use the library

☐   ☐   It is accepted that home-schooled children and their parents may use the library

☐   ☐   The library will be accessible by the public at any time it is open, and through a visible public entrance

☐   ☐   Censorship, Internet access, and filtering issues have been addressed

☐   ☐   It is recognized that the group licensing of electronic products may require special negotiation and investment

☐   ☐   The library provides adequate space to implement the full range of school and public library services and technology

☐   ☐   The library has potential for expansion

☐   ☐   A process for identifying and addressing future space needs is included in the agreement

Yes	No	
☐	☐	The need for some clients to be transported to the library is recognized
☐	☐	The possible need for the library to offer a home delivery service is recognized
☐	☐	The title of the library will make it clear who may use it
☐	☐	The importance of directional and site signage is recognized
☐	☐	Furniture, furnishings, and ambience are as noninstitutional as possible
☐	☐	Public washrooms are available in the library or adjacent to it
☐	☐	A community meeting room is available
☐	☐	Provision is made for people with disabilities

Attitudinal Factors

Yes	No	
☐	☐	Decision makers, administrators, and employees are genuinely enthusiastic about the project and dedicated to making it work
☐	☐	Improving facilities, service, resources, and access—not saving money—is the primary motivation in developing the library
☐	☐	Adults feel comfortable and welcome in the school and are accustomed to using it for public functions
☐	☐	The mixing of preschoolers, children, teenagers, and young and older adults is not seen as threatening or uncomfortable by any of the potential users or the library's partners
☐	☐	All security and duty of care issues have been considered and reconciled

Planning

Two items in the checklist require comment from the perspective of experience. One is that the preliminary feasibility study should be facilitated by a library consultant. At a minimum, it should be someone with no vested interest in the outcome.

Second, at the earliest stage possible, a communication strategy to anticipate and address possible concerns of all client groups about the new facility should be developed. Few joint-use libraries worldwide have been implemented without concern from one or more groups of clients about its impact on them. These concerns may range from senior citizens' reluctance to travel to the school, to turf wars, with students and students apprehensive about "their" resources being used by the public and parents and teachers concerned about unrestricted public access to a facility on school property.

Access to Information and Resources

Internet access policy can be problematic, as schools and their libraries often use filters to minimize exposure to inappropriate materials by their students.

This is generally contrary to public library philosophy and practice worldwide, except in some U.S. states where state funding is unfortunately conditional on filters being used by public libraries. Although this is only the latest iteration of the pressure on school and public libraries from individuals and special interest groups to remove, or limit access to, their resources, it requires early consideration in the planning of a joint-use library. In the long-established system of school community libraries in South Australia, the solution has been to allow students access to only State Education Department–provided filtered Internet access during school hours, and to the public unfiltered terminals after school with the written permission of caregivers.

The Physical Facility

The location, visibility, and ambience of the library is critical to its acceptance by the public. Deficiencies in these were a major factor in the failure of some libraries in Canada—the public refused to use them. Public schools tend not to be located on prime real estate or adjacent to those busy retail, business, or community centers that are the best locations for public libraries. A special effort must therefore be made, with prominent signage indicating the location of the library and that it is a public facility. The lack of this conspicuous signage is a failing in many communities, not only with joint-use libraries but also with public libraries.

The funding, permission for, and erection of directional signage may appear to be a minor issue. It is often an afterthought that falls at bureaucratic local government offices or takes a professional lifetime to achieve. Those school-community libraries in outback South Australia with good directional signage find that this is particularly appreciated by many international tourists, who are pleased to find that the libraries provide free Internet and email access. Good directional and site signage should be built into the initial budget for the new library, and a useful engagement with the new library would be for students in the school to audit their community to identify sign locations.

Terminology also needs careful consideration. For example, the most commonly used term for a library in Australia and New Zealand is *school-community library* or just *community library*. There have been instances of this being interpreted by the general public as "for the school community," not the "for the school and general community." To overcome this, directional signs to some school-community libraries in Australia now unequivocally state, "public library at high school." The lesson is to assume nothing and to take nothing and no one for granted.

Many joint-use libraries, to accommodate the needs of students, teachers, and the public and to minimize congestion, have a feature that is operationally anathema to many libraries—two entrances. From a security viewpoint, in smaller rural communities this is not usually a problem—one rural school-community library in South Australia that can be approached from four directions has four entrances. This may result in costly duplication of electronic or RFID (radio frequency identification) security systems that should be allowed for in planning the library, however.

Public parking for a joint-use library is at least as important as it is for a public library. Not everyone will behave well about parking. If spaces for the public are usurped by teachers and students or visitors to the school, this will deter public use and be a source of never-ending complaint.

Relatively few joint-use libraries are initially provided with new, custom-designed accommodation—most consist of a public library grafted onto a school library, sometimes without additional space. Lack of space, driven often by the needs of technology, is a challenge for many school and public libraries. Such a lack in a joint-use library is particularly detrimental to its acceptance and use as a public library and can be detrimental to library-based student programs. It is the needs of the modern public library, however, that tend to create the most pressure for additional space in joint-use libraries. The assessment of whether an existing school or community college library building can become a satisfactory joint-use library really does need professional judgment. Space standards for school, community college, university, and public libraries exist in various forms and jurisdictions. They may be used in combination, and with allowance for common-use areas, for a joint-use library. There are no space standards for joint-use libraries, however, and they are unlikely to be developed, given the individuality of every joint-use library.

The majority of joint-use libraries are high school or middle school and public library combinations, but in some places such as New Brunswick in Canada, the combination is that of an elementary school library with a public library. In the South Australian scheme of rural joint-use libraries, elementary schools were initially not eligible, but eventually the approval committee did include a small number. These have been less successful than high school–based libraries. The reasons have been the sizes of the elementary school libraries and their furniture, lack of school resources of interest to the public, limited technology, and limited professional and other staffing. An elementary school–public library combination requires especially careful consideration.

Attitudinal Factors

In the first flush of enthusiasm for what may seem to be an innovative, ground-breaking concept, decision makers tend to overstate the advantages and minimize the challenges of a joint-use library. On the other hand, there will always be those, including librarians, who see the challenges and none of the advantages. Open minds and critical faculties are needed. Nothing is as useful as investment in time and travel, email or phone costs to communicate with a range of existing joint-use libraries. Relying on the literature alone to validate or invalidate the concept for local application can be misleading.

CONCLUSIONS

There are several realities about joint-use libraries.

1. Suggestions and proposals for them will continue to arise from politicians, local decision makers, school boards, and community members to whom a

library is a library is a library. They may too-readily assume that a joint-use library will easily meet the needs of all client groups and will save operational, resource, and construction costs. Experience shows that this may *not* be the outcome.

2. Worldwide, the number of such libraries, and experimentation with them, is growing. In Sweden, 40 percent of public libraries are joint-use, as are 40 percent in South Australia, 9 percent in Australia, and 8 percent in Canada (but less than 2 percent in the United States).

3. Given the choice of a mobile library visiting infrequently or a static joint-use library open for longer and regular hours, most people in rural areas are likely to choose the joint-use library.

4. There is now enough experience in their development to identify factors in their failure rate and the resulting poor marks given to them in professional literature since the 1960s.

5. There is also now enough experience in their development to optimize their chances of success.

6. The concept remains most likely to succeed in rural areas of about 3,500 people and in locations where a school library has a professional librarian in charge.

7. The concept may also work well in urban areas.

8. The combination community college–public library often works well, and with more ease than the school-housed public library because of the relative maturity of the student population, the design and technology of the modern community college library, and the utility of its collection to the public.

9. The concept has considerable potential in developing countries with rural populations served currently by neither a school library nor a public library. Despite the increasing urbanization of the world's population, a large proportion continues to live in rural areas. Many of these areas (particularly in Africa, Asia, Eastern Europe, the Middle East, and South America) do not yet have local provision of static, or even mobile, libraries—but they do generally have schools. They do, therefore, offer the potential for a joint-use facility of two complementary but different educational agencies, the school library and the public library.

At their worst, joint-use libraries fail completely or are dysfunctional, do not attract the public, do not advance a school's community profile or access to resources, and result in very stressed library staff. The recorded experience available about joint-use libraries means that there is now no excuse for decision makers to persist in inappropriate joint-use library development.

Many joint-use libraries, however, are a very popular, exciting, and reinforcing manifestation of community vision and professional commitment. This is because, ultimately, what makes good joint-use libraries is the library staff who rise to their challenges and opportunities.

The beginning of this chapter included an observation that joint-use libraries rarely result from advocacy for them by the library profession. Most are an outcome of professional reaction to political and community suggestions. The time has perhaps come when more professional proaction about joint-use libraries—in the right circumstances—would be a better approach.

REFERENCES

Aaron, S.L. 1993. "The Role of Combined Libraries in Florida, Phase I: Surveying the Literature." In *School Library Media Annual,* Vol. 11. Libraries Unlimited, 120–131.

Aaron, S.L., and J.F. Davie, 1977. *A Study of the Combined School Public Library: Phase 1.* Tallahassee: Florida State University.

American Library Association. 2002. *Combined Libraries: A Bibliography.* ALA Library Fact Sheet Number 20. Available: www.ala.org/library/fact20.html (accessed January 3, 2003).

Amey, L.J., ed. 1979. *The Canadian School-Housed Public Library.* London: Vine Press.

Amey, L.J., ed. 1987. *Combining Libraries: The Canadian and Australian Experience.* Metuchen, NJ: Scarecrow Press.

Berger, C. 2000. *Public and School Libraries: Issues and Options of Joint Use Facilities and Cooperative Use Agreements.* Sacramento: California State Library.

Bundy, A.L. 1997. *Widened Horizons: The Rural School-Community Libraries of South Australia* Adelaide, AUS: Auslib Press.

Bundy, A.L. 2001. "Essential Connections: School and Public Libraries for Lifelong Learning." *Australasian Public Libraries and Information Services* 14(4): 142–158.

Fitzgibbons, S.A. 2000. "School and Public Library Relationships: Essential Ingredients in Implementing Educational Reforms and Improving Student Learning." *School Library Media Research 3.* Available: www.ala.org/aasl /SLMR/vol3/relationships/relationships.html (accessed January 3, 2003).

Flagg, Gordon. 1999. "Share and Share Alike? Allan Kleiman and Jane Light Examine the Promise and Peril of Shared Facilities." *American Libraries* 30 (February): 40.

Freeman, A. 2001. "An Innovative Library Partnership. *Planning for Higher Education* 30 (1): 20–26.

Gómez, E., Eila Hulthen, and Uila Drehma. 1998. "A Joint Library Project in Härnösand, Sweden." *Scandinavian Public Library Quarterly* 4: 22–24.

Hamblin, D. 1998. "Method and Madness: The Development of a Tripartite Library in Western Australia." *Australasian Public Libraries and Information Services* 11(4): 181–183.

Harger, E. 1998, December 5. Letter to Professor E. Bruce Edwards, San Jose State University.

Haycock, K. 1979. "Prologue." In *The Canadian School-Housed Public Library*, ed. L. J. Amey. London: Vine Press, 7–10.

Jaffe, L. L. 1982. "The Combined School-Public Library in Pennsylvania." Ph.D. dissertation, University of Pittsburgh.

Rabe, A. 2002. "A Library in Balance." *Scandinavian Public Library Quarterly* 1: 31–33.

Southern Ontario Library Service. 1999. *Best Practices Guide: Public and School Library Cooperation*. Gloucester, Ontario: Southern Ontario Library Service.

South Australia Education Department. 1982. *School-community Libraries in Rural Areas of South Australia: Guidelines for Establishment and Operation*. Adelaide: Education Department of South Australia.

White, R. M. 1963. *The School-Housed Public Library*. Chicago: American Library Association.

Wisconsin Department of Public Instruction. 1998. *Combined School and Public Libraries: Guidelines for Decision Making*. 2nd edition. Bulletin no. 98234. Madison: Wisconsin Department of Public Instruction.

SELECTED BIBLIOGRAPHY

Fitzgibbons, S. A. "School and Public Library Relationships: Essential Ingredients in Implementing Educational Reforms and Improving Student Learning." [http://www.ala.org/aasl/SLMR/vol3/relationships/relationships.html] *School Library Media Research*, 2000, 3.

Southern Ontario Library Service. *Best Practices Guide: Public and School Library Cooperation*. Gloucester: Southern Ontario Library Service, 1999.

Wisconsin Department of Public Instruction. *Combined School and Public Libraries: Guidelines for Decision Making*. 2nd edition. Bulletin no. 98234. Madison: Wisconsin Department of Public Instruction, 1998.

PART V
SERVICES FOR CHILDREN, YOUNG ADULTS, AND SENIORS

11 DESIGNING LIBRARY SPACE FOR CHILDREN AND ADOLESCENTS

Lesley A. Boon

The designing of library space for young people takes specialist knowledge and skills. Most important is a knowledge of behavior and information needs, combined with a love for children and/or adolescents. Adolescence "is a period of time of psychological development which spans the time between the onset of puberty and adulthood" (Frydenberg and Lewis 1991, 119).

Public libraries are changing and "are increasingly taking on social and educational duties, and their traditional role as storehouses of information is expanding exponentially" (Updike 1999, 2). The perception of a public library as a book repository and the librarian as the keeper of books and director of shelves is long gone. So much more is expected. When designing a library or library space for children and adolescents, many questions need to be addressed. For each library facility, the questions may be the same, but the answers must come from local knowledge and expertise about what this particular user group needs. A library for young people should be "a comfortable accessible place, where productive, satisfying things happen" (Cochran and Gisolfi 1997, 26).

FOR WHOM ARE YOU DESIGNING THIS SPACE?

Who your clients are will determine how you go about the process of designing the spaces they use.

- If the space is for children, how will they use it? It should tap into the naturally inquisitive nature of the child and his or her need to explore.
- If it is for adolescents, how will they (or how would they like to) use the space?
- If it is for both, how can you organize it so that both groups can function well and share it effectively?

How Do You Decide What Is Really Needed?

There are steps that will assist in the clarification of answers to these questions. In the preparatory stages of library design it is important to do the following:

1. Look at the needs of children and adolescents. Sandlian (1999) refers to the work of Ashley Montague and his perceptions that children, innately inquisitive and trusting, require a loving environment where the love they give also is returned, in which they can exercise understanding, gain knowledge through learning, and organize what they learn effectively.
2. Read about how children and adolescents use space, particularly in a library setting. Gender is a very important issue. Is the library to be used by boys and girls? It is important to know how boys and girls use space differently and cater for this. "The differences in boys and girls are physical, behavioral, and cognitive" (Boon 1998, 3). Boys tend to be independent and want to study or work alone. Girls tend to prefer working in groups and relying on each other for information and support. Boys take up more space than girls; they are louder and more active. In public libraries, children and (particularly adolescents) may be viewed as a nuisance.

To get an idea of how young adults use space and their perception of the world and themselves, Bernier (1998) suggests looking at their bedrooms. Often the bedroom is the teenager's only private domain. There appears to be a predilection for the chaotic. There are visual statements to indicate a different domain of existence, encouraging adults to keep away. The furniture is not always used in the ways imagined by the designer or manufacturer, and floor space is an important component of work and relaxation.

WHAT IS YOUR VISION?

Visualize how the space you have been assigned could fulfill your dream of the best possible library for children and adolescents.

First, don't think within the constraints of what is happening in your library now; don't be reactive (Kugler 2002). Think, dream, create. Brainstorm all the possible activities, spaces, and attitudes that would serve your client needs best and be identified as best practice within the field. The only limit is your imagination. Not all things may be possible, but this is definitely an excellent start. Prioritize, from what is most important down to what you would love but could live without.

How Do Others View Your Clients?

How do current adult library users view children and adolescents in a joint-use library? Does the Local Council view children and adolescents as an important user group or as a burden that must be endured? Unfortunately, "public libraries give more space to restrooms than to young adults ... who constitute 25 percent of today's library patrons" (Bernier 1998, 52). The adolescent is neither child nor adult and has little power in the adult world. It is up to library staff to advocate for this space to be appropriate and friendly.

This is your opportunity to involve others. Let the adult patrons know what is happening. Explain what you are trying to achieve, listen to their suggestions and grievances, and get them on your side. Encourage ownership of the project. There is nothing like participation to encourage positive outcomes.

COMMUNICATING YOUR IDEAS

Can you communicate your vision to the appropriate bodies? Can you become a liaison with the architects and consult with the experts in designing library space for children?

When an architect has been chosen (and usually, this is not the librarian's decision), arrange for the architect to observe excellent library services for children and adolescents in well-designed library spaces.

Do you have a lot of say in how things should be done? Are you allowed to choose the colors, the furnishings, and the signage? It is important from the outset to have clarification on how things will function and who is responsible for the decisions. The best scenario is for the librarian for children and youth to be seen as a valued member of the planning team.

OTHER CONSIDERATIONS

What is your budget for the project? Lots of creative flair can offset a limited budget. Is it a brand-new library or are you refurbishing an existing one? If you are starting out new, this is your opportunity to participate in the design and realization of a wonderful custom-built space.

Consider Faulkner-Brown's (1999, 13–14) suggestions of what a library building should be:

- *Flexible*, including layout and services that can be adapted
- *Compact*, in its use of space, to make it easier for staff and students to move around
- *Accessible*, both from outside and from within
- *Extendable*, for future growth
- *Varied*, to allow for a wide choice of services and resources
- *Organized*, with an orderly arrangement of the collections
- *Comfortable*, meaning that the library should be welcoming and patrons should feel at home there; Bowcock (1999) suggests that clients found this the most surprising and positive aspect of an experimental library space
- *Constant in environment*, for preservation of material, and user comfort
- *Secure*, against loss and damage
- *Economic*, for maximum use of the dollar

The librarian should give the architect a building program, or brief, containing all the thoughts, ideas, and goals that the librarian would like to achieve, as well as the way he or she envisions that the space should be used. This will be discussed in more detail further on.

At all points during the process, the librarian involved with the project must be informed and seen as an active, valued member of the team.

INFORMATION GATHERING

Once you have the guidelines set, you are ready to go.

Discuss your vision with relevant people. Talk about how it can be achieved. Make sure it fits in with the vision of the total library, if the space you are planning is part of a large complex. Make sure it complies with the mandates of the governing body.

Ask the potential users (i.e., children and adolescents). They will come up with a plethora of ideas not previously considered. "Children provide spontaneous, outspoken points of view" (Sandlian 1999, 5). "Young people seldom get an opportunity to participate in the planning and development of services that affect them" (Rowley et al. 1998, 152). It is amazing how this generates interest and enthusiasm in the project.

You can ask patrons about their preferences in several ways, depending on the clientele and the situation, including the use of questionnaires, setting up focus groups, and targeting specific groups such as elementary and middle school students and teens. Ask if you can talk to students from local schools; use local shops such as popular food outlets and music stores to leave questionnaires or advertise focus groups.

The age group will determine patrons' wants and needs, and they are all very different. In a school library, it is possible to question every student if you wish. If you are catering to a wide age range, a variety of areas will be needed to suit users' specific needs. It is a good idea to separate those areas so that adolescents do not see themselves being perceived as children.

Younger children like to sprawl on the floor or on soft furniture to read and share. They like places they can talk, and quiet reflective places where they can curl up with books and sink into another world.

Adolescents need a variety of places. They need individual study spaces for research and homework. They need places to share information and ideas. They need a space that is obviously their own. It is best to arrange material for children according to the ways in which they think and act. Maybe using the Dewey Decimal Classification System and alphabetizing fiction in shelving areas is not the best way to go; ask them.

Visit other libraries to get ideas. Talk to the library staff about what works and what doesn't work. Talk to library suppliers about what you would like; they can be very helpful. Have a look at other plans. Read the literature about designing specialist spaces for children and adolescents. *Designing and Space Planning for Libraries* by Cohen and Cohen (1979) is very useful in looking at the ways people use library space.

Consider the impact of information communication technology (ICT) in the library. Look at how ICT is being used now in libraries and think about how it will affect future use of library space. Previously, for example, to attain flexibility it was advisable to grid the floors with power and data access. The changes in technology and the use of wireless technology may mean that little or no hard wiring will be required in the future.

PUTTING IT TOGETHER

The architect will require a building program, or brief. This will include a short statement about the community, the composition of its population, and how the library sees its role within it. There should be a statement about how the library will be used and the role of the library staff. A list of preferred configurations should include formal seating, casual seating, story-telling area, technology, shelving or stacks, and workspace for staff.

The brief should include the following:

- Traffic flow considerations
- Need for visual supervision
- Internal space requirements for all services and activity areas
- Services such as plumbing, lighting, heating, acoustics, wiring (including power points and computer outlets), and placement of wireless points, allowing for extreme flexibility
- Construction materials such as brick, plaster, wood, partitioning, windows, storage, furniture, shelving, floor surfaces, color, space between shelves and furniture, and so on
- Noise containment of activities that may be irritating to the general public and therefore must be located out of sight, behind a barrier, or as far away as possible from other patrons; discrete placement of toilets and bubblers (water fountains) out of traffic flow areas

Discuss your ideas with the architect and clarify what you mean. Have as many meetings as necessary to talk through ideas and what is happening.

Details, Details

There is much to consider when planning a library building. Cohen and Cohen (1979) suggest that the square is the best shape to work with. Square spaces are easier to lay out with furniture and equipment. It is not always possible or desirable, however, to plan a perfectly square building, because of limitations imposed by a site or by design considerations. "The arrangement of any space communicates many subtle and not-so-subtle messages about what is valued there" (Carter 1994, 26). Remember the teenager's bedroom? Whatever has physical or visual prominence makes a statement about what is important and valued (Bernier 1998 52). Adolescents will know if you want them there by looking at the area you create for them.

What to Consider

- *How to make this an inviting space*. How would children or teenagers interpret this space?
- *Use of space, open and closed*. Consider user space and space for resources, control, and service units. Make plenty of space for displays and marketing.
- *Signage or "way finding."* Think about different ways to indicate where things are, such as signs, color, symbols (use international symbols), floor layout, and pointers in the flooring. Make them simple, uncluttered, and standard (Robert Sloan 2002).
- *Color* (so important). Study the psychological effects of color. Remember walls can be easily painted but carpets and furnishings are with you for some time. Dark colors may subdue excitable behavior, bright colors will stimulate.
- *Furnishings and fittings*. These should be safe, durable, comfortable, and look good.
- *Shelving*. There is so much scope for shelving. Perspex lit to conduct colored light. Waved shelving. Make the shelving arrangement compliment the learning styles and processes of this century.
- *The collection*. What is the proportion of print to nonprint material? How is technology changing what is needed? Think outside the box when organizing; how do children think? Organize your collection to match. Use educators in the planning process.
- *Technology*. The young are very attuned to use of technology so this is a very important consideration. Discuss this with an expert.
- *Noise*. "Conversation is the beginning and end of knowledge ... the full perception of learning" (Carter 1994, 26). Children and adolescents need to make noise and discuss things with each other (Rowley et al. 1998, 152); allow for it.
- *Lighting*. Lighting can control how the library looks and feels. Good light is needed for study, but intimate lighting may be excellent for reflective areas. Use spot lighting for special effects.
- *Accessibility*. Students may be reluctant to use places that are in the back corner or are accessed by many stairs. Spaces need to be user-friendly and have visual supervision.
- *Flexibility*. Create a space that will allow for change.

Be adventurous and document the learning outcomes. Let's combine our expertise and knowledge and make public libraries exciting, challenging, inviting places for the twenty-first century.

Making Notes   It is a good idea to keep a notebook with you and jot down ideas as you go. Woodward (1999) calls it "tying up the loose ends" (p. 46). Myriad issues may occur to you in the process of planning and construction. It is easier and less costly to revise the building plans to correct oversights than to make changes during or after construction. Woodward gives many excellent examples, such as making sure children cannot access the on/off switches for overhead lights.

FOLLOW-THROUGH

Meetings with the architect are crucial to getting everything the way you envisioned it. The architect may have some good alternative suggestions that are very workable and that you may not have considered. If you seem to have an unsolvable puzzle, ask an expert.

During the process of planning, building, and furnishing, you need to be in constant communication with the others involved, including the architect, the planning team if you have one, the builder, the governing body, the furniture and shelving supplier, and the painter. Keep your supervisor(s) informed. Be there to check every point of progress. Check to be sure that what you assumed would be done is actually happening in the way that you envisioned it. Be prepared to advocate for what you believe is needed. Be prepared to compromise on the less important issues. In planning my building, I fought hard to have a circulation/information desk that was open to all areas of the public library space. I wanted an area that said, "Please come and ask; we would love to help you" rather than the original plan of a fortress-type area with high sides and a small access space that definitely said, "We are busy; it had better be important if you are going to disturb us." I won. I conceded defeat on the issue of using library space to add restrooms accessible from the playground, because inclusion of the restrooms would have held up the building another six months, and there was nowhere to put restrooms in a very restricted play space.

All new buildings have defects, and it is standard practice for the architect to record them and send them to the builder within a standard time frame, usually six months. Make sure this defect notice, or punch list, is done and the repairs are carried out.

THE BIG EVENT

When it's all over, it's good to celebrate. Libraries are "places for celebration" (Andrea Wilson 2002). An opening ceremony gives a high profile to the new library and, it is hoped, will encourage greater use. Everyone involved in the project should be invited to participate.

This is another opportunity to consult your patrons; ask them what they would see as an appropriate way to celebrate. Some suggestions would be to have a party and invite authors and illustrators to talk to the children and adolescents. Have a book launch, if it can be arranged. Have ongoing activities for weeks to keep the focus. Invite the important people, but remember, this is for children and young people, and keep it appropriate. Warn other library users that you are going to celebrate. Enjoy!

EVALUATION

It is a very useful exercise to keep using that notebook after you celebrate. Note things that work well and things that don't. Ask your focus group back to see how they think the new space is working and if it is what they wanted. Survey the other library users and see if they think the new design is working. Document their comments and keep your notes safe; you never know when you will need these pearls of wisdom and hindsight again.

And when it's all said and done, the most important thing to teenagers and children is that you really want them, you really like them, and you really want to help them. You can make your new space work in a concrete basement if your attitude is positive and affirming (Caywood 1997).

REFERENCES

Bernier, Anthony. 1998. "On My Mind: Young Adult Spaces." *American Libraries* 29 (October): 52–54.

Boon, Lesley. 1998. "The Life Concerns of Preadolescent Boys." Master's thesis, University of Technology, Sydney, Australia.

Boon, Lesley. 1999. "Designing Library Space for Teens or 2001 and on a Space Odyssey." *Teens in the Library: 2000 & Beyond.* Young Adult Library Network Annual Seminar, November, State Library of New South Wales.

Bowcock, Tim. 1999. "Library Futures: Striking the Balance." *Australian Public Libraries and Information Services* 12 (1): 31–40.

Carter, Kim. 1994. "Images of Information in a 21st-Century High School." *School Library Journal* February: 25–29.

Caywood, Carolyn. 1997. "The Cinderblock Café." *School Library Journal* 43 (1): 45

Cochran, Sally, and Peter Gisolfi. 1997. "Renovate and It Will Come: Designing a Popular High School Library." *School Library Journal* (February): 25–29.

Cohen, Aaron, and Elaine Cohen. 1979. *Designing and Space Planning for Libraries: A Behavioral Guide.* New York: Bowker.

Faulkner-Brown, Harry. 1999. "Some Thoughts on the Design of Major Library Buildings." *Intelligent Library Buildings: Proceedings of the Tenth Seminar of the IFLA Section on Buildings and Equipment*, The Hague, Netherlands, 24–29 August 1997, *IFLA Publications* 88: 10–31.

Frydenberg, Erica, and Ramon Lewis. 1991. "Adolescent Coping: The Different Ways in Which Boys and Girls Cope." *Journal of Adolescence* 14: 119–133.

Klasing, Jane P. 1991. *Designing and Renovating School Library Media Centers.* School Library Media Programs, No. 11. Chicago: American Library Association.

Kugler, Cecilia. 2002. "Spaced Out in the Digital Age: The Future of Library Design." Presented at The Inside Story: A Library Interiors Forum. State Library of Victoria, Melbourne, 3–4 February.

Rowley, Kyle, Nikki Macor, Tom Ricketts, David Forster, and Emma Toop. 1998. "Creating the Future Library." *Australian Public Libraries and Information Services* 11 (4): 152–158.

Sandlian, Pam. 1999. "Information Playgrounds: Creating Children's Libraries." *Public Library Quarterly* 17 (2): 5–13.

Sloan, Robert. 2002. "Signage." Presented at The Inside Story: A Library Interiors Forum. State Library of Victoria, Melbourne, 3–4 February.

Updike, Robin. 1999. *Downtown Library Space-Age Design Goes Beyond Books.* Available: http://archives.seattletimes.nwsource.com/ (accessed 6 February 2003).

Wilson, Andrea. 2002. "Social Spaces, Social Places? Design Stories." Presented at The Inside Story: A Library Interiors Forum, State Library of Victoria, Melbourne, 3–4 February.

Woodward, Jeanette. 1999. "Countdown to a New Library: A Blueprint for Success." *American Libraries* 30 (4): 44–47.

SELECTED BIBLIOGRAPHY

Australian School Library Association and Australian Library and Information Association. 2001. *Learning for the Future: Developing Information Services in Schools.* 2nd ed. Carlton South, AUS: Curriculum Corporation.

Dahlgren, Anders C. 1998. *Public Library Space Needs: A Planning Outline.* Madison: Wisconsin Department of Public Instruction, Public Library Development. Available: www.dpi.state.wi.us/dlcl/pld/plspace.html (accessed 3 January 2003).

Glick, Andrea. 1997. "Places to Dream: Whimsical New Children's Libraries." *School Library Journal* (February): 30–33

Hillier, Bill. *Space Is the Machine: A Configuration Theory of Architecture.* New York: Cambridge University Press, 1996.

Kirk, Joyce, Barbara Poston-Anderson, and Hilary Yerbury. 1990. *Into the 21st Century: Library and Information Services in Schools.* Artarmon, NSW: Australian Library and Information Association.

Smolders, Nola. 1997. "Radical Changes: Designing Libraries in the Technology-Driven 90s: Buildings as Celebrations." *ACCESS* 11 (3): 17–19.

The Inside Story: A Library Interiors Forum. 2002. State Library of Victoria, Melbourne, 3–4 February. Available: www.libraries.vic.gov.au/downloads/ Library_Network_Unit/newinteriors.htm.

12 USING TEEN PATRONS AS A RESOURCE IN PLANNING YOUNG ADULT LIBRARY SPACE IN PUBLIC LIBRARIES

Sondra Vandermark

Cathi Dunn MacRae (2000) reported in *Voice of Youth Advocates* (VOYA) that a young adult population explosion of more than thirty million teenagers was expected at the beginning of the new century (MacRae 2000). Planning library space for young adult library services is critical to meet the needs of this rapidly expanding population.

RATIONALE

Public libraries can be important in helping a young adult make the transition from childhood to adulthood through an effectively designed young adult library space. Such a space has the potential to provide the resources and environment that promote intellectual, emotional, and social development. An effectively designed young adult space is an environment for the following:

- Encouraging teens to develop the habit of lifelong learning through the library
- Motivating lifelong reading for information and pleasure
- Providing skills for information literacy
- Providing library collections and services for all young adults in the community to meet the following needs: educational, information technology, cultural, leisure/recreational

Having a young adult space not only answers teens' need for independence but also, according to Patrick Jones, author of *Connecting Young Adults and Libraries* (1998) provides a space where exciting things can happen. A young adult space keeps teens from disrupting the entire library because they have their own space to hang out. Jones states, "The most basic thing any library can provide is a place for people to sit and think. Sometimes that is all a YA really needs and wants from us—a place for time alone" (p. 37).

Rebecca M. Wenninger (2000), in Gerard B. McCabe's *Planning for a New Generation of Public Library Buildings*, states that in a typical public library teens make up the largest and most regular users of the public library. There are problems, however. According to Wenninger, it is common that the smallest percentage of the library's budget is spent on materials for young adults. In addition, the number of young adult librarians has decreased. Wenninger argues for allocating greater resources to a young adult space.

Teens need space to socialize and space to study, either individually or in a group. Renee J. Vaillancourt (2000), author of *Bare Bones Young Adult Services*, suggests that a young adult space should have a feeling of seclusion but be visible for supervision. "Most importantly, it should not be located next to the children's department. Many young adults are just beginning to establish their own identity and resent being perceived as children" (Vaillancourt 2000, 31).

Well-designed young adult library space is needed more than ever in public libraries. The young adult area should have certain functional characteristics, including space for needed "materials, comfortable chairs organized so socializing can occur, and an ambience created by posters or other decorations" (Jones 1998, 35).

THE NEED FOR TEEN INPUT

Library managers must plan a young adult or teen space that the target patrons will use. Experts in young adult behavior recommend getting input from teens. There are a number of ways to obtain teen input. They include questionnaires, surveys, focus groups, Junior Friends Groups, and young adult advisory groups. Using input from a young adult advisory committee is one of the best ways to develop a young adult space that will bring them to the library. In addition to young adult advisory groups, librarians can use traditional management tools such as the public library planning (Public Library Association) process and research into how other libraries have planned new young adult services, to identify local library service needs. The teen advisory group can be a key element of these activities.

It is important that the services for young adults be designed not only by librarians but also in cooperation with the target group. The participating young adults must be treated with respect, because they have unique and useful insights. Participants in the young adult advisory group must be willing to realize that their choices could be different from what libraries traditionally choose to do. The librarian working with the young adult advisory group must be willing to consider seriously all ideas that the teens come up with.

The goal of services and programs is to meet the changing needs of the local community of young adults, including all cultural groups and youth with special needs. Young adults must feel that the library space is their own space. It should include library materials teens want, a sense of privacy away from the children's area, comfortable furniture, and a welcoming ambience.

Because the young adult space is intended to meet the needs of teens, it is crucial to get young adults involved in the planning process. These helpful teenagers can be found in a variety of ways. Renee Vaillancourt (2000) discusses the use of junior friends groups and teen advisory boards. She suggests developing the advisory board from regular library users and pages. Other places to find teens willing to be in a young adult advisory group are the National Honor Society, Scouts, school bands, and churches.

It is important to pay attention to suggestions that come from the teen advisory group. Libraries can use the advisory group for many activities, not just planning the young adult space. Vaillancourt (2000) lists the bylaws for the Louisville Public Library Teen Advisory Board, with the intention that management in other libraries may review and use them as a starting point for developing local library bylaws. Some of the key functional elements in the bylaws are mission, membership, meetings, committees, and code of ethics.

COMPONENTS OF YOUNG ADULT SPACE

There is consensus among experts in young adult behavior that certain components should be in each young adult library space. The important issue for library management is to get input from the local teen advisory group about which components are most vital in the local community. Also, the way a component is implemented at the local level might be unique for that library.

According to Jones (1998), Vaillancourt (2000), and other young adult experts, the five essential components of a young adult space are the collection (print), audiovisual materials with an emphasis on music, periodicals, technology (including a young adult area on the library's Web site), and decor (furniture, posters, bulletin boards).

Collection (print) resources are important because teens need books for recreational reading as well as for educational and informational reading. Most young adult collections are predominantly fiction. A small nonfiction collection of hot topics usually can be found there. The location of the young adult space near the adult nonfiction and reference collection makes these materials readily available to teens without duplicating too many titles. Paperback books are the preferred format for fiction. The low cost of paperback books means the library can purchase more copies. Young adult input may affect the specific implementation of a library's use of paperback books, merchandising techniques, or purchase of particular genres such as graphic novels or comic books.

Audiovisual materials are very popular with young adults. Teens are used to learning from a variety of formats. In particular, they like music. Teen marketing guru Peter Zollo writes, "Music is probably the most influential and pervasive medium in teenage lives" (1995, p. 85). It is desirable to provide one listening station or more for the young adult area. Some libraries have cabling in the ceiling that is used with special radio frequency headphones to pick up sound, allowing more freedom of movement within the cabled space. In these situations, teens can listen to music without restraints.

As Patrick Jones (1998) states, having teens choose the young adult music for the library is a process that is inexpensive but has a big impact on teens. The teens get to pick out music that is exciting, choose groups they like and identify with, and see their opinions valued and accepted. In addition, teen input can affect the way in which music is provided in the young adult space.

Young adults like periodicals. The library might duplicate some periodicals that are available in the adult section as well as selecting periodicals that are young adult titles. Young adults have short attention spans; they like magazines because they are timely and cover fads and special interests (Jones 1998). Zollo (1995) also stresses the importance of periodicals: "There is no medium as intimate or directly relevant to teenage girls as magazines. . . . With the exception of friends, magazines are the place where teen girls say they find out about the latest trends" (p. 70).

According to Vaillancourt (2000), short articles, pertinent topics, and photographs are attractive to teens. Display of popular titles will bring teens into the young adult area. Periodicals also are great for nonreaders. Young adult input may affect the location of the periodical collection and the titles selected for the collection.

There is a need to provide a variety of technology for young adults, including online public access catalogs (OPACs), computers with Internet and online access to databases, and word processing. Although it is up to management to decide how many computers to provide for young adults, teens should not have to wait any longer to use a computer than any other library user. Computer use pulls teens into the library (Vaillancourt 2000).

Libraries need to provide as much access to technology as possible. Jones (1998) suggests that libraries must examine the characteristics of their local patrons and identify Internet resources that are of the most use to them, then make those Internet resources accessible through a local Web page. As Jones says,

> YAs like technology. First, because they are growing increasingly comfortable with it, to them it is nothing special. Second, technology speeds everything up, which given the hectic nature of YA life seems to fit nicely. Finally, technology provides YAs with more independence in their library use and, frankly, more excitement (p. 159).

Homework Center

A homework center is an important component of young adult technology resources. One of the uses young adults make of the public library is finding information for homework assignments. Development of a successful homework center includes one-on-one tutoring, telephone and email homework help, quiet study space, and dedicated computers with Internet access, online databases, CD-ROMs, and word processing (Jones 1998). If a library using the Public

Library Association planning process has identified formal learning support, general information, or information literacy service responses as a priority for the library, a homework center can be beneficial in providing the service for the target group. The features and resources of a homework center would be shaped by input from teens.

There are many Web sites for young adults that the library can access. Just a few of the sites with great content include the Internet Public Library (IPL) Teen Division (www.ipl.org/div/teen), which provides titles of good books to read, homework help, entertainment, and other topics of young adult interest; Teen Hoopla, from the American Library Association (www.ala.org/teenhoopla); and some individual public library sites such as the Brooklyn Public Library Info Zone (www.brooklynpubliclibrary.org/default.htm). Library staff should work with the Teen Advisory Committee to identify other sites that benefit local young adults.

Teens can use the library's Web site to develop a local newsletter, write book reviews, or sponsor a teen online bulletin board of local events of interest to the age group. How a library might develop this component of a young adult space will be unique according to local teen input.

The fifth component of a young adult space is the decor. Furniture should reflect the preferences of the young adults. As Vaillancourt (2000) suggests, comfortable furniture including couches, lounge chairs, and coffee tables is desirable to young adults. Beanbag chairs also are popular. Planning should include the selection of heavy-duty, solid furniture. Teens are hard on furniture, leaning back in chairs and sharing a seat for one with several others. A variety of different styles of seating should be available, including carrels for teens looking for a place for quiet individual study. It is also important to provide group study space.

Young adults can get involved with decorating their space through

- selection of furniture,
- selection of color scheme,
- selection of posters and bulletin boards,
- use of YA art collections, and
- use of neon signs.

When a young adult area is being developed, there should be a meeting that includes young adults, the young adult librarian, the architect, and the interior designer. Young adults will be pleased if they are asked for ideas about furnishings and color schemes (McCabe 2000). The color scheme should be different in the young adult area to set it apart from all other areas of the library.

GENERAL IMPACT OF YOUNG ADULT INPUT

Effective implementation of the five components is critical to success of a young adult space. It may be useful to look at how four communities used teen input to determine the characteristics of the five components of their young adult spaces. Three examples examine the impact of teen input on the technology, music, and decor components. The final example discusses teen input on all five components.

Experts on young adult behavior have found that teens need technology. A user survey completed by teens in Santa Cruz, California, indicated that the young adults wanted more technology and longer library hours. The branch library was open only fourteen hours each week (A Place of Our Own 1999). These survey results support the need for technology and a place to socialize and find recreational and educational materials.

One Small Room (1998) is a library space project in Australia. A young adult space was developed using input from a group called young designers. When asked what they would like the library to include, the young designers suggested background music and more contemporary CDs. In the case of the One Small Room example, teens identified the music component as their primary concern. The teen input affected the way music was provided.

Young adults in Edmonds, Washington, focused on the decor component of a great young adult library space. They wanted (1) more comfortable and colorful seating, (2) new shelving to replace old small wooden bookcases, (3) a large bulletin board to display group projects and information of ongoing interest to teens, and (4) a teen volunteer redecoration project for their teen area (Teen Area 2001).

One of the most creative young adult spaces is Teen Central at the Burton Barr Central Library in Phoenix, Arizona. The Teen Central young adult space can be viewed at the library's Web site (http://www.phxteencentral.org). Teen Central includes all of the components of a great young adult library space— new fiction, nonfiction and reference materials, health information center, graphic novels and comic books, lounge chairs, SurroundSound system, soft lounge chairs, CDs and videos, large-screen cable TV, computers, homework help, art gallery, magazines, and a community bulletin board. Teen Central is one of the most sophisticated young adult library spaces. Input from Phoenix teens resulted in a unique design.

SPECIFIC IMPACT OF YOUNG ADULT INPUT

As discussed previously, the five components of a successful young adult space include the collection (print), audiovisual materials with an emphasis on music, periodicals, technology (including a young adult area on the library's Web site), and decor (furniture, posters, bulletin boards). As library planning groups use teen input, the space becomes unique for the local community.

The following are examples of specific young adult impact on young adult space. It is a closer look at three libraries that developed successful young adult space using technology, music, decorating the space, and a look at one library using all of the components. In each of these projects, teen input was gathered in different ways including surveys, interviews, teen focus groups, and teen advisory groups.

The Garfield Park Branch in Santa Cruz California (A Place of Our Own 1999) used teen input collected through a survey to plan for more technology and longer hours. The staff got a Library Services and Technology Act (LSTA) grant to purchase computers and used local funds to renovate and rewire the space and to hire more staff so the library could be open more hours. The tiny Carnegie Building has been a young adult branch for years. The young adult branch now has the desired technology, including an electronic homework center with four workstations with headphones, databases, and CD-ROMs, computer games, word processing, and access to the Internet.

Although teens in Santa Cruz also wanted more technology for their young adult space, the teens also implemented several other components of an effective teen space. The teen advisory committee of the Garfield Park Branch helped with painting the space, after selecting the color. The committee also maintains bulletin boards, designs displays, and recommends materials for the library collection. The teens produce an electronic newsletter available on the library's Web site.

Teen input made this space valuable to the young people who use it. The community and library staff found ways to meet the needs of the target group. Technology support and the homework center encourage kids to be productive in the library. In addition, the teens decorate the space and make it their own through designing displays and maintaining bulletin boards. The use of the Web to address teen concerns through a newsletter mounted on the library's Web site allows for continued involvement by the young adults.

In addition, other ideas from the teens were implemented. A Web space for teens was set up within the library's website that includes an online bulletin board, suggestion box, and review page for young adults. Viewing stations for videos are available in One Small Room. The "young designers" really like listening to new CDs in the young adult space at the library.

This is a special response to the teen input for One Small Room. As Kaye Nunan, executive officer, says,

> The provision of a music collection, which could not be borrowed from the library and taken home, was an important resource as it allowed young people to listen to a variety of the latest CDs during their visit to the room. They did not have to wait two weeks until a current borrower returned it to the library. The provision of local and Brisbane-based bands' CDs also meant that young people had the opportunity to hear music which was unavailable in commercial music stores. The music collection was a major draw card for young people who were not regular library users (One Small Room).

The Teen Area at the Edmonds Library Sno-Isle Regional Library System of Edmonds, Washington is one of the highlighted young adult spaces in the VOYA regular feature, "YA Spaces of Your Dreams." The Edmonds Library invited a teen focus group to answer questions about the original teen area. The most frequent comment was a request to redecorate the young adult area. The staff of the library met with teens to get their ideas for redecorating the library space. According to Tom Reynolds, Adult/Teen Librarian from the Edmonds Library:

The most exciting part of our teen area redesign was ... the approach we took to involve teens in the planning and implementation process. We attempted to accomplish each of the four goals of our 1998 brainstorming group. Although some were modified, such as recovering rather than replacing the stuffed chairs, we were successful in following through with the spirit of their recommendations to make this area more comfortable and teen-friendly. Our process of using teen input in stages could be a model for other middle-sized libraries on a limited budget (Teen Area 2001, 193).

CONCLUSION

When teens are involved in the planning of the young adult library space, they use the space. Teen input can be gathered through surveys, questionnaires, and young adult advisory groups. Libraries can adapt survey questions to meet local needs. Several survey questions from the One Small Room project are useful examples. Among the questions included in that Australian survey were the following:

- What are libraries for?
- Why would you go to a library?
- What kinds of things do libraries offer?
- What other things would you like the library to offer?
- What are your ideas for developing a young adult space?
- How do you think you can attract young people into the library/this space?
- How could we use these ideas in the project?
- What kind of furniture might we need?

These questions encouraged the teens to talk about different components of what became an effective young adult library space without leading them to any conclusions. The young adults identified the components that were important to the teens for One Small Room. Any library can use similar questions (and ones that are unique to their own libraries) to get good results.

As stated earlier, the goal of services and programs is to meet the changing needs of the local community of young adults. Young adults must feel that the library space is their own space. Input from young adults is the best way for a library to meet this need.

REFERENCES

"A Place of Our Own, Garfield Park Branch, Santa Cruz Public Libraries, Santa Cruz, California." 1999. *Voice of Youth Advocates* June: 100–101.

Jones, Patrick. 1998. *Connecting Young Adults and Libraries.* 2nd ed. New York and London: Neal-Schuman.

McCabe, Gerard B. 2000. *Planning for a New Generation of Public Library Buildings.* Westport, CT: Greenwood Press.

MacRae, Cathi Dunn. 2000. "YA Radar: Youth Experts Screen the Teen Climate at the Dawn of 2000." *Voice of Youth Advocates* February: 384–387.

"One Small Room: What Would Young People Do to Make Library Spaces and Services More Appealing to Other Young People?"; "Resources"; "Appendix C: Young Designers and Initial Design Notes." 1998. *The One Small Room Report*. Brisbane State Library of Queensland, Public Libraries Division. Available: http://www.slq.qld.gov.au/pub/onesmall/contents.htm.

"Teen Area: Edmonds Library Sno-Isle Regional Library System, Edmonds, Washington." 2001. *Voice of Youth Advocates* August: 192–193.

Vaillancourt, Renee J. 2000. *Bare Bones Young Adult Services: Tips for Public Library Generalists*. Chicago: Young Adult Library Services Association.

Wenninger, Rebecca M. 2000. "A Place To Call Their Own." In *Planning for a New Generation of Public Library Buildings*, ed. Gerard B. McCabe, 63–66. Westport, CT: Greenwood Press.

Zollo, Peter. 1995. *Wise Up to Teens*. Ithaca, NY: New Strategist Press.

13 CREATING A SENIOR-FRIENDLY LIBRARY

Rebecca Wenninger

Older adults tend to be a large and dedicated group of library users. These are the people who grew up without television and computers and who remain avid readers. They value libraries and free access to books, information, periodicals, and traditional library services. Older adults like to educate themselves about current issues (Second World Assembly on Ageing 2002). They also vote in higher percentages and are growing in political influence (Dychwald 1999). In the eleven years I have been a librarian, I have seen the focus of library services shift more and more toward children and youth. Although this is very important in trying to encourage literacy, build lifelong readers, and assist with academics, services to older adults are often neglected. People are living longer and remaining active in their older years, and libraries need to establish better relationships with them. This group of people is large and growing. In fact, by 2050 the number of people age 60 and over will exceed those under 15 for the first time in history (Second World 2002). Such rapid growth of this population demands that libraries make the necessary adjustments to buildings and services to accommodate them. These are the people who make up our library boards, Friends groups, and volunteers. They are a vocal and strong group whose donations of time and money keep libraries going. They love libraries and what we stand for, and without their support, a lot of our work with today's youth would not be possible. We can no longer assume that we are meeting older adults' needs simply by supplying them with bestsellers and large-print books.

Because libraries have always been an important part of most communities, older adults know that the library is there and do not need as many incentives to visit as do those in other age groups. But even though this group may be aware of traditional services and even be regular users of the library, we must still address their changing and special needs and interests. We cannot assume that because someone is of a certain age, he or she would not be interested in a particular service. The increasing number of people over 60 using computers and attending computer-training classes is proof of this. Someone who has been a regular customer for years may still be unaware of everything the library has to offer. When developing these relationships, we are also gaining support for the library in other ways.

When planning new libraries or renovating existing structures, care should be taken to provide a senior-friendly theme throughout. This will benefit other users as well, including those with disabilities. Assuring the comfort of older adults is not going to cost any more than providing for any other population age group. Thoughtful planning will provide a pleasant atmosphere, which in turn will encourage use. A lot of seniors' needs will be met by following Americans with Disabilities Act (ADA) guidelines, and common sense will likely cover the rest. As always when planning libraries, valuable input can be gained directly from the customers themselves, and they should be involved in the planning. Often their wish list is something that may have been overlooked by staff planners simply because librarians don't have the same point of view as patrons.

Older adults are most often seen in libraries in the morning and early-afternoon hours. Some may visit as just another stop while running errands, some may come in daily to read the newspaper, and still others may come in and spend an hour chatting with neighbors. Morning visits can be attributed to many factors: transportation issues, inclement weather, health issues, crime, and wanting to avoid the after-school crowds of noisy kids. Regardless of the reasons, older adults' tendency to visit the library early in the day should be noted when planning lighting in libraries for maximum comfort. Skylights that let in direct light should not be placed over seating or reading areas that may cause a glare. Direct lighting from skylights can also cause visibility problems when placed over stacks and displays. Depending on the layout of the building, "wall-washing" lighting can be used to illuminate displays, bulletin boards, and the like. A well-lit perimeter will also add a spacious feeling to the room (Siems and Demmers n.d.). Special consideration should also be given to floor-level shelving to ensure that it is illuminated well. (Those bottom shelves can be hard to see.) Because of safety issues for seniors as well as all customers, exterior lighting should provide a sense of security to those visiting the library after daylight hours. Well-lit parking lots, walkways, and doorways are a must.

All buildings should be compliant with ADA standards, whether they are renovations or new structures. This will address many issues of importance to seniors. Not all seniors are frail or sick, but as we age we tend to slow down; by making accessibility easier, the library is shown to be responsive to seniors' needs. Parking lots should have parking places designated for people with disabilities, and sidewalks should have ramp cutouts. Entrance doors should either be sliding or slow-open. This allows easy access for wheelchairs or people with ambulatory problems and is also a good idea to accommodate the customer with an armload of books. If turnstiles are used at entrances, they should turn easily, and there should also be some provision for those who cannot go through a turnstile for whatever reason. Restroom entrances should have wide doorways, both at the entrance and in the stalls, for wheelchair access. Handrails should be present inside stalls. Sinks, soap, and paper towel dispensers should be of wheelchair height and close to each other. Thought should also be given to installing a family restroom that would be useful to those who may need help from a caregiver. Circulation and information desks should be easily accessible to those in wheelchairs, and also easy to place books and materials on. Walkways and aisles between stacks should accommodate wheelchairs comfortably. Exact measurement requirements for restrooms, doorways, aisle widths, and shelving heights are provided in the *Americans with Disabilities Act Handbook* (1991) guidelines for libraries (appendix B).

Placement of materials should be logical, and once it is known what senior patrons tend to use, place these subject areas in as close proximity as possible. For example, new books/bestsellers, large-print books, audiocassettes, and biographies could be in close proximity to each other with the travel path easily flowing from one area to another. Placement should be determined by use of the collection. As mentioned before, seniors are not the only ones who use specific areas or collections of materials, so careful arrangement of materials based on use statistics will benefit all library users. Signage should be large and understandable, without a lot of "library lingo." Often customers are unfamiliar with terms librarians use, even though to us they are basic terminology. There are many customers who may not think of the circulation desk as the desk where you check out books. Signs should be placed at eye level to assure that they will be seen by those who need them.

Shelving for seniors and also for customers with disabilities should not be too high or too low. In some cases, this will be unavoidable and assistance from library staff will be necessary for customers to get what they need, but if there are specific areas, such as a large-print collection, that will be primarily used by seniors, keep accessibility in mind when selecting shelving. No one of any age wants to have to bend down too far or be forced to stand on kick stools to reach materials. Circulation and registration counters and information desks should have at least one space low enough to meet the needs of those in wheelchairs. Counters and desks should also be low enough so that books and materials can easily be placed on top.

Special seating is probably not necessary for seniors. Use of comfortable chairs in conversational groupings in areas such as spots near bestsellers and magazine collections will more than likely already be planned. As long as there is a place that seniors can meet with friends to chat, away from the children's area and quiet study area, this should be sufficient.

As can be seen across the country, many libraries have incorporated senior community rooms into library buildings. Some are dedicated for senior use only; some may be used by other groups as well, with storage for senior groups' supplies and so on. The library is an ideal meeting place for seniors, as most members of this group are familiar with the location of the library, hours and parking are accessible, and they are regular users anyway. This is another way to increase library use and attendance at programs and events. The needs of the community should be assessed before deciding whether or not to dedicate a room specifically for senior use. If there is no interest or funding available for a community room, a bulletin board specifically for seniors can also be placed in a prominent area. This is a great way to advertise library-sponsored events as well as services and programs in the community for seniors.

More and more seniors are interested in and becoming proficient in using technology. When purchasing equipment, thought should be given to large screens and audio devices that will accommodate those with visual or hearing disabilities. A special mouse can also be purchased for those who may have trouble manipulating the traditional mouse. Classes specifically for seniors are also gaining popularity, and if staff resources are available, these should definitely be added to library programming. Seniors are a valuable resource to libraries, and we as librarians should provide them with comfortable and accessible surroundings.

REFERENCES

Americans with Disabilities Act Handbook. 1991. Washington, DC: U.S. Government Printing Office.

Dychwald, Ken. 1999. *AgePower: How the 21st Century Will Be Ruled by the New Old*. New York: Jeremy P. Tarcher/Putnam.

Second World Assembly on Ageing. 2002. "Building a Society for All Ages: Population Ageing: Facts and Figures." United Nations Department of Public Information DPI/2264. Available: http://seniors.tchnet.org/articles%20population_ageing.htm (accessed 3 January 2003).

Siems, Earl, and Linda Demmers. n.d. "Library Stacks and Shelving." Libris DESIGN Project. Available: www.librisdesign.org/docs/stack_shelving.html (accessed 3 January 2003).

PART VI
TECHNOLOGY

14 WIRELESS NETWORKING IN THE LIBRARY: CREATING NETWORK CONNECTIVITY THROUGHOUT THE LIBRARY—A DECISION-MAKING GUIDE FOR PLANNERS

Kenneth D. Clipperton

In the summer of 2000, Buena Vista University (Storm Lake, Iowa) created a campuswide wireless network that includes complete coverage of its library facilities. Wireless connectivity enables the university to provide access to electronic resources, including the card catalog, from everywhere within the facility. It has been very well received by our clients and has made a positive impact on the way they use the library and library resources. This chapter provides a decision-making guide for planners and describes the design considerations that might be useful to those considering the provision of wireless network access in their facilities.

THE IMPACT OF STANDARDS

Someone has quipped, "One of the great things about standards is that there are so many of them." The following paragraphs describe some of the history of wireless networking standards. The main thing I hope you will take away from this is that there is one standard for wireless networks that has won in the marketplace. That standard is 802.11b (http://standards.ieee.org/catalog/olis/index.html). The Institute of Electrical and Electronic Engineers (IEEE), using working groups of engineers, tests and establishes standards for industry. Future winning standards will almost certainly be backward compatible with that standard. This means that organizations can deploy networks based on the 802.11b standard with a high degree of confidence that the networks will be useful for several years.

Wireless networking has been around for many years, but its use was once confined mostly to vertical applications, for example, in situations such as warehouse management, or in hospitals. That all began to change in 1997 when the Institute of Electrical and Electronics Engineers (IEEE) adopted the first 802.11 standard. Unfortunately, this standard had a maximum data rate of 2 megabytes per second and allowed for two different and incompatible radio technologies. The 802.11 working group also identified a path toward 11 megabytes-per-second and 54 megabytes-per-second wireless networks.

The 11-megabytes-per-second 802.11b standard was ratified on September 30, 1999. The 802.11b standard passed without any inherent incompatibilities. As the standard was approaching finalization, an industry group called the Wireless Ethernet Compatibility Alliance (WECA) was formed to certify the interoperability of 802.11 products and to promote Wi-Fi (the designation for certified products) as the global wireless local area network (LAN) standard.

Several factors led to rapid adoption of 802.11b by organizations. First, WECA called the technology "Ethernet." This was smart, because networking folks are comfortable with Ethernet networks. The use of the term Ethernet also communicated the idea that this standards-based wireless network equipment would perform at approximately Ethernet speeds. Second, WECA's Wi-Fi interoperability testing meant that organizations would be able to buy any Wi-Fi certified wireless cards and be assured they would work with any Wi-Fi certified access points. The 802.11b/Wi-Fi standard has done for wireless networking what the original Ethernet standard did for wired networks and what the Group 3 standard did for fax machines. Assured interoperability led to widespread adoption and to rapid price drops as a robust competitive marketplace developed.

WHY GO WIRELESS?

There are many reasons to implement wireless networks in libraries. These include access, cost, timeliness, flexibility, aesthetics, asbestos, and historic buildings.

Access

Wireless networking puts full network access everywhere the people are. It literally puts networked resources within arms reach—in the stacks, in the study carrels, in the conference rooms, perhaps even on the lawn. Putting the online public access catalog (OPAC), the databases, and the Internet within reach changes the relationship between electronic and paper resources; it creates new opportunities for integration. Wireless technology takes access to a whole new level, providing access everywhere people want it.

Cost

Planning a new facility that incorporates a wireless network combined with portable and/or small-footprint client computers effectively makes your building bigger. You can go from 40 square feet of space per person to 30 square feet per person in some instances. Therefore, planning for wireless can have a large positive impact on the budget for a new facility.

Installing a wireless network infrastructure in a new facility can cost much less than does a fully wired infrastructure. Even the best planning efforts fail to anticipate every future use of certain spaces within a library. Needs and expectations change over time. When planning a wired network infrastructure, generally we balance the additional cost of installing extra network drops during initial construction with the much higher cost of installing network drops later on an as-needed basis. With wireless, we can plan complete coverage of every space in a building up-front. Because the cost of adding network drops in an existing facility is so much higher than during new construction, wireless technology is even more cost effective when expanding network access within an existing building.

Flexibility

With a wireless network in place, network access can be created anywhere there is power for a computer. If clients are using portable computers, network access exists everywhere there is a place to sit down. Rather than dedicating a significant percentage of study carrels as computer access spaces, each carrel can be used according to patrons' needs by checking out portable computers on request.

Timeliness

Installing a wireless network in a small building may be as simple as plugging a single access point into power and a live Ethernet jack. There are other considerations that may complicate this scenario, but it truly can be that quick and easy.

Aesthetics

Beauty may be in the eye of the beholder, but very few people would argue that surface-mount cable molding and Ethernet jacks are beautiful. A wireless network infrastructure can be completely invisible. In our library at Buena Vista University, a truly beautiful facility, the wireless access points were installed above the drop ceiling to create invisible access. Aesthetic considerations may be especially important for landmark structures. In addition, since the client machines connect via wireless, there is no need for patch cables to be draped from computers to the nearest network jack. In environments that include portable computers, this also enhances safety by eliminating the risk of people tripping over the cables.

Asbestos

Any construction work that would disturb existing asbestos can be costly, time-consuming, and disruptive of normal use of the building. Implementing wireless may allow you to create more long-term access without disrupting access in the short term.

Historic Buildings

The installation of a traditional wired network may simply be disallowed in some historic buildings. A wireless network can create the opportunity to continue to use these wonderful buildings without impairing your ability to provide clients with the access and services they need from a library today.

WHY NOT GO WIRELESS?

In spite of the many advantages of wireless, there are some trade-offs. Depending on your situation, these may or may not be significant. These trade-offs include performance, interference, security, and obsolescence.

Performance

Wireless networks are slower than current wired networks. Although the 802.11b standard operates at a theoretical 11 megabytes per second, current wired Ethernet is commonly deployed at 100 megabytes per second, and we are beginning to see client systems ship with 1,000 megabytes per second (Gigabit Ethernet) wired ports. Worse, all the wireless clients connected to an access point *share* that 11 megabytes per second. Even worse, most access points achieve a real throughput of around 5 megabytes per second to share among the connected computers. Most wired networks provide each computer with its own dedicated (switched) Ethernet connection.

Whether the slower data rates of wireless networks makes a significant difference in any network environment depends on the type of traffic and the size of files that are routinely moved across the network. If the files most clients use are under several megabytes in size, the perceived performance difference will be negligible. At Buena Vista University, all full-time students and faculty are equipped with wireless portable computers. These 1,400 computers connect to the campus network exclusively via wireless Ethernet. Many faculty report that the wireless network feels as fast as the 100-megabytes-per-second switched Ethernet connections their previous computers used. If your users will routinely work with files larger than four or five megabytes, however, they will notice the speed difference. For our faculty and students, these occasional delays are more than outweighed by the access and convenience that wireless mobility enables. Network-performance-monitoring tools are readily available to help understand the traffic in a network environment. Understanding your own traffic is the key to an intelligent decision about whether or not the performance limitations of wireless technology matter in your environment.

Interference

Other devices operate in the same 2.4 GHz radio spectrum that 802.11b uses. It is possible for those devices—some wireless phones, wireless speakers, wireless video cameras, poorly sealed microwave ovens, medical devices, industrial devices—to interfere with a wireless network if they are operated in proximity to network devices (access points or client machines). It is also possible for someone to intentionally disrupt a wireless network by building a radio transmitter that operates in the 2.4 GHz range and then placing the device in the environment as a form of denial of service attack. Although unlikely, such attacks are possible and would be effective until the device was found and disabled or removed. Interference has a negative impact on performance, no matter what its source.

A site survey is an important prerequisite to any wireless LAN deployment to identify any existing interference issues. In most cases, no substantive interference will be encountered.

Security

Wireless networks are not very secure. The standard encryption included in the 802.11b specification (Wired Equivalent Privacy [WEP]) is easily broken. This means that unless you install additional encryption technology, your wireless network traffic is more susceptible to interception than is traffic on a wired network that employs switched Ethernet. (Network security is a many-fanged animal. There is much more that could be written here.)

Since many libraries are interested in providing public access, encryption may not be a significant consideration, and implementing encryption of the wireless network infrastructure might prove to be counterproductive. Many organizations have implemented enhanced security through virtual private networks (VPNs) and other technologies. At Buena Vista University, we use the standard WEP encryption, but don't rely on WEP alone for security. We also embed encryption in the applications that need it. An example of encryption in the application is a sure sockets layer (SSL)–enabled web page that prompts for a username and password. By incorporating encryption into the application, we protect our clients' private information no matter how they get to the application—via the wired network, the wireless network, or the global Internet.

Obsolescence

Wireless technology is evolving. Equipment designed to the 802.11a standard is already available from some vendors. The 802.11a equipment operates in the 5 GHz range and supports data rates up to 52 megabytes per second. Also, a faster 2.4 GHz standard called 802.11g is rapidly moving toward finalization. It is also expected to operate at 52 megabytes per second.

The new 802.11g products will be backward compatible with 802.11b. This means that 802.11g access points will serve 802.11b clients and that 802.11g clients will be able to use an 802.11b network. Also, 802.11a equipment manufacturers are working on dual-band 802.11a/g devices. These dual-band devices are expected to dominate the 802.11a market, because they would interoperate with 802.11a, 802.11g, and 802.11b devices. In other words, any 802.11b deployment on either the network infrastructure or client side is likely to be useful for as long as an 11-megabytes-per-second connection speed feels fast enough in use. It will not be made obsolete by the emergence of the next generation of devices.

WIRELESS NOW OR LATER?

The case for wireless will eventually be compelling for most organizations. This is especially true for those who seek to offer public access to networked resources and information. Given the existence of the 802.11b global standard for wireless LAN technology, the commodity pricing that this technology has achieved, the expected longevity of this technology, and the opportunities a wireless LAN creates to increase service and improve flexibility, it makes sense to incorporate a wireless LAN into almost any library construction project.

HOW TO IMPLEMENT WIRELESS TECHNOLOGY

There are a number of decisions that need to be made for any wireless network implementation. These decisions are reasonably straightforward and include access point placement, site survey considerations, required network services, and other decisions about how open your wireless network will be.

Access Point/Antenna Placement

Generally speaking, it is good to place the access point, or an external antenna connected to an access point, as high as possible within the area being served. For reasons of aesthetics and security, it is also good to place access points where library patrons will not see them. Good alternatives for access point placement include nonpublic spaces such as communications wiring closets, storage areas, technical service areas, staff offices, and above ceilings. Wiring closets are ideal, because using them places your wireless network infrastructure in the same space as your wired network infrastructure, and there is a good chance that clean AC power is already available. One disadvantage of above-ceiling installations is the need to run an Ethernet connection, and possibly AC power in small implementations, to these odd locations. Another disadvantage of above-ceiling placement is the need to use a ladder when doing installations or service.

Site Survey Considerations

A wireless site survey is an essential part of almost any wireless network implementation. Whether the survey is contracted out or done in-house, the survey involves temporarily placing one or more access points in planned locations and then verifying the resulting wireless connectivity coverage area by systematically walking through the desired coverage area with a radio signal measurement device and a diagram of the facility, marking coverage boundaries. Generally speaking, wireless network adapters come with free software that allows any portable computer equipped with a wireless adapter to function as the survey instrument.

The wireless signal degrades primarily due to two factors, reflection and absorption. As a radio signal encounters various objects it is either reflected or absorbed. The more a signal is reflected, the more difficult it is for the receiver to discern the original signal from its accompanying reflections. Water is especially adept at absorbing 2.4 GHz radio signals; this is what makes water boil in a microwave oven. Both reflection and absorption can make wireless networking within the stacks problematic. Some libraries have seen no problems at all in the stacks, whereas others had a tough time getting a decent signal to all points in the stacks. That's why a site survey is so important. If a given library experiences large seasonal swings in humidity, it is conceivable that the wireless radio signal will be more readily absorbed in the library environment during the high humidity season, particularly in the stacks. The survey should be performed during the high humidity season or allowances made in the coverage boundaries.

The survey might also include scanning for preexisting radio frequency (RF) interference in the 2.4 GHz range. This is most likely to be an issue in situations where the library shares a building with other organizations, though proximity to buildings with certain industrial, scientific, or medical devices may also yield interference. Because the use of the spectrum is unlicensed, no one has special rights to its use. Resolution of conflicting use generally involves working out an agreement to use different channels and unique network names.

A key decision is whether you are designing the wireless network for maximum coverage area or for maximum performance. Most libraries will design for maximum coverage and minimum cost. Enterprise-class access points generally have settings for large-, medium-, small-, and even microcell coverage areas. The large-cell setting is appropriate for maximum coverage. Be sure to set this parameter in the access points prior to doing the site survey.

If your library includes multiple floors, be sure to test each access point's coverage area on all floors. The standard access point coverage area is three-dimensional and generally globe-shaped. It is not uncommon for a radio signal to penetrate two stories in either direction.

Required Network Infrastructure Services

Except for the smallest implementations, a wireless network rides on top of a wired network infrastructure. If the wireless network is to be used for Internet access, the minimum services required of the network infrastructure include TCP/IP protocol support, either a DHCP service to provide Internet provider (IP) addresses to wireless clients or an assigned range of IP addresses, and appropriate network bandwidth back to library servers and to the Internet. In very small implementations where these services do not already exist, a single broadband router/access point/firewall device may provide a low-cost and simple solution.

Client Decisions

A decision that will influence other choices is whether only library-owned devices or both library-owned and patron-owned devices will be allowed to use the wireless network. If only library-owned devices will be allowed, then it is advisable to use a specific network name, also called a service set identifier (SSID), rather than the default. Furthermore, if the access point supports the feature, make it a closed network. This means that the access point will not broadcast the network name. Also, use the WEP encryption option and assign an encryption key. With these settings enabled on your wireless infrastructure, only someone who knows your network name and encryption key will be able to connect a computer to the wireless network.

If you intend to allow patron-owned devices to use the wireless network, you should probably use the default network name, use the open network option, and leave encryption turned off. Most wireless access points come with these settings as the default. With these settings, anyone who has a wireless device will easily be able to configure their device to utilize your wireless network. In most cases, their devices will be able to autodetect these settings and begin to use your network immediately.

Many organizations place their wireless access points outside the firewall. This is probably an especially good choice if you are going to allow patron-owned devices on the wireless network. This will work well if your library system is Web accessible. On the other hand, if your library system is not Web accessible and requires specialized client software, placing the wireless network outside the firewall may require you to open up the firewall so much that it no longer protects your key networked assets from the global Internet. Consult with someone who understands your complete technical environment to assist you in making this decision.

CLIENT ACCESS ALTERNATIVES AND CONSIDERATIONS

Once a wireless network is in place, it opens up several client access alternatives. A particularly attractive option is a portable computer lab. This consists of a number of computers on a cart. The cart provides charging adapters for all the computers, so they can be recharged simply by plugging the cart into the wall. A setup like this allows individual computers to be checked out and used in any location in the library yet also allows for the creation of a computer lab for library instruction or other purposes simply by rolling the cart into a conference or community room and putting the computers out on the table(s). The cart also provides an easy way to secure the computers by locking the cart or storing it in a secured area.

Another option for patron access is to provide a small number of computers available for checkout. For libraries with six or fewer computers, this may be almost as convenient as the portable computer lab, without the extra expense of the cart.

Some libraries that allow patron-owned devices to use the wireless network are providing just the wireless cards for checkout. The cost per card is now under $100; much less than the cost of a computer. Providing the cards implies support from the library staff in configuring computers to use the cards. This is something to clarify via written policy before offering the service.

Again, some libraries have created wireless networks primarily to meet their own access requirements but do allow patrons to configure patron-owned devices to use the wireless network. Establishing a clear policy and rationale prior to rolling out the wireless network is a good idea. If your library allows patron-owned devices, establishing a clear policy on what technical support will and will not be provided is strongly recommended.

LIST OF WIRELESS STANDARDS

802.1x
802.11
802.11a (not allowed in Europe)
802.11b (International standard)
802.11g
802.11h (802.11a plus spectrum and power management)
802.3af (Power over Ethernet)

15 CONSIDERATIONS IN PLANNING AND MANAGING COMPUTER SERVICES

Cathan Cook

When you plan to renovate or to design a new library, you will want to consider computer services for the patrons. This chapter guides you through considerations in deciding what services to offer and what will be involved in planning and supporting them.

TYPES OF COMPUTER SERVICES

As technology becomes more prevalent in society, more people are interested in using computers as part of their research or sense of community. Therefore it is not unusual for a community library to provide a small multipurpose computer area. Although it is a fairly simple matter to set up a couple of personal computers (PCs) with Internet connectivity, maintaining even such a small section can become a challenge when many different people use them for a variety of purposes. Careful planning is needed to ensure the success of the computer area. The first aspect to consider is what services you will offer and what purpose they serve in the library.

Just as you would consider and plan which books to purchase on a specific topic, you should consider how a computer area will enhance your patrons' experience of the library. A formal statement of this purpose will drive the design and planning and influence your choices along the way.

The following sections consider different computer services, how they contribute to the library, and any special considerations they introduce.

General Connectivity

One of the first things to come to mind in providing computer services is providing access to the Internet. Through use of the Internet, email, and online chats, modern technology allows us to communicate with people all over the world. This is bound to be a popular service, because exploring the Internet, communicating in emails, and chatting online are never-ending sources of entertainment and education. But what is the purpose of providing this generalized connectivity? The Internet, one of the best general research tools available today, is a worldwide community, made up of posted documents and multimedia materials. Its greatest strength, and greatest weakness, is that anyone can post and maintain a Web site (a group of posted materials) on any topic. It can be a fabulous research tool, especially on subjects that are obscure or very recent. It can also be a tremendous waste of time. So, perhaps a good question to ask is how do you focus the use of the Internet to the goals of the library?

First, we must acknowledge that providing connectivity may be the goal in itself. This service is beyond the budget of many patrons who do not own the requisite hardware or cannot pay for monthly connectivity fees from their homes. As a result, you will probably find that providing this service in the library will attract more patrons, some of whom would not otherwise have darkened the library's door. For this reason, you should advertise other, more standard library services in your computer area, in the hope of luring these patrons into exploring the stacks. At best, you will attract people who want to email friends and relatives, students who are working on projects, and those looking for information on a specific research topic or hobby interest. At worst, you may attract people with somewhat reprehensible interests or habits. More information on controlling Internet access is provided later in this chapter. Note that, by providing Internet access, you also provide email access at no additional expense; chat capabilities usually require specific chat-related software, although much of this is free. In addition, because there are sites on the Internet that allow a person to create a Web site for free, by supplying connectivity you also are providing a simplistic means for your patrons to create their own small Web sites. This can be enhanced by providing a scanner as well, so that they can scan in graphics.

Another purpose of providing connectivity is to create a sense of community that contributes to the value provided by a public library. By becoming the place where people can keep in touch with their local community (through local Web sites and email) or the larger world community, the library can come to be viewed as the place to go for keeping in touch with current events.

More in line with traditional services, connectivity can provide patrons with the ability to do research on their own. There are many Web sites, called search engines, that provide a simple interface for searching through existing cataloged Web sites for specific keywords. These can be specialized to a specific topic or a specific audience, or they can be very generalized. Some contain rated content, others use some complex algorithm to value content, and others simply list every entry found. Providing the patron with an opportunity to do research on the Web also provides another hidden opportunity as well: that of educating the patron on better search skills. Especially in the case of students, this is a valuable skill, and one that would not usually be sought out individually. If students are searching unsuccessfully for materials, they will be more inclined to ask for help with searching skills, especially if a sign near the computers points them to a research librarian. In some cases, extensive research needs might also lead to further use of the research librarian's abilities.

Simple Office Services

Another service is providing simple word processing and similar office-type software. This is popular among people who do not own computers and students who are working on research projects in the library.

In addition to word processing, however, there are other office services to consider. One that is bound to be popular is the ability to create presentations, or digital slide decks. This will appeal to students, to individuals active in the community, and to businesspeople as well. And as a result, this service may increase library use.

General word processing can often be implemented through free software, although purchased software allows a wider variety of file formats. This can be a significant factor, depending on how flexible you want the service to be. Limited file formats could prevent patrons from working on all but the most basic documents. Presentations are created by using software specifically designed for this purpose, and this adds an additional software expense. But it may have great promotional value in reaching out to the business-oriented members of the community.

Provision of either of these services implies that the patron will either print out what has been created or save it to a file for later use. Providing a printer is an additional maintenance consideration, a point that will be addressed later in this chapter. Allowing patrons to save the files they create requires both a piece of hardware in the PC (such as a 3.5-inch floppy disk drive or a CD-ROM burner) and the storage media (diskettes or CDs). It is a good idea to provide storage media for sale on the premises, if at all possible.

Multimedia Materials

Providing the ability to use multimedia materials on the computers can be a tremendous enhancement over providing print materials only. Many topics, such as music and language, are related better through sound and pictures than through print. Additionally, many topics easily addressed in print can be more easily absorbed when the presentation is enhanced with multimedia. A classic example of this is an encyclopedia. In print, these are cumbersome, expensive, and quickly outdated. In multimedia format, the encyclopedia is less expensive and therefore easier to keep updated; it contains enhancements such as sound, moving pictures, and diagrams; and it allows the patron to electronically search for topics. If you are also providing simple office services such as printing and word processing, the patrons can print relevant sections or transfer sections to their own documents via software cut-and-paste features.

Supplying multimedia services can greatly improve the type of information available from the library; it does require some special considerations, however. Computers that easily run multimedia software must be more robust in hardware and are therefore more expensive. Multimedia software also tends to become dated; generally, five years old is considered outdated in terms of what will function effectively in current PC hardware/software. In addition, using multimedia means that the PC must be able to create noise, so it also means that you need to supply a nonintrusive way for patrons to hear the sounds, such as headsets.

Multimedia applications are also very appealing to children, and a great deal of software is available to help children learn to read or do math, for example, in the form of educational games.

There is an additional benefit to multimedia support that is worth emphasizing. The latest software accepts voice commands as a means of input. This means that if you supply your computers with headsets that have microphones, you can also add voice recognition capabilities to your list of computer services. With the correct software, voice recognition can be used to enter a word-processed document without continuous use of keyboard and mouse. Some foreign-language programs even allow users to speak aloud to evaluate the effectiveness of their pronunciation.

Other Software Services

A complete coverage of this topic is beyond the scope of this chapter, but here are some ideas for services that can be offered simply by providing software:

- Creation of reports, resumes, or letters
- Creation of presentations
- Exploration of online atlases
- Research through online encyclopedias
- Organization of research
- Travel planning and map searches
- Creation of Web sites

Note that if you need a computer that "speaks" a different language, this can also be accomplished by installing software in the required language. Simply request language-specific copies of software from your software vendor.

Portable Catalog Services

New wireless technology also allows libraries to provide additional services such as loaning out laptops or even creating wireless access to the catalog via handheld or palm-sized computers. These wireless computers, which are connected via a wireless network (not via cell-phone connections) can be set up to also allow Internet access. These are extremely flexible tools, but because they are so new, you would probably need a specialist to help you maintain them.

Wireless catalog access needs to be designed to work with your catalog system, so if you believe this would be a good option for your library, work with consultants or with your own information technology department. (See also chapter 14, which covers this topic in detail.)

Services to Help the Library

In a larger library system, you might also plan to provide computer services that help the library. A couple of examples are a library intranet and analysis of library usage patterns. An intranet is a Web site that is only available to staff members. Usually, an intranet contains information such as calendars, forms, announcements, lists of resources and contacts, and so on. It can even be set up to allow employees to add their own materials to the intranet, so that research or other information can be more easily shared between groups. If you would like to make it easier for library teams to collaborate in reaching common goals, you should investigate the possibility of using Sharepoint Team Services, a Microsoft product that turns the creation of a team site into a very simple nontechnical process. For more information (both technical and nontechnical), visit the Microsoft Sharepoint Technologies Web site (http://www.microsoft.com/sharepoint/).

Analysis of library usage patterns can be accomplished through another Microsoft product, SQL Server Analysis Services (www.microsoft.com.sql). This type of analysis can reveal trends in patron interest and relate these trends to demographical information. Additionally, this type of tool could be used to recommend book selections to a reader, by listing books that interested similar readers (that is, books checked out by readers who also checked out the book being viewed).

PLANNING CONSIDERATIONS

There are several aspects to be considered when planning your computer center, including the decisions regarding software, establishing facilities, and procedures.

Software: A Business Solution

The software solution you select should meet your service goals. It is important to select the right software, and there is a key to making this more manageable. Above all, you need software that is easy for your organization to maintain and that provides the solution you need. You should evaluate whether the software will assist you in accomplishing your business goals. Rather than viewing a list of features for each software package, evaluate how the addition of each software package will add to all of the software you are planning to use together.

The term for software that works together, or with what you already own, is *integrated solution*; the opposite of an integrated solution is a *heterogeneous system*, which is more expensive to maintain. You might ask to see a demo or, even better, ask for a trial software package. Make sure to take advantage of the trial by thoroughly testing what it can do, and if possible, by allowing users to try it as well.

Deploying an integrated solution is also important for another reason: manageability. If you build a system of many unrelated parts, the result will require those using the system to have a wider variety of skills, and thus it may require more support personnel as well. If your library system is already using a particular technology, you should consider using that first and only discard that idea if it does not help you achieve your business goals. A good example of a well-known integrated solution is the Microsoft product line.

The Bill and Melinda Gates Foundation has a set of projects and services related to promoting public access through libraries (http://www.gatesfoundation. org/libraries/). Their U.S. library program is dedicated to providing computer and Internet access to library patrons in low-income communities. And they have additional programs for libraries in other countries, as well. Visit their site for more thorough updated information on these topics and more.

The software you choose, which will be used by the library patrons, should be easy to learn and use. A graphical interface can be of great help, although novice users may still need assistance. Ideally, there should be a way for the patrons to train themselves on the software via some tutorial feature or introduction that comes with the product. Otherwise, or in addition, you can consider offering training classes on key areas of interest. This would, of course, require a member of the staff who was willing to learn the material and deliver the short class on it. Such a class could be used to draw more people into the library and could perhaps also be coordinated with other promotional events or target audience groups. For example, you might offer a class for teens in creating a simple Web page, and simultaneously set up displays of interesting teen fiction materials, or even career-planning information.

Because you cannot train your patrons in every aspect of using a computer, you should also require that your software come with easy-to-use documentation. Also, consider storing computer-use reference items (handbooks, pamphlets, quick reference guides) in the computer area.

Another essential evaluation point is what type of support will be required to implement and maintain the software. First, you must consider what kind of support you can offer. Can you hire an employee who specializes in computers? Do you have an employee already who is able to take on the responsibility? If so, what impact would that have on his or her normal role? Or, do you already have someone assigned to computer support? If so, collaborate with that person to make sure your computer area meets his or her recommendations.

Another aspect of software maintenance is storage. You need to store the original software CDs in a safe location. Record the license numbers, phone numbers, support account numbers, and Web site information with the CDs and in an additional area.

Also, look for self-supporting features. For example, Microsoft's Windows XP operating system can be configured to automatically install software updates and also has a simple interface for assisting with support issues—you don't need to be a computer expert to get help on this platform. Microsoft has excellent product support (contact 1-800-microsoft or http://microsoft.com /support). Whatever software you buy, always make sure that you understand how to get assistance if you need it and what kind of service you should expect. If your software vendor tells you about a Web site you can visit for help with that vendor's product, visit it before you need to, just to make sure you understand what it can do.

Security and customizability should also come into consideration when setting up a computer center. How much privacy will your patrons have when using the computers? How will you prevent them from leaving personal materials on areas of the PCs that are available to others? How will you prevent them from viewing undesirable Web sites, if you choose to do that? Remember that the location of the computers, the orientation of the screens, and the visibility of the keyboards all play into security. Also, some users like to customize "their" areas of the computer by installing wallpaper (background pictures), changing settings, or installing software from the Internet. Consider what your policy on this will be and how you will enforce it. Although a full discussion of these issues is beyond the scope of this chapter, keep in mind that it is possible to provide a basic amount of customization while also securing your computers. You would need a technical expert (for example, a Windows Operating System Infrastructure professional) to set this up (for advice, contact www.gates foundation.org/libraries). For example, using Windows, you could configure *roaming profiles* that would allow patrons to log in at any desktop and retain their original settings. This type of implementation is a bit more complex than one in which each person logs in as a *guest* (or does not log in at all), but it is good to know what is available if you find that this best suits your needs.

Multimedia Software as Part of the Library Collection

Software needs more evaluation than other materials. Often there is more than one software title available on the same topic. In addition, the software may have features that add value beyond merely storing information digitally. Make sure you understand the differences when you place an order. Read reviews online, visit the company Web site, and look for demos. Tip: While you are there, look at their support articles to see if many people have problems with the software. Also search for the software title on the site that supports your operating system. Record what you find, but also be aware that finding no entries is not always good because it might indicate that the problems are not well documented, which in turn would indicate a lack of support for the product.

Unlike print materials and audiovisual materials, software is licensed. This means that you have a usage agreement with the software company. Normally, over-the-counter software allows either one or two simultaneous users of the software. You will need to develop policies and procedures on installation and use of the discs.

The license and packaging also include information you need to protect your investment. Unlike other types of materials, if your discs become damaged and you have properly maintained your registration, replacement discs are usually available for a nominal fee. Call to find out the policy for replacing lost software. All software information—including licensing, software version, registration codes, support policies, and numbers—should be documented in a secure place.

Remember when you are purchasing any software that you must check it for compatibility with systems in use at your library or in use at home by those who will be checking out the software.

Facility Planning

There is more to developing a computer center than simply setting up the software. Computers and their use also relates to the environment. Here are some considerations about the physical location of computers and how that relates to their use.

First, computers have wires to be dealt with. The organization of wires is called the *wiring infrastructure*. Even if there is only one computer available and it isn't on a network, it has wires connecting the different parts. If it is on a network or connects to the Internet, there are most likely wires to make this happen, or connections are made via wireless technology. When you are at the planning stage, obtain the advice of an expert on laying out wiring for a computer center. This person will need to know how many computers (and other devices) will come into play, and what they will be used for. The expert can then develop wiring and network bandwidth requirements and physical diagrams for you.

It is a good idea to create and maintain updated documentation on the wiring. Label connections on both ends of each wire, so that if it becomes unplugged, even a nontechnical person can reconnect it. Label the wire with a specially made tag or with a simple address label folded around the wire. Also label the socket the wire should go into. Consider using colored marks to coordinate the two. This is very easy to do by sticking matching colored label dots or squares on the unit next to the port and on the end of the connecting wire.

Also, keep a document that lists wiring connections. Obviously, you don't need to write up how the computer parts plug into each other, although you could include a diagram that came with the computer (many manufacturers include very simple graphics showing how to hook up their computers), and many new computers come with color-coded ports and connection cables. It is wise to keep a list of network *drops* (the sockets in the wall where the network cables are connected from the computers), however, and a list of which ones are *live* (turned on) and what machines are using them. Refer to each machine by its network name designation or IP address, either of which should be unique, and place a label on each machine with that address. Also, you can add a user-friendly name to each machine, for example, Station 1 or Unit 1. Your wiring expert should be able to create this information for you, perhaps in diagram form, but make sure that you have the original electronic document in updatable form.

Computers also require ventilation. They produce heat but do not tolerate heat over long periods of time. The computer will last much longer if it is stored in a very cool dry location. Also, the computer generates enough heat to change the temperature around it. This is not as noticeable with one machine as it is with many. So, if you are setting up several machines, make sure they are in an open area with good cross-ventilation, or add extra ventilation to keep the equipment and the patrons comfortable. Keep in mind that the computer has internal fans to keep it from overheating, and these blow air through vents on the computer. Do not block these vents, and be aware of where the air is going so it is not, for instance, blowing on a seating area. (Note: The air is not harmful in any way.)

It is also a good idea to keep a list of what is installed on each machine. One good way to do this is to store a copy of this information along with the original installation disks. You may need an additional copy of this information available for easy access, either to do a quick verification or to help patrons decide which machine to use. The stored document or collection of information on the computer's software and setup is called *configuration management*.

Computers also generate noise, in three ways. First, the machine itself generates electronic *white noise*. This is louder behind the machine than in front, because of the vents. Second, the computer can make noise as part of the software (for example, music software). Windows software makes sounds as part of its interface. You should adjust the volume on the machines to keep this from being overloud. It is a good plan to include headsets if you do not intend to manage sounds in another way, however. The mouse and the keyboard make clicking sounds that, although not very loud, can be a repetitive-noise annoyance to someone trying to concentrate. The third way that a computer generates noise is by the user's speaking to someone nearby, speaking with someone online (via a microphone), or speaking to the computer itself (as in the case of dictation). (Note that, although you can establish policies regarding people having conversations in the vicinity of the computer, you may not want to completely eliminate speech, because this is one way that a disabled person can interact with a computer.)

One way to overcome a lot of these issues is to isolate the computers in a closed-off room. This may make it difficult to supervise those using the machines to prevent damage to the equipment, however, and may also discourage them from getting up to use other library resources. And, although a closed-off area provides privacy, this may not be what you want.

There has been some question recently of privacy and security in a public computer environment with regard to how the PCs are used. A simple way to discourage undesirable computer behavior is to place the machines in highly visible, well-traveled areas, preferably within view of a librarian who is normally at a desk. If a new building is being planned, a glassed-in computer room will help with this. Also be aware that if you have a robust computer environment in your library, you can also configure security that can limit what can be transferred to the machine via the Internet. Additionally, software can be used to electronically "snoop" on what users do at the computer. Although this is viewed by many as an infringement of their rights and therefore not desirable for implementation, you want to be aware of what is possible. Give careful consideration to security and privacy policies established in your library, how they will be enforced, and what is being monitored by the network system (if anything).

Whether to place the machines in a public area or a closed-off section has other implications as well. For example, a closed-off room lends itself well to the concept of providing computer-training facilities. If this appeals to you, then you should also consider your policy on what may be taught using the computers. For example, you might want to specify that no software may be loaded on the machines by patrons. The reason for mentioning this is that setting up a computer classroom in which software is installed before each class usually means that additional tasks are required to configure the classroom for use and after it has been used (to restore the original configurations).

If you prefer the idea of making the computers available in a large public area, you can consider placing the machines side by side to create an easily visible but somewhat isolated area. Because computers already generate noise, you could easily locate this in a traffic area of the library. This arrangement simplifies wiring; the more computers you have in one spot, however, the more heat and noise and traffic you will create.

Alternately, consider placing machines at strategic points throughout the library: some in the children's areas, some in reference, and others in the adult sections. If the areas are relatively small, you could place two or three machines together in each area. Or, if you have a very large library, you might place the computers at regular intervals, for example, near the elevators on each floor. Scattering the machines reduces heat and noise and allows patrons to use the machines while still roaming the stacks. This idea may be a success if your computer system allows access to an online catalog. But if you are using a hardwired network (i.e., not wireless), then you will need to run network cable to each area. A wireless network can overcome this problem but introduces its own problems, such as signal strength and lower bandwidth.

If your implementation involves a significant number of computers, you should consider hiring a consultant to help plan the infrastructure and deployment.

Policies and Procedures

Once you have a clear idea of the services you will be providing, take time to consider what processes must be in place to support the smooth operation of the computer center. It may be that you will need to involve trustees as well as library staff. You may wish to prohibit food and drink near the computer equipment. Most people, however, will eat and drink at the computers. Preserving the equipment is as simple as making sure the computer unit or monitor is not in direct range for a spill and, optionally, covering the keyboard with a protective plastic film (available commercially). Keyboards and mice, however, wear out on a regular basis and are cheap to replace in most locations, so this should not be the driving concern.

In order to improve the sustainability of the computer area, arrange for training of the librarians who will be a part of the computer areas. This may simply include training on basics such as what is available through these services, where the patron can find more information, and how to arrange for technical support if necessary.

To make the new implementation more supportive of the community, arrange a formal method of filing suggestions and complaints. The feedback you collect from the patrons can be extremely useful in determining what changes, if any, are necessary. For example, if a significant number of users have questions about some aspect of the services, you might schedule training related to those topics. Or, if you find that many patrons are complaining about Internet access to pornographic content on Web sites or in news groups, you might either hold a seminar to educate the community on the benefits of the Internet, or you might investigate other ways to address this concern. Since this is bound to be a common complaint, it bears some discussion. One way to filter out pornography might be to preselect sites that are available to patrons, or at least sites available to children; another way would be to use a content-filtering service, although these are not always perfect. Although this may sound like censorship, it might be the only solution available; there is an intrinsic difference in library materials that may be checked out and viewed privately, and Internet materials that are displayed on a screen for everyone passing by to see. After due consideration, you may elect to simply post a disclaimer regarding Internet content. Your solution will most likely depend on your geographic location.

This leads into another topic related to policymaking: privacy. Although you may not want to allow too much privacy for computer users, for a variety of reasons, there are some privacy issues to be considered. If your computers are set up to simply allow one patron after another to use the same *session* (in other words, they do not have to log in individually), then you should be aware that a savvy computer user can determine what sites have been visited by the previous user. Or, if a user leaves personal information saved to the hard drive, other users may access that information as well. Therefore, you might set up the computer to disallow storing personal information in the form of Web sites-visited history, documents viewed, and so on. And, although most e-commerce Web sites offer secure connections for credit card transactions, the security of the connection will not prevent another patron from looking over the computer user's shoulder. Again, you may elect to simply post a sign, and whether this is necessary may depend on your community location.

CONCLUSION

Many issues were raised here for your consideration, without providing an exact method for addressing each of them. The purpose of this is to increase your awareness of what goes into running a successful computer area so that you may be better prepared to deploy one or to improve the services you already offer.

SELECTED BIBLIOGRAPHY

Ensor, Pat, ed. *The Cybrarian's Manual 2*. Chicago, American Library Association, 2000.

Janes, Joseph, Annette Lagace, Michael McLennen, Sara Ryan, Schelle Simcox, and David S. Carter. *Internet Public Library Handbook: A Guide for Building and Monitoring Virtual Libraries*. New York: Neal-Schuman, 1999.

Joint Reference and User Services Association and Association for Library Collections and Technical Services Institute. *Virtually Yours: Models for Managing Electronic Resources and Services: Proceedings of the Joint Reference and User Services Association and Association for Library Collections and Technical Services Institute, Chicago, Illinois, October 23–25, 1997*. Edited by Peggy Johnson and Bonnie MacEwan. Chicago: American Library Association, 1999.

Molz, Redmond Kathleen, and Phyllis Dain. *Civic Space/Cyberspace: The American Public Library in the Information Age*. Cambridge, MA: MIT Press, 2001.

16 THE IMPORTANCE OF LIGHTING

James R. Kennedy

A successful library facility today must incorporate both the best of natural light and internal-lighting techniques to produce a truly flexible facility, one that will provide a custom visual experience for every user. This statement sounds like a tall order, and it is. It is also very necessary, because library facilities support activities for computer researchers, for aging baby boomers and their parents who are making the shift from dim coziness to needing light to read, to children in a light-controlled environment intended to support their program and craft activities.

The best single step a librarian can take is to overplan for lighting. Uses of the building built this year will change throughout its history much more than in libraries built in the past. Better to overplan than to underconfigure and fall short in meeting future needs.

NATURAL LIGHTING FIRST

Early U.S. libraries of the late 1800s and early 1900s featured tall arched windows to let in as much natural light as possible. Such designs were seen in the first Carnegie libraries constructed. The first of these buildings was built in Fairfield, Iowa, in 1893. Many Carnegie libraries used a combination of vertical rectangular windows alternated with arched windows. Many libraries of the early twentieth century mimicked the broad expanse of glass featured prominently in the Boston Public Library designed by architect Charles McKim.

Many libraries emphasized daytime use to save on electricity. The Middleboro Public Library and the Walpole Public Library in Massachusetts were two of many to use opaque glass flooring between levels of book stacks. This glass flooring made it possible for light to filter down from the skylights above, enabling retrieval of needed volumes without artificial lighting in the daytime. Note that when the Middleboro Public Library undertook expansion/renovation in 1990, it sold opaque bricks cut from the library's stack areas as a fund-raiser.

The original Jonathan Bourne Public Library in Bourne, Massachusetts (built in 1895) featured brass whale-oil lamps that were discovered, complete with chimneys from McBeth Glass, still stored in the since-electrified building in the early 1970s. This type of lighting was most fitting, as the library had been built by Miss Emily Bourne in memory of her father, a New England whaling captain.

Beyond electrification, lighting continued to be a function of necessity more than of beauty. Libraries designed with lighting to complement striking architecture succumbed to the budget restrictions of the Great Depression, and later, to the cautious blackouts of World War II. Most libraries relied heavily on incandescent bulbs in ceiling, sconce, and task lighting. Green globe table lamps became fashionable. Brass and bronzed lamps graced many a reference table. Libraries such as the Bapst Library at Boston College featured fluorescent reading lamps at long reading tables in the early 1960s. (Lighting in the elevator at the Bapst Library, too, was dim, but not so dim that one could not read the word HEAVEN placed next to the top floor button.)

The early 1970s marked a time when libraries moved from a traditional design to one more contemporary, reflecting the straightforward influences of Frank Lloyd Wright, I. M. Pei, and others who used broad expanses of glass. Newer libraries such as the Lawrence Public Library in Lawrence, Massachusetts (1973), the Jennie King Mellon Library at Chatham College in Pittsburgh (1973), and the Cedar Rapids Public Library (1985) in Iowa all featured broad expanses of tinted glass, brick or block, and concrete. Library design themes had shifted from closed buildings to structures of openness and added dimensions of beauty. Architects provided attractive vistas within and without to enhance lounging opportunities in the library. Their objective was to make the library attractive from the outside so that passersby could identify the building's function by seeing volumes and readers at work. Chatham College undertook an extensive renovation of its library in 2001, replacing all of its windows and upgrading its interior lighting. Lawrence's building remains a visual showpiece, with views of the historic Campagnon Common, an adjacent stone church, and Robert Frost's alma mater, Lawrence High School, visible through 433 expansive glass panes (190 panes measuring 52 inches by 87 inches and 143 panes measuring 21 inches by 52 inches). Steel clips on the window corners provide support.

Massive expanses of glass appeared at a time when more and more libraries were air-conditioned, and (to minimize cost) these windows were inoperable. Air-conditioning systems were turned on earlier in the spring and ran later into the fall season. Inoperable windows eliminated the opportunity to save energy in these transitional seasons by simply opening windows.

Using large glass windows called for planning slightly bigger buildings, as the amount of wall space that could be relegated to single-faced shelving, art displays, and signage was reduced. The plan didn't work completely. Glass, even tinted glass, conducts heat. The plate glass windows, their edges secured by double-faced tape instead of stainless clips, began to fog like the windshield of an old automobile. Buildings were expensive to heat and to cool. Opened just before the OPEC oil embargo of 1974, the attractive Lawrence, Massachusetts, Public Library all-electric 55,000-square-foot building had a utility bill that in one year eclipsed the library's budget by $20,000. The library trustees wisely converted the heating source to natural gas. The Middle East oil embargos of 1974 and 1979 led many small communities to follow a strategy used in public school buildings, that of reducing the size of or eliminating completely a number of windows. Turning the heat down made buildings cold. Casement windows and brushed-aluminum panels replaced windows. Some libraries replaced operable windows with glass blocks. The Somerville Public Library just outside Boston turned to airplane-window thickness in major renovation of its city library as a security measure.

Librarians implementing computer terminals for their online catalogs and working with microfilm reader printers encountered glare problems. Sitting with one's back to a window produced glare on computer screens. Many libraries added transparent fabric drapes. Older patrons in large city libraries moved, like house cats, to follow the sun's warmth during the day. Others moved in the opposite direction to avoid heat and glare.

As big window themes passed from favor, U.S. librarians were faced with new challenges: how to accommodate the computer terminals, personal computers, and laptops that have transformed and will continue to transform libraries forever.

Atriums and Skylights

Early U.S. libraries used skylighting to naturally illuminate book stacks in the inner library. Others did so as part of an architectural feature, bringing openness to buildings whose interiors were dark and monotonous.

In some instances, such as in the libraries of the University of Minnesota in Minneapolis and Buena Vista University, glass light wells, or inverted atriums, brought natural light to a library's underground levels. Light wells, when coordinated with an effective internal system of corridors, can do much to eliminate the underground bunker feeling found in below-grade levels. Underground libraries are a necessity in areas where land is in short supply; examples include the Nathan Pusey Library at Harvard University and the Park University Library in Parkville, Missouri.

ARTIFICIAL LIGHTING

Lamps

Built in 1895 by Miss Emily Bourne in honor of her sea captain father, the original Jonathan Bourne Public Library, Bourne, Massachusetts, featured brass lamps outfitted with Pennsylvanian McBeth chimneys. This library and many others relied on oil lamps until electric lamps became widely available. Libraries then used incandescent and, later, fluorescent tubes to brighten darker areas of the library in daytime and to open up the library for evening use. Incandescent electric lights came first, and in many cases were nothing more than electrified oil lamps. Libraries used bare bulbs in chandeliers and in wall sconces, with many of the former providing ambient light at heights of 15 feet or more. Today's incandescent bulbs may be found in attractive fixtures of many types.

Incandescent or halogen spots are often used in recessed-can lighting intended to accentuate particular areas. It is important that these fixtures make changing bulbs easy. Also, when using incandescents, the core of the bulb must be of the same metal alloy as the socket—bronze with bronze, aluminum with aluminum. Mixing of types will cause the two metals to bind and make bulb changing more difficult.

Task lighting in the form of table lighting brought brighter rays to those studying maps or newspapers and those working with fine print. Bridge lamps were not as common. In some cases, task lighting became a substitute for that provided by hanging fixtures. Often, planned levels of illumination were not sustained, because custodians used whatever bulbs were handy when changing them. Not all bulbs in a fixture provided the same wattage.

Long-Life Lighting

Lighting options are more numerous today. Bulbs and fluorescent tubes can now be ordered to provide specified qualities of desired intensity, color enhancement, and durability. When planning a new or renovated building, it is important to include the best-quality products possible. Bulbs and energy modulating ballasts last up to five years. (A ballast stabilizes current in lighting circuits.). With this longevity, there is less danger of inadvertently mixing bulb colors. Please remember, however, that long life does not mean forever. Funds to support a major change-out of bulbs must be included as part of long-range planning.

The use of fluorescent lighting in public libraries increased greatly after World War II. Fluorescent lights brought much higher wattage at a lower cost and the long, thin bulbs were longer lasting. Fluorescence replaced incandescent lighting for general lighting but did not provide the enriching warmth of color. Most fluorescents were mounted at heights requiring tall ladders or stagings for access. Maintenance was difficult.

Normal Maintenance

Maintenance of existing lighting in a library is just as important as installing new fixtures. In many libraries, bulbs or tubes are installed and never touched again till they are replaced. Careful washing of lamps and fixtures should be an annual maintenance task.

Fluorescent bulbs are available in a variety of shapes, sizes, and tints. Many are decorative, and most practical. In recent years, general lighting has called for an overall light level of 55 *footcandles* (fc), with lower levels at the bases of stacks (15 fc) and in areas near computer screens (25 fc). Fluorescents are most frequently found in stack areas, placed parallel to book stacks over each aisle. Where compact shelving is used, lighting should be placed perpendicular to a range of stacks to ensure even lighting.

Some libraries have placed fluorescent lighting directly on the book stacks, with a single 3-foot-tube shielded fixture protruding from the frame or top canopy of each shelving section. Such fixtures provide good light, but they do so via a trade-off. Their presence limits the full use of the top shelf when occasional oversized volumes must be placed in sequence.

Libraries making use of suspended ceilings often employ extensive fluorescent fixtures. It is generally wise to select fixtures that will provide broad, diffuse light as opposed to task-specific fixtures. There should be no shadows appearing in spaces not directly covered by a fixture. Even lighting provides a warm, inviting atmosphere and will enable the library to maximize its plan for later reuse of space. The best library consultant in the world can tell you with great certainty how a library can best support the needs of its patrons for five years and may come very close to a similar prediction into the tenth year. But with rapid technological changes mirroring those of the past decade and anticipating the next score of years, the planning picture becomes fuzzy.

The use of computers in libraries is perhaps the greatest example of such change. Typical desktop computers featuring 13-inch by 17-inch color monitors call for placement in areas where there is little glare. Computer placement required an increase of reader space from 30 square feet per person in the 1970s and 1980s to 40 square feet per person at study carrels. This mirrored the need for carrels big enough for each to hold a computer central processing unit (CPU), monitor, keyboard, and peripheral equipment, along with books, legal pads, handbags or book bags. Most library computers were linked via a network to a centrally located printer or printers, but for those with smaller accompanying printers, the necessary workstation size crept toward 48 square feet. Lower levels of lighting in computer carrels were needed at different times of day, and many libraries employed dimmer switches on their lights.

In the year 2000, libraries saw greatly increased use of laptops and wireless technology to accommodate laptop users. Laptops promise to bring the greatest flexibility in reader space. Patrons bring them to lounge chairs, to reading tables, to steps where users sit, or on the floor. Less space is needed (only 35 square feet per person for laptops). As laptop screens are hinged to the combination CPU/keyboard, they may be individually adjusted to compensate for possible glare.

In libraries where barrel vault, trapezoid, cathedral, or other shapes are used, indirect light can be used most effectively to yield glare-free illumination. Many libraries use recessed fluorescents (the tubes are not visible), spot lighting, and indirect lighting, often called up-lighting.

Wall sconces in late 1930s art deco style have seen a revival in public and academic libraries. So, too have retro-style halogen chandeliers. Halogen bulbs give a bright glow and burn at a very high temperature; in the fixtures, these bulbs require a protective shield to prevent setting fire to any paper or other flammable material that may come into contact with them. When changing or handling halogen bulbs, it is best to wear gloves to avoid getting skin oils on them. Canister and pod lights make use of incandescent lights to highlight special exhibits. Track lighting is useful to showcase library art displays.

Security Lighting

Security lighting must comply with state and local building codes, providing exit signs with directional arrows as needed to facilitate egress. Fire alarm systems today feature flashing platinum lighting (wall lamps affixed to red wall features). These flashing platinum strobe lamps are impossible to miss and provide guiding directional lights from the building in case of fire. Libraries must also be equipped with independent emergency and security lighting that stays on at all times, even when the library is closed, and that supports safe passage during power outages.

Lighting the Outer Library

The library should be easily identified in daylight by its unique design and proper signage. Special care is needed to both identify and secure the library at night.

If a library is located on a site featuring gardens, ground-level lighting must be placed to protect patrons entering, leaving, or waiting outside the library at night. Lights set on delayed timers must be used to protect patrons and staff leaving the building at closing. Outside lights should remain on for at least fifteen minutes after closing, and longer for facilities in urban areas. Spotlights aimed upward from the base of the library can highlight unique architectural features while providing enhanced security. A public library is both art and function, and quality lighting will positively reflect the building's architecture. Walk lights in surrounding gardens and parking areas provide enhanced access and security.

The library's main entrance and supplemental entrances should be easily identifiable by day. Identifying signs both near and on the building must be illuminated. If the library features a drop-off drive with an overhang, this should be well lit. A professional lighting designer can produce a quality new look or replicate traditional lanterns with better-than-original quality. Planners should take time to assure that lighting schematics comply with state and local codes, and that new lighting complements both the facility and adjoining areas.

17 NEW CONCEPTS FOR TECHNOLOGY IN LIBRARY DESIGN

Gerard B. McCabe

INTRODUCTION

A library building must be attractive and aesthetically pleasing to the eye. Internally, it must be functional and current in the use of technology supporting services to its community. Architectural design features provide for the physical appearance. Careful review and analysis of features offered by various technologies provide the remainder of our planning concerns. The descriptions that follow will appear to meld issues of attractiveness and effectiveness, because sometimes they are inseparable. The descriptions are applicable both to new buildings and to buildings requiring retrofitting or renovation.

At the beginning of this twenty-first century, today's theme is "green" for library buildings and other types, too. As industry adapts new technologies to its buildings, new energy-efficient and labor-saving applications are entering into the affordability range for library buildings of all sizes. The Library Administration and Management Association's Building and Equipment Section has been presenting green-themed programs at annual conferences of the American Library Association. With our attention focused on energy efficiency and greater effectiveness for our services, it is time to review our planning for our library buildings and how we can bring about more efficient and effective services while making our own contribution to environmental concerns. We must work with our architect/engineer teams to make library buildings environmentally friendly and greater contributors to the general welfare of our communities.

LIGHTING AND WINDOWS

An attractive building has windows tastefully planned with a concern both for the exterior appearance and for the light admitted to the interior. The benefits of natural light for a few hours daily are immeasurable (van den Beld 2000). Interior lighting coordinated by sensors with that coming through the windows provides for effective functional use of the interior space. For libraries and other places where work is performed, the combination of lighting sources into an effective and useful aid to what is being done in the building is of high importance.

The critical objective is providing the best possible lighting adjusting and maintaining even intensities through all hours of the day, for public areas, and controllable lighting for staff at their workplaces. In the typical workroom, each person can adjust lighting at his or her workspace to suit personal requirements. Competitive technologies now on the market offer these advantages through the combination of lighting units controlled by software installed in personal computers and sensors placed near windows and similarly controlled by computer software. The ability to control lighting intensity has the side effect of reducing utility costs without depriving people of suitable levels for their use of library materials or their work.

Improvements in window glazing now provide effective screening out of ultraviolet rays, important in all buildings where people work and read. C. Greg Carney, technical director of the Glass Association of North America (GANA), has spoken on this subject: "As GANA's Carney points out, 'From the perspective of the glass industry, the biggest impact of green building design has probably been the increased awareness of the energy performance capabilities of today's insulating glass units with low-emissivity (low-E) coatings, spectrally selective substrates and low-conductance spacers.'" He adds that programs such as Energy Star have helped to educate designers and consumers about the virtues of glass, and the greater awareness has led to continual product development. "For example," he points out, "Energy Star frequently notes that the labeled windows of today are twice as efficient as the typical windows produced just ten years ago" ("The Impact of Energy Issues on Glass" 2002, 47).

Other design features where appropriate are the use of atria and skylights. In certain climates, either or both can be effective in providing natural light. In the past, atria were once thought wasteful for space-deprived library buildings. This has changed as better understanding of the need for natural light has been gained. Concepts for using atria space beneficially through a series of options are now available. These include beverage services, displays of art works (notably, sculpture), browsing areas, or simple places for relaxation and reading casual magazines or newspapers.

Skylights were once thought to be a source of problems such as glare and leakage. Librarians often were reluctant to agree to their use. Industry can and will respond to complaints and the challenge raised by dissatisfaction with a product. New skylight designs (tubular is one example) are now available to address these problems and allow the admission of natural light in a thoroughly diffused way that enhances a building's interior and helps reduce energy costs. With some of these skylight designs, natural light can be brought into areas very distant from windows. By so doing, both the healthful advantage noted by van den Beld (2000) and the energy-saving advantage can be obtained.

Glass

In my book published in the year 2000, there is a section on glass (McCabe 2000, 97–98) in which I encourage more use of glass and project some interesting future developments. The following are some glass developments that will affect libraries in a beneficial way.

In a special section called "The Glass Guide for Architects and Specifiers," the June 2002 issue of Glass Magazine, offers a series of articles on "Energy and Green Building Issues." The section culminates with a "Green Glazing Checklist, Design Considerations for Energy-Efficient Glass Constructions and the Optimum Use of Natural Light."

In the same issue, Jim Plavecsky (2002) describes the design and use of glass windows for sound attenuation. A single page with a photograph describes a new glass canopy 120,000 square feet in size at the Portland (Oregon) International Airport ("Portland International" 2002). Libraries can use smaller glass canopies to brighten their front entries and make them more attractive.

The days of considering glass as a hard surface reverberating noise are gone. Now we must consider the beneficial aspects of glass usage in library environments. It isn't just to see through anymore.

Photovoltaic Metal and Vision Glass

The Mary Ann Cofrin Hall Academic Center at the University of Wisconsin, Green Bay, is being hailed as one of this nation's "most energy-efficient buildings ever constructed" ("Why Glass" 2002, 47). It makes use of two new technologies described as building-integrated photovoltaic (BIPV). A review of the university's Web site (http://www.uwgb.edu/maps/buildings/cofrinhall.htm) tells why this Leadership in Energy and Environmental Design project (LEED) is so outstanding.

> UW-Green Bay's bold, bright new building is the first in Wisconsin to deploy two new technologies together—standing seam metal roof and "vision glass"—to generate electricity. In simple terms, sunlight falling on specially designed roof and window areas generates power. . . .
>
> The Winter Garden atrium is site of the first vision glass installation of its kind in the United States. Semi-transparent panels allow some daylight to pass and harness the rest for electricity. Energy flows through power-conversion equipment to feed alternating current to the building's electrical loads.

The Web site continues with this description of the roof: "Photovoltaic Metal Roof—The standing-seam metal roof is the most productive building-integrated photovoltaic feature. Light harnessed by the roof is expected to generate 15,000 kilowatt hours of electricity annually, slightly more than the Winter Garden."

This building also has a solar wall and makes great use of recycled materials. The Wisconsin Public Service Corporation, on another Web site (http://www. buildingsolar.com/design.asp), gives more details. Following its description of the standing seam metal roofing, this site goes on:

> The other section incorporates a thin-film BIPV vision glass product. The vision glass product is the first installation of its kind in the United States. . . . In total, about 4,300 square feet of BIPV material were installed, which will generate approximately 27,500 kWh annually.
>
> Daylighting, energy-efficient lighting, and SolarWall technology are three additional energy features that add to the uniqueness of Mary Ann Cofrin Hall. . . . Power conversion systems and utility interconnections are other devices that function behind-the-scenes to ensure that BIPV and PV technologies are running accurately, efficiently, and safely. (Wisconsin Public Service Corporation 2002)

The Wisconsin Public Service Corporation's Web site gives further details such as this description of vision glass:

> Photovoltaic (PV) vision glass substitutes a thin-film, semi-transparent photovoltaic panel for the exterior glass panel in an otherwise traditional double-pane glass window or skylight. (Wisconsin Public Service Corporation 2002)

For daylighting in this academic building, the report continues:

> The design includes skylights, clerestories, borrowed light, daylight diffusers, and direct sunlight. Glazings were selected based on their abilities to reduce solar gain, provide insulation, ensure meeting performance goals, and permit a "looking in on learning" atmosphere. Photosensors and mechanical shading devices were also utilized. (Wisconsin Public Service Corporation 2002)

Cofrin Hall cost $20 million and is 120,000 gross square feet in size. Librarians planning similar large buildings, and even smaller buildings, should consider adapting similar features for their buildings. We are moving toward the day when power independence will become an achievable dream. Librarians in the early stages of planning a new or renovated building should raise these issues with their architect/engineer design teams.

Confirming my point about industrial applications, the San Francisco International Airport recently placed BIPV roofing panels capable of generating 20 kilowatts on the roof of one of its support buildings. These panels will supply a part of that building's power requirement ("California Skies" 2002). As industrial use becomes commonplace, costs will lower to the affordability range for most libraries.

POWER INDEPENDENCE—AN ACHIEVABLE DREAM: ELECTRIC POWER GENERATION

It should be the goal of every public library to be "off the grid." Libraries today are power dependent for most aspects of their operation. Open or closed, the library's need for power continues. Public libraries cannot endure brownouts and other interruptions to their power supply. Independence is a solution. This issue is critical. In an article entitled "Making the Switch to On-Site Electricity" (Dang, 2002), the *Baltimore Sun* reported that the University of Maryland, College Park, has a science building (the Chesapeake Building, 52,000 square feet) for which "almost 30% of the electricity is generated in a box the size of a large industrial freezer outside the building's back door" (p. 1). The article stated further, "The concept is called distributed generation (DG). It means generating electricity on-site for use in a small area or by a small company instead of relying on a huge power plant that might be hundreds of miles away" (p. 1).

The presence of a natural gas supply makes feasible the consideration of a gas-powered generating system. There are other means of generating power under development; solid oxide fuel cell generation is another example. If not included in this project's planning, care should be taken to provide for a future development.

Industrial buildings with their own power generation systems are now operating. Competitive technologies are under development and have been developed to free power-dependent industrial buildings from the inconsistencies of electrical supply and to ease the pressure on overworked power plants. Costs are dropping as these technologies improve and are adapted more frequently, and as manufacturing costs decrease. It is becoming reasonable for power-dependent libraries to consider the adaptation of economical power generating systems and to look forward to the day when the library's power requirements are produced on-site. For projects in process, it isn't too late to move toward some power generation. Library buildings must become contributors to the environment, not takers from it.

I recommend using the power-producing technologies now on the market and providing for eventual future adoption of a system that will meet requirements for full production. It is part of thinking green. In the meantime, there are some technologies that are well worth considering, as noted in the following sections.

Solar Power

In suitable climatic areas, solar panels can be used to generate supplemental power and aid in reducing dependency and thus lowering the cost of power. The federal government is promoting energy saving and encouraging the use of alternative power sources. *Architectural Record* reported on one project:

The National Park Service (NPS) installed the first solar electric system at the White House Compound this past fall. The system, installed in August

[2002], went online in September and was officially unveiled in January [2003]. NPS also installed two solar-hot-water systems—the first since former president Carter's and the first one ever fully integrated into a White House building design. . . .

The 8.75-kW photovoltaic (PV) system feeds into the White House complex's electrical distribution network, supplying a fraction of power at the 55,000-square-foot White House, the 600,000-square-foot Old Executive Office Building, and other structures in the 18-acre compound. ("Solar Panels Installed" 2003, 56)

Fuel Cells

Solid-oxide fuel-cell systems are appearing, with the promise of meeting limited needs and eventually the full power needs of small businesses. These are moving toward the day when full capability of meeting a library building's power needs becomes a reality.

Librarians may not be aware of the power crisis that the world is facing. This quotation from the annual report of Fuel Cell Technologies Corporation (2001) will prove enlightening:

> Over the next decade, the evolution of fuel cell technologies will converge with a doubled world demand for electricity to effect a revolution in the delivery of power. World demand for power and the characteristics and constraints of incumbent power sources are pulling the evolving fuel cell industry and its developing fuel cell products into commercialization. The traditional response to demand for power has been to build huge power facilities and string transmission lines between towering pylons. This response is increasingly costly financially, politically, and environmentally. Stationary fuel cell products and distributed generation may be the timely and efficient way to supply the growing need for power. (p. 4)

Fuel cell systems that should prove attractive to the library market are coming. In a few years, these systems are expected to be competitive in cost with currently available power supply systems.

Natural Gas Turbine Systems

Natural-gas-powered systems are now available for the partial generation of electric power on-site. If gas is available, then this technology should be considered.

Distributed Generation

The power supply is generated on the premises for a small building or for the supplemental supplying of power for a power-intensive building. If natural gas is available, this option is quite viable.

COMPUTER TECHNOLOGY: HARDWIRED AND WIRELESS

Librarians must be current on both hardwired and wireless computer service requirements. For retrofitting older buildings and avoiding concerns with asbestos, installing wireless computer service can be cost effective. The asbestos is undisturbed, and patrons still will have very good access to the Internet. For new buildings, a combination of hardwired and wireless computing will meet the needs of patrons. Those patrons using their own computer equipment will have no difficulty with wireless service.

ROBOTIC STORAGE

For large libraries with collections from one-half million to over one million volumes and equivalents in size or higher, robotic storage is a viable option. This idea or concept has been attempted in the past with some limited success. Two new systems are now on the market and in use in several academic libraries that provide high-density compaction, quick retrieval of requested materials, and appear very cost effective in use of space.

COMPACT SHELVING

For some situations, compact shelving remains a quite viable solution in view of its space-saving features and ease of accessibility. Materials on the interior shelves of a typical range of compact shelving are shielded from light and from dust.

SELF-CHECK CIRCULATION SYSTEMS

At the New Orleans midwinter conference of the American Library Association in January 2002, I saw three vendors demonstrating Radio Frequency Identification Systems (RFID) systems for circulation of library materials. At the following annual conference in June 2002 in Atlanta, I saw five companies demonstrate their systems. These systems feature high-speed self-service checkout by library users. Check-in on return also is very fast, requiring little human intervention.

Under the heading "What is RFID?" the trade association, Automatic Identification Manufacturers (AIM), provides this response:

> The object of any RFID system is to carry data in suitable transponders, generally known as tags, and to retrieve data, by machine-readable means, at a suitable time and place to satisfy particular application needs. Data within a tag may provide identification for an item in manufacture, goods in transit, a location, the identity of a vehicle, an animal or an individual. . . . A system requires, in addition to tags, a means of reading or interrogating the tags and some means of communicating the data to a host computer or information management system. (AIM 1999)

Self-service checkout stations at Clinton-Macomb Public Library South Branch, Macomb, Michigan. To the right is the customer service desk. There is no circulation counter.

Library vendors have adapted RFID to library purposes, primarily for circulation. It can be used for inventory control (shelf reading) as well. With its wide applicability for industrial purposes, it can hardly be said that it hasn't been field-tested. Now, librarians have a choice of two systems: bar-code or RFID technology. Depending on the perception of needs, a decision can be made.

Using self-check circulation systems, libraries save space by reducing the size of the traditional counter. Establishing goals for self-check activity by patrons frees proportionate staff time for other related work. Two examples of self-check adaptations follow.

The Clinton-Macomb Public Library in Michigan has two new branch libraries designed for self-service check-out using RFID. With double-sided machines, library staff at a customer service desk can see one side of the unit while the public sees the other; if a patron has a check-out problem, staff assist without leaving their station. The library's eventual goal is 90 percent of all checkouts through self-service by patrons. These branch libraries are South Branch (7,400 square feet, opened in summer 2000) and North Branch (14,000 square feet, opened in summer 2001). See the library's Web site (http://www.cmpl.org) for these and other features.

Clinton-Macomb is building a new main library of 82,000 square feet that will also have self-check as the main method of circulation. The new main library will open in the fall of 2003 (Christine Lind Hage, email communication to the author, July 2002).

Close-up view of the Clinton-Macomb Public Library self-service checkout stations. Books requested on hold by patrons are on shelving on left for self-service pick-up.

Using bar-code technology, St. Louis County, Missouri, Library has installed self-service check-out in three branch libraries: Daniel Boone, Thornhill, and the new Sachs Branch completed near the end of 2002. The goal is to have self-check handle at least 50 percent of the transactions, freeing staff time for other circulation-related services.

COMMUNICATION

Telephone Service

Librarians have long used hardwired telephone systems with various added features. In service areas where mobility is essential, cordless telephones were adapted. Now librarians must think about the advantages of cell phones as the wireless capability and added features of these devices become more attractive for use in daily work. Models with Internet access features are attractive to patrons and make consideration of wireless computer service imperative.

CONCLUSION

As new technologies develop and are adapted and costs decrease, public libraries have much to look forward to as this new century advances. It can only hold a brighter future for libraries.

REFERENCES

Automatic Identification Manufacturers. 1999. *Radio Frequency Identification—RFID, A Basic Primer*. Pittsburgh: AIM USA. www.aimglobal.org/technolgies/rfid/resources/papers/rfid_basics_primer.htm (accessed 13 February 2003).

"California Skies." 2002. *Architectural Record* (May): 344.

Dang, Dan Thanh. 2002. "Making the Switch to On-Site Electricity. *Baltimore Sun,* Business, 24 March, 1.

"Energy and Green-Building Issues." 2002. *Glass Magazine* (June): 43–49.

Fuel Cell Technologies Corporation. 2001. "Powered by Fuel Cells, Driven by Experience." FCT Annual Report. Kingston, ON: FCT Corporation.

"The Impact of Energy Issues on Glass." 2002. *Glass Magazine* (June): 47.

McCabe, Gerard B. 2000. *Planning for a New Generation of Public Library Buildings*. Westport, CT: Greenwood Press.

Plavecsky, Jim. 2002. "Designing Windows to Control Sound." *Glass Magazine* (June): 59–63.

"Portland International Airport's New Glass Canopy." 2002. *Glass Magazine* (June): 68

Van den Beld, Gerrit. 2000. Light and Health. *International Lighting Review*. Eindhoven, The Netherlands: Philips Lighting. www.eur.lighting.philips.com/ilr/ilr011/health.shtml.

"Why Glass Is the Red-Hot Green Building Material." 2002. *Glass Magazine* (June): 46–48.

Wisconsin Public Service Corporation. 2002. "Energy Features." Available at www.buildingsolar.com/design.asp (accessed January 3, 2003).

SELECTED BIBLIOGRAPHY

Audin, Lindsay. "A Brainy Luminaire for the 21st Century." *Architectural Record*, November 2001, 208.

"Daylighting: Many Designers Are Still in the Dark." *Architectural Record*, June 2002, 161–165.

"Fingertip Comfort: Automated Control Systems for the ABN AMRO, Netherlands and Germany." *International Lighting Review*, 2000. www.eur.lighting.philips.com/ilr/ilr011/abnamro.shtml.

International Lighting Review. See at www.eur.lighting.philips.com/int_en/prof/about/ilr/online.html.

PART VII
NOTABLE BUILDINGS

18 PUSTAKA NEGERI SARAWAK: SARAWAK STATE LIBRARY AND MULTIMEDIA CENTRE

Donald Bergomi

BACKGROUND

Sarawak is the largest state of Malaysia and is located at the northwestern corner of the island of Borneo. Sarawak, approximately the same size as Peninsular Malaysia, has a colorful history enriched by its diverse ethnic mix. The kingdom of Brunei lies to the east, the Indonesian province of Kalimantan to the south, and the South China Sea north and west.

In Sarawak today, a rich mix of indigenous cultures is blended with Malay and Chinese traditions and the vestiges of a private colonial past that live on in place and street names, lifestyles, and cultural and religious manifestations.

Indigenous oral as well as Moslem and Chinese literary traditions are widespread and historic. During the nineteenth and early twentieth centuries, Sarawak was ruled by a series of English "White Rajahs," beginning with James Brooke. The White Rajahs were accompanied by expatriate British staffs who brought extensive collections of printed material to Sarawak. A government printing office was established in 1870, and the *Sarawak Gazette* was first published.

A subscription library and reading room was also established in the 1870s in Sarawak's capital, Kuching. This institution was reserved for the exclusive use of those who could afford to subscribe. The era of the White Rajahs ceased at the end of World War II, and Sarawak became a British Crown Colony. During the colonial period, library development was actively fostered by the British Council. In 1955, the colonial authorities funded the establishment of libraries throughout the state. The development of these libraries was slow due to the population spread in this very large state and the difficulties of travel via jungle rivers. Even today, libraries in remote settlements and longhouses are supplied by helicopter.

In 1962, the Carnegie Foundation donated a collection of 350 works to the Sarawak Central Library, as it was then known. When the colonial period came to an end with the formation of the Federation of Malaysia in 1963, the Sarawak Central Library's collection exceeded 35,000 volumes. Many students from Sarawak studied at British, Australian, New Zealand, and U.S. universities. English print material was extremely popular. In 1970, the Sarawak State Library came into being.

During the 1980s and early 1990s, there was growing recognition that if the library system was strengthened, it could contribute greatly to the educational, social, and economic development of Sarawak. Libraries were funded and expanded all over the state. At the same time, authorship and printing of books in the national language, Bahasa Malaysia, expanded dramatically.

With the approaching millennium, the government of Sarawak decided to develop an entirely new resource center in the state capital, Kuching. The Sarawak government, led by its chief minister, the Right Honorable Datuk Patinggi Tan Sri Dr. Haji Abdul Taib Mahmud, and its state secretary, the Honorable Tan Sri Datuk Amar Dr. Haji Hamid Bugo, passed legislation establishing the Pustaka Negeri Sarawak (PNS) or Sarawak State Library and Multimedia Centre. The PNS later became the Sarawak government's millennium project.

In 1993, the government commissioned a senior Australian library consultant, Dr. David J. Jones of the State Library of New South Wales, to write a brief, or building program, for the new facility. His plan was approved by the Sarawak State Cabinet in June 1994.

The choice of architect was a critical one. With so many local and international architects available, the rationale behind the selection process was that the architect should be a firm with very strong credentials in library planning and design, because the functionality of the new PNS was a paramount concern. The building was to be designed from the inside out; the required facilities were not to be shoehorned into a preconceived envelope.

It was also agreed between the Sarawak government and their library consultant that a medium-sized architectural firm (in which the principals could be directly involved throughout the master planning, design, construction, and commissioning stages) would be favored as principal consultant. This strategy proved to be a sound one, because the two principals of the selected firm were immersed in the project for the following seven years. It was also agreed, for the sake of clear contractual lines of responsibility, that a principal consultant would be appointed to carry out or coordinate all aspects of the planning, design, and administration of a construction contract. Thus, all of the many disciplines required for the project would be woven together into a team under a single leader.

Representatives of the Sarawak government, led by the state secretary and director of the state planning unit, visited Sydney in September 1994, interviewed a number of short-listed Australian firms, and visited their completed library projects. Stephenson & Turner International was selected, and its representatives were invited to submit a technical proposal, including the choice of local consultants who would form the strong team required to execute this ambitious project.

The master plan. State Mosque is at upper left and Pustaka Negeri is near lower right overlooking lake.

The Vision

The city of Kuching has a developing government quarter called Petra Jaya located on the north bank of the Sarawak River. The zone is historic, in that the Palace of the White Rajahs (Astana) and one of the two forts that controlled the seaward approaches to the city, Fort Margherita (now the police headquarters), are located on the north bank. The commercial center of Kuching is located on the south bank. It was the vision of the Sarawak government that the PNS and the existing State Mosque be co-located in a large and beautifully landscaped park in the approximate center of Petra Jaya. It was their wish that the park would be inviting to all, but especially to families. The State Mosque and the PNS would each be the focus of two distinctive precincts within the park.

The master landscaping plan encompassing the State Mosque and the PNS precincts was appropriate to the natures of each. The former is peaceful and inspiring, whereas the latter possesses a spirit of contemplation and inquiry. The active recreational zone between them is oriented to the activities of families.

Due to its location and the general topography of the site, which is low-lying and swampy, the park was planned around an artificial lake that forms an integral part of the Petra Jaya storm-water management system and provides detention during periods of high storm-water runoff. An artificial platform was created, on which the buildings now sit.

The Building Program

The functions of the PNS are wide ranging and ambitious:

- Acquiring, organizing, and making available information resources in all formats relevant to the economic, social, and cultural well-being of the state of Sarawak
- Collecting, organizing, and making available special collections in specific subject areas, such as works on Borneo and Sarawak and government publications
- Developing and contributing to relevant bibliographic databases, with particular reference to materials published in Sarawak
- Facilitating and coordinating the information process by developing itself as the hub of the library and information network of Sarawak
- Participating in local, national, regional, and international networks of libraries and information services
- Assisting in the dissemination of information originating in participating state, federal, local government, higher education, and private-sector organizations
- Promoting the use of information and know-how flowing from industries and products in which Sarawakians have specialized knowledge or expertise
- Providing an educational environment, through programs and exhibitions, to raise awareness of the importance and the potential of information services, and to teach information and research skills
- Supporting the public library sector by the provision and processing of library resources, and providing opportunities for training of personnel, specialist consultancy, and advice
- Providing specialized information services to the business community
- Promoting and providing facilities for cultural and literary activities at the local, national, regional, and international levels

PLANNING

The site for Pustaka Negeri Sarawak was chosen shortly before the design team was appointed and some time after the completion of the design brief. The site was a vacant block of land, initially some 40 acres in extent. It was subsequently enlarged to include the adjoining State Mosque site and finally totaled 200 acres.

The PNS site is close to the central business district of Kuching as the crow flies, a relatively long way away by road due to the location of existing bridges over the Sarawak River. A new bridge, currently under construction, will bring it closer to the central business district. The few relatively tall neighboring buildings are all some distance away; such is the scale of the site. In the early stages of planning, there was no real limit to the extent of the building footprint, beyond considerations of the inefficiency of too large a building on one floor.

Thus, the planning process was indeed able to begin with block planning of functional groupings with desirable proximities. The actual position of the facility on the site was determined by the existing contours. The need for stormwater detention suggested an artificial lake, with a building constructed on a platform at the lake's edge and reflected on its surface. This had the additional benefit of dramatically reducing the requirement for imported fill and enabling the creation of an artificial hill in the park.

The PNS had a number of design objectives in common with many other building projects:

- Accessibility, an easy issue to address at the entrance, as level access could be designed after the final site contours were determined
- Access to natural light for users and staff alike
- Maximum flexibility
- Enticement of users into the building by an exciting appearance, and from closer up by glimpses into the building
- Similar functions to be grouped together
- Ancillary functions, including the exhibition gallery, auditorium, cafeteria, and seminar rooms, to be accessible independently

From this, it can be seen that there was little to prevent form from following function. Very few compromises were required in translating the brief, feature by feature, space by space, into a design. Fixed elements, such as elevator shafts and stairs, could be located where they worked best functionally and would least inhibit the building's adaptability. A module could be selected that would work well with open public areas, closed stacks, open stacks, ceiling tiles, partition lengths, and so on.

Cultural factors intervened, however. The Moslem religion is strong in Malaysia, and the co-location of the PNS with the State Mosque led the government to request that the designers respect Islamic architecture. We were more than willing to do this, because Islamic architecture was not only appropriate, but also allowed us to give the desired scale to the building and to satisfy many elements of the physical building plan.

Naturally, there was the usual experience of functions that had an affinity with the entrance foyer all clamoring for positions on the entrance floor. Deciding on the right layout was not simple, but there was the opportunity to look at a number of different permutations.

The process benefited from the involvement of the Sarawak state secretary, the director of the state planning unit, and an interdepartmental steering committee established to facilitate and guide the process. Much reliance, however, was inevitably placed on the ideas of the architects, who had designed a number of major libraries in Australia.

Ensuring that what was evolving at this stage of the planning was true to the brief was only part of the challenge. As spaces began to take shape in two dimensions on plan and started to become a little more real, it was important to ensure that the client was comfortable with what was emerging.

An evening view of Pustaka Negeri.

The building attracts a great deal of attention from passersby. As far as prominence is concerned, its positioning, visible across a lake from a major road, on the route to the Sarawak State Stadium in a city with many soccer enthusiasts and near the State Mosque, is impeccable. It is the place to go for Kuching's high school students. The building's café, called Windows-on-the-Lake, is full of teenagers in their blue-and-white school uniforms every afternoon and evening and most weekends during the school year.

Bus stops were provided on all nearby roads, one of which has been renamed Jalan Pustaka in honor of the PNS. The parkland setting for the PNS is also enticing, with bicycle trails, passive and active recreation areas, and very creative landscaping features including fountains, cascades, and waterfalls, all of which help to aerate the lake's water and keep it clean.

The building itself is on two floors, the entrance floor containing public areas with extensive multimedia facilities, including services aimed specifically at children. On this floor are also an exhibition gallery, shop, café (with a lakeside terrace), administration, staff work areas, and stacks.

The auditorium is accessible from the first floor, and nearby are seminar rooms and serving areas, making this a suitable venue for conferences or workshops. The great reading room is located on this floor, with open-access shelving and a number of spaces for specialized services such as a business information service, information technology training, in addition to an informal reading area and a large separate area for rare books reading, digitizing, and storage.

Building services (including cooling towers, chillers, substation, fire pump, emergency generators, satellite dish, and so on) are located in an adjacent service building. This compound is similar to the main building in appearance and external colors but was erected at a fraction of the per-square-foot cost of the main building.

Pustaka Negeri in a daylight view, illustrating its colonnades.

A drop-in and extended-hours day-care center was also provided. This facility provides care for the preschool age children of library users and PNS staff.

ARCHITECTURAL EXPRESSION AND FORM

As project director for Stephenson & Turner International, I had extensive experience working in Australia, the United States, Europe, North Africa, and the Middle East, and I knew that the level and sophistication of building techniques and trade skills could vary widely.

Therefore, Design Director Geoff Larkin and I spoke extensively with the local consultants and visited every available building site in Kuching to determine what levels of skill were to be expected in the local building industry. Final design and detailing of the components, finishes, and joinery were developed accordingly.

The building is based on classical Islamic design principles, using the 5-centered arch expressed in the form of external colonnades. An articulated rhythm of solid masonry and deeply shaded recesses provided by the colonnades gives expression to the long, low form of the building. The two-story-high colonnade provides the scale appropriate to a building of statewide significance that must command attention from across the park and the lake.

Passive Solar Design

The building is oriented with its longest axis running from east to west, thus minimizing the length of wall facing the sun. The building's external walls are set 4.6 yards behind the colonnades that shelter them and shade the large windows to public spaces. These large windows provide extensive outlooks on

Computer laboratory workstations.

the lake and park and the landscaped environs of the Sarawak Golf Club opposite the PNS site.

The designers faced two challenges with respect to the roof. High thermal-insulation values, along with equally high sound attenuation characteristics, were required. The resulting roof is of composite construction with a profiled-steel inner liner, dense-mineral-wool insulation, and an aluminum outer skin. Gutters are very large, and syphonic drainage is used.

External Finishes

The blue-green Kynar 500–finished aluminum roof of the building is a unifying element, simple and strong when seen from a distance across the park or when looked down on from the tall office buildings in the vicinity. An octagonal dome, the same color as the roof, is located symbolically over the center of the upper-floor main reading room.

The walls of the building are finished in natural, warm, off-white Shanghai plaster. Shanghai plaster is a mixture of finely crushed marble and cement, and with a spray-applied acrylic coating, it is highly resistant to the fungal growth common to Southeast Asia and to Sarawak, in particular, which has the world's highest levels of rainfall and very high temperatures.

Interior Design

Stephenson & Turner International was separately commissioned to provide interior design services for the building. One of the requirements of the brief was

The main staircase—beauty in glass.

for the designers to showcase the beautiful tropical rainforest timbers of Sarawak. The same firm was responsible for the design and selection of all shelving, compact shelving, built-in, and movable furniture. Reader tables, computer desks, and multimedia carrels were all fabricated locally to our designs.

The main two-story entrance foyer links the two functional halves of the building. Its floors and walls are finished with Italian marble in three main colors. A fountain in black marble is located at the center of the foyer. The basin contains a hemisphere clad with gold Venetian glass mosaic tiles. Water from a single low-velocity jet spills over the surface of the tiles and symbolizes the fountain of knowledge.

An elegant polished-stainless-steel space-frame structure supports the glass treads and balustrades of the main staircase. A second, less elaborate, glazed staircase wraps around the shaft of a glass elevator in the library's security zone. This links the ground-floor multimedia and staff zones with the main reading areas above.

The building contains many elaborate ceilings. The main reading room ceiling steps up from 12 feet along the windows to almost 16 feet generally. The ceiling of the transverse barrel vault is 36 feet above floor level, and the main domed ceiling rises to more than 52 feet. The main and tower domes are lined internally with ascending rows of copper, aluminum, and gold-metal-faced plastic laminate triangles. These are lit from below and are quite spectacular.

The walls separating the main reading space from and leading to the special collections area are paneled with Sarawak timber veneers. Early in the design process, it was determined that the best floor finish for the major public areas would be carpet tiles. Based on an earlier project in Australia, Stephenson & Turner International designed a series of carpets unique to the PNS.

The first, used on the upper level (especially in the main library, special collections area, and ancillary spaces), was based on the theme of the twisting rivers of Sarawak, the all-pervading jungle, and the human settlements that we had seen many times from the air. Nine separate tiles were designed. These were laid at random in some areas and linked to form intricate river patterns in others.

The second, used in the main adult and children's multimedia areas as well as administration and staff areas, is based on the pixels from which images are electronically created.

The third is based on sunlight sparkling on shallow water moving over stones that is so typical of the jungle streams throughout the state. This carpet tile is used in the Exhibition Gallery. (These carpet designs won Stephenson & Turner International a Dupont Antron Design Award Asia 2000.)

Artwork

The interior of the building showcases the rich arts, crafts, and materials of Sarawak, just as the collections and multimedia facilities provide access to information about its natural beauty, culture, and industries. Works by indigenous artists will eventually embellish the building, its surrounding terraces, and the park beyond. The artworks will take the form of paintings, frescoes, tapestries, weaving, etched and appliquéd glass, sculpture and carving.

A large exhibition gallery has been provided. The gallery is artificially lit with a track-lighting system at 4-foot centers in both directions. The gallery will be used to display the permanent PNS collection, as well as traveling exhibitions.

Construction

A local construction company, Jurudaya Constructions, won the bid in the face of stiff competition from a number of contractors from Peninsular Malaysia and overseas. The foundation stone was laid by the prime minister of Malaysia, Dr. Mahathir Mohammed, and the chief minister of Sarawak.

Stephenson & Turner International's two directors took turns traveling to Kuching for one week every month. The visits included briefing the steering committee and the state secretary on progress, consultants' coordination meetings, site meetings with the contractor, quality control inspections, and ongoing applications and approvals from the many governmental authorities having jurisdiction over various aspects of the project.

The construction period for the project was contractually established at eighteen months. But difficulties encountered with piling (including a 200-foot cavern in the underlying limestone precisely beneath one of the most heavily loaded piles supporting the dome), as well as alterations and additions to the scope of the project requested by the government, meant that completion was delayed by five months.

Nonetheless, with almost superhuman effort on behalf of all concerned, the project was completed for the scheduled opening, although it was a close shave. The PNS opened with tremendous fanfare and a two-hour historic and cultural show under the auspices of the chief minister and state secretary of Sarawak, at midnight on December 31, 1999. It was truly Sarawak's millennium project.

ACKNOWLEDGMENT

Some of the information in this chapter is based on the book *Fountain of Knowledge: The Story of Pustaka Negeri Sarawak* by David J. Jones, published by the Pustaka Negeri Sarawak, Kuching, 1999.

19 HISTORIC LIBRARIES AND THEIR ENDURING VALUE: BROOKLYN PUBLIC LIBRARY RENEWS ITS HISTORIC BUILDINGS

Elisabeth Martin

The preservation of historic library buildings has an intrinsic value that cannot be quantified. In contrast to a commonly held misconception, historic libraries are inherently flexible. Restorations of these grand and evocative civic buildings can preserve and transform their awe-inspiring spaces to serve generations to come. Early in the twentieth century, Brooklyn was fortunate in receiving a grant from Andrew Carnegie for twenty-one library buildings (Jones 1997). Many of these libraries serve neighborhood communities not dissimilar in their own right from small towns across the United States. I have the rewarding responsibility for planning the renovations of all Brooklyn's historic buildings and preserving the qualities that endeared them to the neighborhood residents when they were first constructed.

During the course of my research and work on library design, I have frequently heard heartfelt testimonials that recount the impact historic libraries have had on an individual's growth and how integral they were in inspiring that person toward success in future endeavors. Equally present are stories about how a local library has been integral to the growth and history of a community. Witnessing these personal and collective testimonials, one cannot help understanding the power of these buildings to make a critical difference in the lives of individuals and their respective communities. The earliest libraries in communities were private lending libraries; the transition from private libraries to free public libraries broadened access immeasurably and transformed the library into a major civic facility. Far more than just repositories for resources, the buildings themselves have come to symbolize the concept of free and open access to learning.

The magnificent portal of Brooklyn's Central Library welcomes visitors.

There are some libraries that will always inspire and have an eternal appeal; for instance, the extraordinary Bibliothèque Ste-Geneviève in Paris, designed by Henri Labrouste, has been the basis of inspiration for many libraries over time. Fortunately, many paradigms of library design of this stature have never been poorly renovated. There are, however, many historic libraries around the country, by far the majority, that may be underestimated, because their attributes have been occluded by poor renovation or changing perceptions of needs. The flexibility of these buildings is often overlooked. Although I have relished my opportunities to create dynamic library spaces in new buildings, I find each opportunity I am given to restore luster to an historic library remarkably compelling. When a well-meaning elected official in Brooklyn, New York recently suggested that I consider bulldozing the 18 remaining Carnegie branches among

Flatbush Branch Library, Brooklyn, New York; its atrium in 1905.

Brooklyn Public Library's 59 buildings and start afresh, I was truly taken aback. I politely declined his offer and shared my thoughts regarding the benefits preservation can bring. In my years of designing and renovating libraries, I have never come across a historic library that, when approached intelligently and sensitively, could not produce results that either met or surpassed anyone's renovation and restoration expectations.

This chapter discusses key features that greatly affect the renovation of libraries in general and historic libraries in particular. The following are general truths to remember in creating all successful library spaces:

- The library is an eternal but evolving place.
- The best library layouts seem natural; they feel rooted and function well.
- Great library layouts respond to cues from their space or site. Their forms, volumes, and contents work with the space's unique features.
- Great design approaches take advantage of potential benefits and compensate for perceived deficiencies in sites or spaces.
- The importance of a cohesive design, where layout, form, materials and function embrace each other, cannot be overemphasized.
- Volumetric variety, without undue gymnastics, creates inviting spaces.

Brooklyn's DeKalb Branch has been successfully rescued and fully restored.

Pendant lighting illuminates shelving at DeKalb Branch.

The entry sequence extends into the building defining connections and enticing the visitor.

Multiple factors that can influence the outcome and create awe-inspiring libraries:

- Entry sequence: its visual impact and its relationship to the other spaces
- Coherence of the proportional relationships, forms, and spaces
- Finishes: material and color palette selection and coordination
- Furnishings: layout, coordination, form, and finishes
- Lighting: natural and artificial lighting opportunities
- Options for seamless integration of new building systems (lighting, heating, cooling, etc.) and technology
- Integration of new architectural elements within the historic envelope
- Integrating innovative program elements that add spark and beckon
- Merchandising approaches—showcasing available collections and services

ENTRY SEQUENCE

Historic buildings frequently have enormously appealing entries. A building's approach and entry sequence is its first cue to visitors; it must be inviting, secure, and also accessible. Altering buildings to meet current accessibility

Dekalb's restored façade again attracts visitors.

requirements is often a challenge. Whether treated as elements seamlessly integrated into the materials and detailing of the original historic facade or skillfully designed to act as a visible but elegant new insertion, new accessibility features such as ramps and portals require great design sensitivity. Although a challenging task, it can always be accomplished and should not be considered an obstacle to the successful reuse of historic library buildings. Starting at the exterior, the entry sequence extends past the portal and into the building—defining connections and continuing to beckon the visitor. Within the spatial envelope, a central organizing element serves to orient the user and give needed visual cues regarding the hierarchy of internal relationships. In historic buildings, this organizing element is often a tall central space or atrium that plays a key role in defining spatial relationships and lends clarity to its internal organization. The development of the central circulation desk, often an anchor in this organizing element, was a modern and extraordinarily functional idea that continues to serve well to this day.

COHERENT INTERIOR RELATIONSHIPS

Multiple factors define the interior of the building. The best renovations manage to harmoniously integrate new elements into the existing historic build-

An atrium as a central organizing element in the restoration.

ing interior—with each of the elements working in concert with the others to create a cohesive product. In the newly renovated sections of Brooklyn's historic Central Library on Grand Army Plaza, furnishings and materials refer to the Moderne style of the elegant 1930s design yet provide for comfort and twenty-first century functions. Factors such as material and color choices, scale and proportional judgments, relationships between the existing palette and the newly introduced elements—all work together to influence the success of the resulting renovation. These factors are eternal and affect the design of both new and historic libraries. They are not prescriptive, and careful consideration of these relationships permits immense freedom in stylistic choices and approach. There is no one way to approach the renovation of an historic interior.

THE INTEGRATION OF NEW INFRASTRUCTURE SYSTEMS

As perhaps the single most significant change in historic libraries, the integration of new climatic systems brought new levels of comfort to staff and

The visual impact of the materials palette and stylistic choices is key to the successful renovation of historic library interiors.

patrons. Their early integration into buildings also brought about some of the most egregious examples of poor-quality renovations. All eighteen of the Brooklyn Public Library's extant Carnegie branches and its landmarked Central Library were host to renovations in the mid-1960s that hid or removed beautiful historic details while increasing comfort. Early systems were often insensitively placed, noisy, and inefficient. On both the interior (exposed ductwork weaving through suspended fluorescent lighting grids) and the exterior (visible concrete bunkers and rooftop cages), the new heating, cooling, and even lighting systems were not skillfully integrated into the historic envelope. This early approach, whether inspired by an infinite zeal to improve comfort or whether brought about by an insufficient focus on critical architectural needs and goals, was not the result of irremediable conditions in the buildings themselves. Historic buildings can accommodate very elegant heating, ventilation, and air-conditioning (HVAC) systems and lighting solutions. Preservation-sensitive state-of-the-art window replacements now replicate the beauty of the historic window with efficient draft-free systems (with double glazing, thermal properties, and glare control). Subsequent recent renovations at Brooklyn's Carnegie branch libraries and portions of its Central Library provide excellent examples of successful integration of infrastructure improvements in landmark quality structures.

Variation in the lighting plan and ceiling plane.

LIGHTING

The impact of decisions regarding both natural and artificial lighting choices is too frequently underestimated. The larger primary spaces and the smaller-scale support areas in historic libraries provide infinite opportunities to combine varied lighting sources with great success. The inherent variety in the scale of the spaces and the detail that often exists in the beamed and vaulted ceilings enhance the design opportunities and the results. Although the appearance of today's lighting products may often resemble historic fixtures, modern lighting products developed over the last decade bear little relationship to earlier products. Photometric data examined during the design phase can assist design professionals in the development of a balanced and varied lighting plan that will provide adequate lighting levels, appropriate glare control, and desired energy efficiencies.

Natural lighting also improves the quality of spaces greatly; spaces formerly deprived of natural light can be transformed by the delivery of natural light to those areas. The vast majority of historic libraries have generously proportioned window openings that once were the primary source of light for the interior. Even well-lighted interior spaces are significantly enhanced by the presence of

Central Library's custom carrels.

natural light. Its powerful positive visual and psychological effects have been the subject of painters and theorists for centuries.

INTEGRATING TECHNOLOGY

If one is evaluating the difficulty of integrating technology into an existing historic building as compared to one built more recently, it is clear that the task is considerably easier in most historic buildings. The typical construction techniques of the 1960s, 1970s, or 1980s—on grade floor slabs, block walls, and limited ceiling cavities present far greater obstacles. The basement spaces, spaces between joists or studs, wall cavities, and attic spaces found in most historic

Custom desks and carrels can reflect the style and finishes of the individual buildings.

buildings all provide convenient pathways for the conduits and cabling required to deliver technological improvements.

Although there are many technology furniture products on the market, custom carrels and public service desks may prove to be an aesthetically preferable and economically viable solution. Carrels and desks designed with concealed wiring troughs facilitate the delivery of wiring to public service points. The ability to choose among available wood species and grain choices (i.e., rift-cut oak) and the ability to match site-specific detailing (i.e., recessed panel proportions) and stain requirements at individual locations enable the creation of a custom product that better reflects the architectural style of the individual building's existing millwork.

INTEGRATING NEW ELEMENTS

Renovation with preservation sensitivity is not merely a re-creation of the library building as it existed when it was built. Renovated historic libraries must provide for today's collections and services, climatic controls, comfort levels, ergonomics, accessibility standards, and desired amenities. Yet, as with the integration of technology, historic buildings have proven enormously flexible in accepting changes. The skillful integration of inviting new spaces and uses can actually enhance the existing historic building. Even eternal library elements such as circulation desks, stacks, and staff workrooms can function far

Brooklyn's Central Library café.

Reading rooms transformed for comfort and today's functions.

Meeting rooms now serve new conference functions.

more efficiently than ever before with the integration of both visible and invisible functional improvements.

Historic reading rooms may have provided a warm and dry place to access materials, but they were not always designed with patron needs and comfort in mind. Newly restored reading rooms are still inspiring spaces that offer resources of all kinds; yet today's tables and chairs, age-appropriate displays, user-friendly layouts, signage, casual seating, and public access computer workstations have transformed the comfort and nature of their usage significantly.

Rather than compromise the character of the existing structure, the new essential or desired functions enrich them. Entirely new program areas and elements, such as digital distance learning centers, multimedia conference centers, thematic collection areas, galleries, teen spaces, children's program rooms, merchandising library material displays, cafés, retail ventures, reading gardens, and an infinite number of other possibilities have brought sought-after amenities to the library. Each element brings multiple benefits, often making it difficult to imagine the building prior to its integration. As just one example, lush new reading gardens enhance the approach to and quality of the sites at many Carnegie branches in Brooklyn, New York. These oases in an urban environment are a visual delight, accommodate story-hour programs and

Central's new Youth Wing: (a) magazine area, (b) computer area, (c) children's area, (d) book area.

Merchandising displays boost circulation.

The Saratoga Branch Reading Garden created by the Horticultural Society of New York.

poetry readings, inspire dedicated garden-tending volunteers, serve community events, and are even reserved by community residents for photography settings for special family events such as weddings. These new program elements only serve to reinforce the idea of the library as the locus of learning and culture in its community. The ease with which expanded services can be integrated is a testament to the innate flexibility of these profoundly civic structures.

CONCLUSION

Historic library buildings afford infinite renovation possibilities. The spirit of free access to materials and the characteristics that inspired citizens to take advantage of their great resources in order to enrich their lives is still present. Inspirational buildings that exude a civic presence serve a vital purpose in connecting and enriching communities. Careful planning, skillful design, and community support can transform our historic library building resources into ever-valuable twenty-first-century centers of learning. Whether through modifications in the existing buildings or through expansion and integration of new uses, their grace endures as their space and functions transform.

REFERENCE

Jones, Theodore. 1997. *Carnegie Libraries Across America, a Public Legacy.* New York: Preservation Press/Wiley.

PART VIII
BIBLIOGRAPHIC ESSAY

20 ANNOTATED BIBLIOGRAPHY: PLANNING, DESIGNING, AND BUILDING PUBLIC LIBRARIES

Sandra D. Trezzo

American Library Association, Library Management and Administration Association, Buildings and Equipment Section. *Library Buildings Consultant List,* 2001. [https://cs.ala.org/lbcl/search/].

A biennial print publication for the past twenty years, the current list is published in an electronic format. It remains a valuable resource for librarians who wish to hire a qualified consultant to prepare a building program and guide librarians through the design process. Searching instructions for this fee-based list are on the Web site; the next revision is scheduled for June 2003. Information provided includes how long the consultant has been in business, the number of projects the consultant has completed, five most recent projects, areas of expertise, details on fees, and time and geographic limitations. (Note: The Library Management and Administration Association [LAMA]) cautions that consultants provide their own information and pay LAMA a fee to be to appear in the list, and inclusion does not constitute any endorsement or approval by LAMA.)

Brawner, Lee B., and Donald K. Beck Jr. *Determining Your Public Library's Future Size: A Needs Assessment and Planning Model.* Chicago: American Library Association, 1996.

This work, authored by a well-known building consultant and an architect, provides a step-by-step description of the library space analysis and planning process. Using a typical medium-sized public library as a model, the authors demonstrate how to evaluate present services and determine future needs in terms of services and size and type of building needed. Among the topics covered are selecting an assessment team, assessing site alternatives, and making design and space recommendations. The many tools, surveys, and models included can be tailored for each individual library, making this an invaluable resource for librarians involved in the planning process.

Brown, Carol R. *Planning Library Interiors: The Selection of Furnishings for the 21st Century.* Phoenix, AZ: Oryx Press, 1995.

This is a very helpful resource for selecting furnishings for a new or existing library facility. Brown provides comprehensive information on a wide variety of furnishings, ranging from shelving, service desks, chairs and tables, carrels, and computer workstations to furnishings for children's areas and sign systems and displays. Explanations of the bid process and the library furniture market, as well as numerous diagrams and photographs of furnishings and useful lists of manufacturers and associations, are included.

————.*Interior Design for Libraries: Drawing on Function and Appeal.* Chicago: American Library Association, 2002.

Brown has again produced a useful book. The first three chapters provide fundamentals that should be helpful to people just beginning to get into building planning. The remaining six chapters go into planning and selection details and give some excellent advice. This is most apparent in her chapters on signs and lighting and acoustics. These chapters also will serve more experienced planners as refreshers by covering measurements for certain furniture, color selection, and lighting preferences for library buildings. The concluding chapter presents a series of questions intended to gather concerns and desires from staff members.

Cirillo, Susan E., and Robert E. Danford, eds. *Library Buildings, Equipment, and the ADA: Compliance Issues and Solutions.* Proceedings of the Library Administration and Management Association, Buildings and Equipment Section Preconference, June 24–25, 1993, New Orleans, Louisiana. Chicago: American Library Association, 1996.

This series of papers provides many insights into the intent of the Americans with Disabilities Act and offers constructive ways for libraries to comply with the law and meet the needs of users with disabilities. Of particular interest are contributions on issues of building design and accessible seating for libraries. The publication also features a comprehensive bibliography and an instructive appendix, "Questions and Answers on the ADA."

Crawford, Walt. "Library Space: The Next Frontier?" *Online.* March/April 1999, 61–66.

In this thought-provoking article, Crawford makes a compelling case for the continued need for library buildings, both for the services they provide and the public places they represent. Despite earlier predictions that digital, access-based library service would lead to the demise of library buildings, the opposite is true. Physical collections are continuing to grow; meeting rooms, study spaces, research areas and places for quiet reading are more necessary than ever. The popularity of "new mains" (massive centrally located city libraries), as well as continued support for diverse branch locations, also attests to the continued need for library service and the function of the library as place in the community.

Curry, Ann, and Zena Henriquez. "Planning Public Libraries: The Views of Architects and Librarians." *Library Administration & Management*, Spring 1998, 80–90.

This well-written, concise summary of the process of planning and building public libraries is based on numerous real-life experiences of architects and librarians involved in the building process. The authors contend that, because architects and librarians have divergent views on the form and function of library buildings, library professionals must be cognizant of these differing perspectives and take an active role in the building process. They offer many suggestions to help librarians and architects work together to produce a better product—a library building that would both be visually appealing and serve the needs of the library's staff and users.

Dahlgren, Anders. *Planning the Small Library Facility.* 2nd ed. Small Libraries Publications, No. 23. Chicago: Library Administration and Management Association, American Library Association, 1996.

Dahlgren's practical booklet provides a concise overview of the facility-planning process for libraries in smaller communities and institutions. He summarizes the basic steps in preparing for a building project and cautions against using space formulas too rigorously. Emphasis is placed on incorporating new technology and adapting furniture and equipment sizes and space needs. A short bibliography and resources for additional assistance are included.

————. *Public Library Space Needs: A Planning Outline.* [http://www.dpi.state.wi.us/dlcl/pld/plspace.html]. Madison: Wisconsin Department of Public Instruction, Public Library Development, 1998.

Dahlgren, a consultant for public library construction and planning, developed this step-by-step method by which library planners can obtain a general estimate of their libraries' space needs based on their underlying service goals. Formulas and examples for calculating the area required in six broad types of library space—collection, reader seating, staff, meeting, special use, and nonassignable space—are explained. The author stresses the need to obtain accurate population data and forecasts in order to plan for the actual population to be served by the library system. The planning outline can be accessed on the Web or downloaded as a Microsoft Word 6.0 or PDF file.

———. "Solutions in Hand, Planners Earn High Marks from Their Peers." *American Libraries*, April 2001, 65–70.

This article features the eight winning libraries of 21st Library Buildings Awards chosen biennially by a panel of librarians and architects. Although the designs, methods, and ideas employed in these buildings are not applicable to all library projects, these award-winning projects can provide insight into current trends in library design and restoration.

Dahlgren, Anders, and Erla P. Heyns, comps. *Planning Library Buildings: A Select Bibliography*. Chicago: American Library Association, 1995.

This work presents a detailed list of books and articles on library facilities planning published between 1980 and 1994. The bibliography is divided into "General Works" and "Special Topics." A variety of subjects, ranging from "The Planning Team," "The Architect's Role," "The Consultant's Role," and "Space Planning and Programming" to "Standards and Recommended Space Allowances," "The Library Building Program Statement," "Site Selection," "Lighting," and "Interior Design" are covered. Although some works cited are dated and of limited use, many are still useful and provide an excellent overview of the many topics to be considered in the facilities planning process.

Dancik, Deborah Bloomfield, and Emelie Jensen Shroder, eds. *Building Blocks for Library Space: Functional Guidelines*. Chicago: Library Administration and Management Association: Buildings and Equipment Section, Functional Space Requirements Committee, American Library Association, 1995.

This handbook presents detailed formulas for calculating the square footage required for each function, item, and area in a library building. Although rigid space formulas have been somewhat superseded by more flexible planning methods, the work remains useful for the practical guidance it offers for planning space allocations in both new and existing library facilities.

Hagloch, Susan B. *Library Building Projects: Tips for Survival*. Englewood, CO: Libraries Unlimited, 1994.

This slim volume is a practical, easy-to-read collection of tips, warnings, and hints compiled from the author's experience as the librarian in charge of an expansion and renovation project for a public library. The work is divided into the planning, financing, construction, and postconstruction phases and includes floor plans and elevations for a number of public library buildings, along with general information about these projects.

Hall, Richard B. *Financing Public Library Buildings*. New York: Neal-Schuman, 1994.

This thorough explanation of the financing process should be required reading for all library officials responsible for obtaining funding for new projects. The author explains how to plan the library construction project and the project cost estimate and explores the wide range of available potential funding sources, from local, state, and federal governments to private funding.

Henry, Clyde. "Building the Road to Success." *Library Journal 2001 Buyer's Guide and Web Site Directory*, December 2000, 8–10.

An architect provides an insider's view of the three main steps in a typical library project—planning, design, and construction—in this brief but informative article.

Jones, David, and Geoffrey Larkin. "Securing a Good Design: A Library Building Consultant and an Architect Consider Library Security." *Australasian Public Libraries and Information Services*, December 1993, 164–171.

The authors address security in libraries, an often-overlooked aspect in the design and planning of library facilities. They contend that it is most effective to address security concerns as an integral part of the design process in both new and renovated library facilities. Studying designs from a security perspective at the planning stage can lead to a safer, more secure library, without significantly adding to building project costs. Security issues for specific areas such as book drops and entrances are also discussed.

Koontz, Christine M. *Library Facility Siting and Location Handbook*. Westport, CT: Greenwood Press, 1997.

Koontz's work provides a comprehensive reference for those library planners whose first concern is where to locate a new library facility. Koontz reviews the history of library siting and library location research and discusses the advantages of using geographic information systems for determining public library locations. She provides facility location models and offers advice on how to locate library facilities where they will most effectively serve the local population. Although not required reading for all projects, it would be very helpful when choosing a location is the first phase of the building process.

"Library Buildings 2001." *Library Journal*, Architectural Issue, December 2001, 48–61.

Since 1946, the December Architectural Issue of *Library Journal* has presented a summary of library construction and renovation projects in the United States in the public and academic sectors. In addition to color illustrations of many library facilities, the issue features numerous charts that detail project costs, size, capacity, the project architects, and funding methods for each project. A six-year nationwide cost summary and an alphabetical directory of architects are additional helpful resources.

Lushington, Nolan, and James M. Kusack. *The Design and Evaluation of Public Library Buildings*. Hamden, CT: Library Professional Publications, 1991.

The authors advocate that libraries engage in a comprehensive planning and evaluation process to help develop libraries designed with users in mind. Part I of the work offers practical guidance for designing a library. Book stacks, furnishings, the children's library, staff work areas, and special considerations such as graphics, lighting, and energy are among the many areas discussed. Many site plans, diagrams, and architects' sketches are featured in this useful book. Part II details how a postoccupancy evaluation should be conducted to determine whether the building has actually achieved its goals.

Martin, Ron G., ed. *Libraries for the Future: Planning Buildings That Work*. Proceedings of the Library Administration and Management Association, Library Buildings Preconference, June 27–28, 1991, Atlanta, Georgia. Chicago: American Library Association, 1992.

These proceedings consist of papers presented by contributing experts with a broad base of experience in both public and academic libraries. Issues addressed include the planning process, the roles of the consultant and the planning team, the building program statement, technical requirements and building criteria, functional requirements and space relationships, and selecting the design team. (Note: The selected bibliography is somewhat dated.)

McCabe, Gerard B. *Planning for a New Generation of Public Library Buildings*. Westport, CT: Greenwood Press, 2000.

This work provides a good starting point for librarians wanting to familiarize themselves with the process of planning and building a new library. It covers all aspects of the process from start to finish in a concise, easy-to-follow style. The checklists and appendixes are of practical value, and the annotated bibliography includes a variety of other helpful sources.

McCarthy, Richard C. *Designing Better Libraries: Selecting and Working With Building Professionals*. 2nd ed. Fort Atkinson, WI: Highsmith Press, 1999.

Written by an architect who also serves as a public library trustee, this thorough, straightforward guide will help library board members and administrators learn more about the building process and the professionals who will make a new library building a reality. Three broad topics are covered: who architects are and what they do, what the parts of a typical architectural project are, and how to find and hire an architect. The second edition has been updated to reflect recent changes in standards and procedures for the architectural and building professions. McCarthy includes many tips and warnings throughout the work that could help a library avoid many unnecessary legal and financial problems during design and construction; he also provides useful checklists for key stages in a project. This work should be required reading for any librarian or board member involved in the building process.

Oehlerts, Donald E. *Books and Blueprints: Building America's Public Libraries.* New York: Greenwood Press, 1991.

This intriguing historical overview of public library design from 1850 to 1989 focuses on a number of major metropolitan library facilities. The evolution of book stack design, the addition of children's rooms to public libraries, and the role of library boards in building design are among the interesting topics covered. Many illustrations of public library buildings past and present are featured.

Sannwald, William W., ed. *Checklist of Library Building Design Considerations.* 4th ed. Chicago: American Library Association, 2001.

This recently updated checklist is a very helpful, easy-to-follow tool for librarians, architects, and all members of the building team. It contains an almost exhaustive array of questions concerning all aspects of the planning and building process, from start to finish. Site selection, building planning and architecture, general exterior considerations, internal organization, compliance with ADA accessibility guidelines, communications, electrical and miscellaneous equipment, interior design and finishes, book stacks and shelving, safety and security, maintenance of library building and property, and groundbreaking ceremonies are among the many areas covered. New topics explored in the fourth edition include environmentally correct design, alternatives to new construction, young adult and children's areas, remote storage, and technology issues.

———. "Espresso and Ambiance: What Public Libraries Can Learn from Bookstores." *Library Administration & Management,* 1998, 12, 200–211.

Sannwald examines some of the successful features of large bookstore chains and suggests ways in which libraries can duplicate their merchandising and design ideas. He contends that, when designing new spaces, libraries should consider shelving and other fixtures that will allow them to market their collections effectively. The importance of making the library a place people will want to visit often, through both the atmosphere and the layout of the library itself, is stressed. This is an interesting concept, but the article failed to explain how libraries could afford to put these merchandising suggestions into use.

"A Sense of Place." *American Libraries*, Annual Facilities Showcase, April 2002, 45–59.

Each year the April issue of *American Libraries* showcases the latest in library design, featuring new construction and renovation projects at public, academic and school libraries. The information provided is much less comprehensive than *Library Journal*'s December Architectural Issue; however, the color illustrations alone should provide inspiration and provoke envy for many librarians.

Wiley, Peter Booth. "Beyond the Blueprint." *Library Journal*, February 15, 1997, 110–112.

Wiley examines the experiences of several large public libraries built in the past ten years, among them those in Chicago, Phoenix, San Francisco, and Denver. The author notes that new libraries are never finished; they must constantly adapt to meet changing technology and changing public needs. Increased budgetary constraints, greater usage, and demands for meeting and study space are among the challenges discussed. The necessity of clear signs, easily understandable layouts, and flexibility in building design are also emphasized.

Woodward, Jeannette. *Countdown to a New Library: Managing the Building Project*. Chicago: American Library Association, 2000.

An insider's guide to the building process that will be certain to help other library professionals through the stressful process of new construction or renovation. Woodward urges librarians to become as familiar as possible with all aspects of the complex process of planning, designing, and constructing a new library building to ensure that the new library meets the needs of both users and staff. Woodward's work familiarizes librarians with "the world of architects and contractors," planning, building details, technology and security issues, selecting flooring, wall coverings and furnishings, construction, and "moving and getting settled." The "Tips and Tales" sections contain invaluable advice from librarians who have survived their own building projects. Each chapter concludes with helpful sources for additional information such as professional organizations and supplemental readings.

APPENDIX: PREQUALIFICATION FORM FOR LIBRARY FURNITURE MANUFACTURERS

CUSTOM FURNITURE FOR THE _____ LIBRARY

PART I - PREQUALIFICATION QUESTIONNAIRE

1. Name of business: _____

   Address: _____
   City _____ State: _____ Zip: _____
   Telephone: _____ Facsimile: _____

2. Contractor's License No.: _____ State: _____
   Certificate of Insurance No.: _____

   List other states in which this organization is licensed to do business:

   _____   _____   _____
   _____   _____   _____
   _____   _____   _____

3. List those individuals, as applies, involved in this business:

   CEO or Partners: _____
                                                 _____
   Officer in charge of estimating (name & title): _____
                                                 _____
   Officer in charge of production (name & title): _____
                                                 _____
   Contact or Project Manager: _____
                                                 _____

4. How many years has your organization been in business? _____

5. Indicate the percentage of custom wood library furniture (as distinguished from your standard lines) that your firm manufactures regularly: % of yearly production _____.

6. Indicate the average number of library projects that your firm manufactures in one year: _____.

7. Is yours an Architectural Woodwork Institute (AWI) member firm?
( ) Yes   ( ) No. If no, to what quality guidelines or standards does your firm subscribe? _____
Is yours an AWI Certified firm? ( ) Yes   ( ) No. If yes, please submit a copy of your certification.

8. Has this organization, or another organization with which the officers or partners were involved during the past five (5) years, ever failed to complete work awarded to it? ( ) Yes   ( ) No   If yes, please provide explanation on a separate sheet.

9. Claims and suits: If the answer to either question is yes, please provide explanation on a separate sheet.
   a. Are there any pending or outstanding suits, claims, judgments or arbitration proceedings that involve your organization or its officers?

   b. Has your organization requested arbitration or filed suit regarding projects or contracts within the last five (5) years?

10. Capabilities:
   a. What is your monthly production capacity? $ _____
   b. What size job are you most comfortable producing, given typical contract time constraints? $_____ Time Period _____
   c. Total dollar volume currently under contract: $ _____
   d. What was your annual volume over the last 3 years? $ _____
   e. Indicate, in dollars, the largest single project your firm successfully completed in the last 5 years: $_____
   Project: _____
   Location: _____ Date completed: _____

11. Attach audited Financial Statement, current to within one year.
   Assurances:
   a. Name of Bonding Company: _____
      Contact:_____ Phone Number: _____
      Normal Bonding Limit (total projects/any one project): $_____

   b. Insurance company: _____
      Contact: _____ Phone Number: _____
      Normal General Liability Limit (total projects/any one project)
      _____

   c. Your state's Worker's Compensation Insurance Experience Modification Rate for the last three (3) years:
      Year/EMR ___/___   Year/EMR ___/___   Year/EMR ___/___
      Based on last year's Cal/OSHA No. 200 log, provide your incidence rates:
      _____

12. List 4 major suppliers: Contact:

_____
_____
_____
_____

13. Bank References:
     Bank: Address: Contact: Phone:

_____
_____
_____

Physical Profile:

14. a. Total square feet of plant space: _____
     b. Total number of employees: _____
     c. Total number of production employees: _____
     d. Total number of journeyman installers on payroll: _____

15. List the manufacturing processes your firm performs in-house:

		Yes	No
a.	CAD engineering	_____	_____
b.	Veneering (clipping, stitching, and panel pressing)	_____	_____
c.	Finishing under positive pressure (dust-free) conditions	_____	_____
d.	Installation of electrical components and wiring	_____	_____
e.	Integration of related materials (metal, glass, stone, fabric, leather, solid surface material, etc.)	_____	_____
f.	Warehousing (square footage:_____)	_____	_____
g.	Other: (List) _____		

16. Facilities: (Briefly describe these facilities if you have them)
     In-house positive pressure finishing:

_____
_____

     CAD Engineering: _____
_____

     Software in use: _____
_____

17. List the major library furniture projects in which this organization is currently
     involved citing required quality standard. (Indicate standard other than AWI if
     applicable):

     Project name: _____ Location: _____
     Architect: _____ General Contractor: _____
     Contact: _____ Contact: _____
     Phone: _____ Phone: _____
     Contract Amount: _____ % Complete_____
     Expected Completion Date: _____
     Bonded? ( ) Yes ( ) No AWI Grade: ( ) Premium ( ) Custom

     Project name: _____ Location: _____
     Architect: _____ General Contractor: _____

Contact: _____   Contact: _____
Phone: _____   Phone: _____
Contract Amount: _____   % Complete_____
Expected Completion Date: _____
Bonded? ( ) Yes ( ) No   AWI Grade: ( ) Premium ( ) Custom

18. List major library furniture projects which this organization has completed in the last 3–5 years:

Project name: _____   Location: _____
Architect: _____   General Contractor: _____
Contact: _____   Contact: _____
Phone: _____   Phone: _____
Contract Amount: _____   Date completed: _____
Bonded? ( ) Yes ( ) No   AWI Grade: ( ) Premium ( ) Custom

Project name: _____   Location: _____
Architect: _____   General Contractor: _____
Contact: _____   Contact: _____
Phone: _____   Phone: _____
Contract Amount: _____   Date completed: _____
Bonded? ( ) Yes ( ) No   AWI Grade: ( ) Premium ( ) Custom

Project name: _____   Location: _____
Architect: _____   General Contractor: _____
Contact: _____   Contact: _____
Phone: _____   Phone: _____
Contract Amount: _____   Date completed: _____
Bonded? ( ) Yes ( ) No   AWI Grade: ( ) Premium ( ) Custom

Project name: _____   Location: _____
Architect: _____   General Contractor: _____
Contact: _____   Contact: _____
Phone: _____   Phone: _____
Contract Amount: _____   Date completed: _____
Bonded? ( ) Yes ( ) No   AWI Grade: ( ) Premium ( ) Custom

19. Referring to items 17 and 18 above, cite specific projects that, in your estimation, required unusual technical capability, adaptability, or production capacity. Respond to the items that apply to the work of your firm:

   a.   Example of large volume project under tight schedule constraints:
       Project name: _____
       Comments: _____

_____

   b.   Furniture custom-designed to meet customer's unusual needs or requirements:
       Project name: _____

CUSTOM FURNITURE FOR THE _____ **LIBRARY**

PART I - PREQUALIFICATION QUESTIONNAIRE

1. Name of business: _____

    Address: _____
    City _____ State: _____ Zip: _____
    Telephone: _____ Facsimile: _____

2. Contractor's License No.: _____ State: _____
    Certificate of Insurance No.: _____

    List other states in which this organization is licensed to do business:

    _____ _____ _____
    _____ _____ _____
    _____ _____ _____

3. List those individuals, as applies, involved in this business:

    CEO or Partners: _____

    Officer in charge of estimating (name & title): _____

    Officer in charge of production (name & title): _____

    Contact or Project Manager: _____

FURNITURE FOR THE _____ **LIBRARY**

PART II – PREQUALIFICATION MOCK-UP

The drawings and specifications that follow represent elements of design and function important to the library and pose some of the technical problems that you as a prospective bidder/manufacturer will need to solve in order to be admitted to the approved bidders list.

Please submit the mock-up illustrated on the following page, demonstrating compliance with the specifications below, and using your best skill and craftsmanship in its execution.

    I.   QUALITY STANDARD
        A. All materials shall meet or exceed the Architectural Woodwork Institute (AWI) standard for Grade I.
        B. All workmanship shall meet or exceed the Architectural Woodwork Institute (AWI) standard for Premium Grade.

    II.   MATERIALS
        A. Options for table and carrel tops
            1. Wood species for solid edges: _____ ; cut:_____
            2. Wood veneer species for tops:_____; cut_____
            3. Core material: medium-density fiberboard (MDF)
            4. Wood species for legs, aprons:_____; cut_____

    III. FABRICATION
        A. Apply wood joinery solutions complying with AWI Premium Grade.
        B. Face-fastening of exposed members is not permitted.
        C. Closely match solid wood to adjacent wood veneer for color and grain.
        D. Veneer for tops shall be sequence-, book-, and center-matched.

    IV. FINISHING
        A. Stain: Match library's control sample for color.
        B. Finish: AWI System TR-6 catalyzed polyurethane.
          1. Match library's control sample for texture and sheen.

EXAMPLE
PART II - MOCK-UP PREQUALIFICATION

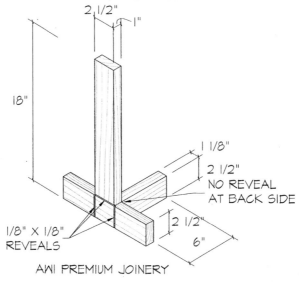

2 1/2"
1"
18"
1 1/8"
2 1/2"
NO REVEAL
AT BACK SIDE
1/8" X 1/8"
REVEALS
2 1/2"
6"

AWI PREMIUM JOINERY

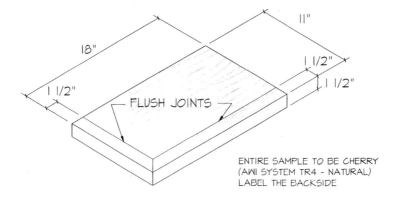

11"
18"
1 1/2"
1 1/2"
1 1/2"
FLUSH JOINTS

ENTIRE SAMPLE TO BE CHERRY
(AWI SYSTEM TR4 - NATURAL)
LABEL THE BACKSIDE

ABOUT THE EDITORS
AND CONTRIBUTORS

DONALD BERGOMI, Fellow of the Royal Australian Institute of Architects, was born in New York City. As a member of the U.S. Air Force, he served for two years in Central Australia and later trained as an architect at Sydney University. His project experience includes work in the United States, Europe, the Middle East, Southeast Asia, and Australasia. He is Managing Director of Stephenson and Turner International, a Sydney-based architectural and interior design practice specializing in libraries. He is married and has one son.

LESLEY A. BOON is Teacher-Librarian in a Jewish day school in Sydney, Australia. She has been teaching for many years and has been a librarian for eighteen of them. She has worked as a librarian in schools, universities, and the New South Wales Health Department. She has designed several libraries and is a consultant in library design to a Sydney architectural firm. She has a passion for literature and helping others along the information highway.

ALAN BUNDY, Ph.D., is University Librarian at the University of South Australia, Adelaide. He is a past president of the Australian Library and Information Association and is known internationally as an authority on joint-use libraries.

JAY CAROW studied architecture under Mies van der Rohe. He was a Peace Corps volunteer in Malaysia and a visiting Fulbright Professor at the University of Baghdad and was Dean of the first university-degree-granting programs in architecture, planning, and building technology in Malaysia. He has planned and designed libraries for thirty years. He served as Evanston (Illinois) Library Board Trustee and Building Committee Chairman, as President of the Evanston Library

Friends, and as a participant in the American Library Association's LAMA Building and Equipment Section.

KENNETH D. CLIPPERTON, Managing Director of University Information Services at Buena Vista University (Storm Lake, Iowa), is involved in implementing the nation's first wireless community through the eBVyou initiative. He serves on the board of the Iowa Research and Education Network and is a member of Gateway Computer Corporation's Higher Education Advisory Council.

CATHAN COOK works for Microsoft doing strategic consulting for system architecture. She works from her Florida home or customer sites throughout the country. Her personal Web site with up-to-date contact information is www.wildcoast.org/people/cathan.htm.

ROBERT W. FETZER is with Fetzer's, Inc., a custom library furniture manufacturer in Salt Lake City, Utah. His expertise is in furniture ergonomics emphasizing durability and quality of design. He can be reached at rwfetzer@fetzersinc.com.

JAMES J. "JIM" FLOTT is Urban Forester for the city of Spokane. He has previously held positions as Nursery Manager at an 800-acre wholesale nursery; Teaching And Research Associate at the University of Illinois, Urbana-Champaign Horticulture Department; and Campus Horticulturist at the University of Nebraska in Omaha. He received a B.S. degree in horticulture from Iowa State University and an M.S. degree in forest pathology from the University of Arizona.

MERRI A. HARTSE is Branch Manager for Spokane Public Library. She received her library degree from the University of Denver and spent the first part of her library career working in academic libraries in New Mexico, Arizona, and Illinois. She most recently coordinated the 2001 Washington Library Association conference.

JAMES R. KENNEDY is University Librarian at Buena Vista University (Storm Lake, Iowa). He has both academic and public library experience. Active in the Library Administration and Management Association, he has served as chairperson or member of several American Library Association Building and Equipment Section committees. He is an active library consultant and contributes to professional publications.

ALEXANDER P. LAMIS, AIA, has been Partner-in-Charge of library projects throughout The United States. He has lectured and written on the use of technology in libraries and sustainable design issues. He is a member of the Architecture for Public Libraries section of the American Library Association and the Building Design section of the International Federation of Landscape Architects. A graduate of MIT and Columbia, he is a partner at Robert A. M. Stern Architects in New York.

ELISABETH MARTIN, AIA, is Director of Planning, Design, and Facilities for the Brooklyn Public Library System in New York City. Her responsibilities include establishing a vision for the course of the system's facilities goals and setting standards for renovations and facilities-planning design, construction, and maintenance. She is a published author and is a frequent speaker on library design issues.

GERARD B. McCABE retired as Director of Libraries at Clarion University of Pennsylvania. He is the author of *Planning for a New Generation of Public Library Buildings* (2000, Greenwood Press). An active library consultant, he is also a past chairperson of the Building and Equipment Section Executive Committee, LAMA.

VALERIE L. MEYER is the Director of Library Services for the City of Mission Viejo, California. She has been an active member of, and consultant to, design teams for several public libraries in Southern California. She has managed public libraries for over twenty years.

ANDREA ARTHUR MICHAELS, IIDA, President of Michaels Associates Design Consultants, Inc., has 28 years of experience in an international practice of planning and designing public, academic, and special libraries—creative solutions for staff and users based on efficiency, effectiveness, and the potential for graceful change. She is an active member of the LAMA Building and Equipment Section.

WILLIAM W. SANNWALD, Assistant to the City Manager and Manager of Library Design and Development, San Diego, California, formerly was City Librarian of the San Diego Public Library, 1979 to 1997. A consultant and an author on library architecture and management, he is a past president of the Library Administration and Management Association.

CAROL SPEICHER is Administrator of the Northeast Nebraska Library System. Twenty-one member communities have undertaken library construction or remodeling projects during her fourteen years of service, and another thirteen are in the planning or fund-raising stages. She is an active library consultant and presenter of a wide variety of continuing education topics, including all aspects of library construction.

JOHN STANLEY is the owner of John Stanley Associates, based in Western Australia. His retail consultancy business started in 1976, and he is a recognized international conference speaker and consultant, with clients in sixteen countries. He is the author of the bestselling book *Just About Everything a Retail Manager Needs to Know* (1999, Plum Press). He has worked with numerous libraries to improve their retail technology skills and hence their book lending. John can be contacted via his Web page (www.jstanley.com.au) or email (info@johnstanley.cc).

SANDRA D. TREZZO has a B.A. in political science from Union College and an M.L.S. from Indiana University. She has experience working in public libraries as a reference librarian, branch manager, and manager of Extension Services.

SONDRA VANDERMARK is Regional Administrator of the Metrowest Massachusetts Regional Library System located in Waltham, Massachusetts. She was Library Director during two public library construction projects in Massachusetts. In her spare time, she is a library building consultant.

REBECCA WENNINGER is Branch Manager with the Enoch Pratt Free Library in Baltimore, Maryland. She is coauthor of *The Coming Generation of Computer Proficient Students: What It May Mean for Libraries* (1994) and author of "A Place to Call Their Own" in Gerard McCabe's *Planning for a New Generation of Public Library Buildings* (2000). She received an M.S.L.S. from Clarion University of Pennsylvania in 1990.

JANET C. WOODY is Manager of Tuckahoe Area Library, Henrico County, Virginia. A librarian since 1978, she has held positions in public and technical services in a school library, an academic library, and at the Library of Virginia. She can be reached at jwoody@henrico.lib.va.us.

INDEX